The WPA
Guides

The WPA Guides

Mapping America

Christine Bold

University Press of Mississippi
Jackson

www.upress.state.ms.us

Copyright © 1999 by University Press of Mississippi
All rights reserved
Manufactured in the United States of America

07 06 05 04 03 02 01 00 99 4 3 2 1

Library of Congress Cataloging-in-Publication Data
Bold, Christine, 1955–
    The WPA guides : mapping America / Christine Bold.
        p.   cm.
    Includes bibliographical references and index.
    ISBN 1-57806-194-6 (cloth : alk. paper). — ISBN 1-57806-195-4
(pbk. : alk. paper)
    1. Federal Writers' Project—History.   2. American guide series.
3. United States Guidebooks.   I. Title.
E175.4.B65   1999
917.304'929—dc21   99-26871
                                                                        CIP
        British Library Cataloging-in-Publication Data available

For Wesley and Lewis

CONTENTS

Illustrations

Acknowledgments

This project began as someone else's good idea. In 1982, Frank McMahon headed up a research team at what was then Ealing College of Higher Education in London to work on the Federal Writers' Project and hired me as research assistant. I left that study after a year to begin teaching, and the Ealing group's work and my own interests diverged increasingly from that point. Nevertheless, I want to thank Frank for introducing me to this critical moment in U.S. cultural history as well as to the pleasures and challenges of interdisciplinary, collaborative work.

It has been a long journey—geographically and intellectually—since then, and I have accrued more debts in the process of this book's formulation and completion than I can recall. Colleagues who have lent particular support at various stages include Michael Fellman, John Fondersmith, Mick Gidley, Bob Lawson-Peebles, Ian McLaren, Laura Murray, Gerald Schwartz, Mark Simpson, Maurizio Vaudagna, Chris Wilson, David Wright, and Seetha Srinivasan, Elizabeth Young, and Anne Stascavage at the University Press of Mississippi. I am currently blessed with a remarkable community of scholars in the School of Literatures and Performance Studies at the University of Guelph, who, over the years, have listened and contributed to this work with signal interest and incisiveness. Without my women's writing group at the University of Guelph I would not have finished the book; I am especially grateful to Susan Brown, Diana Brydon, Donna Palmateer Pennee, and Ann Wilson for the huge amounts of time, attention, wisdom, and good humor they contributed to this project. And Ric Knowles, who came to this work in its final stages, showed it a generosity of attention and acuity of response that I don't have words enough to thank.

The research for this book was made possible by generous grants from the Social Sciences and Humanities Research Council of Canada, the U.S. Embassy in Canada, the University of Alberta, and the University of Guelph. I am also extremely grateful for the patience and skill of the many archivists who made my research possible: at the National Archives and Records Administration, Washington, D.C.; Library of Congress, Manuscripts Division; Boise State University Library; Idaho State Historical Society; University of Idaho Library, Special Collections and Archives; Western Historical Manuscript Collection–Columbia, at the University of Missouri, Columbia; Municipal Archives of the City of New York; Southern Historical Collection and the University Archives, Library of the University of North Carolina at Chapel Hill; North Carolina Department of Cultural Resources, Division of Archives and History; University of Rochester Library, Department of Rare Books and Special Collections; and Washington State University Libraries, Manuscript, Archives and Special Collections.

Parts of this book have been presented in earlier versions at conferences organized by the Association of Canadian College and University Teachers of English, American Studies Association, British Association of American Studies, Canadian Association for American Studies, European Association for American Studies, and Netherlands American Studies Association, as well as in forums at the University of Alberta and the University of Guelph. Earlier versions of parts of Chapters 4, 6, and 7 have appeared in *American Studies* 29 (1988): 5–29; *Modern American Landscapes*, ed. Mick Gidley and Robert Lawson-Peebles (Amsterdam: VU University Press, 1995), 172–96; and *"Writing" Nation and "Writing" Region in America*, ed. Theo D'Haen and Hans Bertens, European Contributions to American Studies (Amsterdam: VU University Press, 1996), 197–216.

This book is dedicated to Wesley Wark, extraordinary scholar, and to Lewis Bold Wark, our boy, for the precious memories of all the trips you made possible (by your presence and your strategic absences), for the conversations, the fun, and the support.

Introduction

I was going to the Pacific Coast and we happened to reach the Great Horseshoe Bend on the Great Northern. It's magnificent. If you've never seen it, you don't know what a tremendous spectacle it is. . . . And so I saw this and I was very struck by the magnificence of America and all of a sudden it occurred to me, "What the hell you lookin' at? This don't belong to you."

—Theodore Ward

This anecdote by Theodore Ward, African American playwright and Federal Theatre Project employee, exposes all the issues that engage this book: the mapping of American identities—national, regional, and local—onto the landscape; the struggles over cultural ownership, dispossession, and citizenship provoked by that process; and the federal government's role in brokering the politics of representation.

In 1935, Franklin D. Roosevelt's administration embarked on the largest governmental intervention into cultural production in the history of the United States when it put forty thousand unemployed artists to work in four Federal Arts Projects (for visual artists, theater workers, musicians, and writers). Amid the lively and contentious debates around government funding of the arts today, the New Deal experiments tend to get forgotten or brushed aside as unique to the economic and political conditions of the Depression. Yet the Works Progress Administration (WPA) Arts Projects were on the cusp of the modern bureaucratization of culture, at the moment when the federal government exponentially extended its reach into people's daily lives. They make peculiarly vivid the imbrication of publicly funded art in the governmental making and regulation of a national citizenry—with all the benefits, limitations, complicities, and power relations that process implies.[1]

The Federal Writers' Project's main contribution to this process was the American Guide Series, more than four hundred volumes touted as America's first indigenous guidebooks to every state, most regions, and many cities, towns, and villages across the country (Scharf). In August 1935, $6,288,000 was allotted to the Writers' Project, under the aegis of the Works Progress Administration, to employ sixty-five hundred writers from the relief rolls in every state, with a central office in Washington, D.C., directing their work (primarily the collective composition of the American Guide Series). In September 1939, Congress voted—in the face of both political and fiscal concerns—to devolve the project into state-sponsored programs with greatly reduced federal control. When the renamed Writers' Program closed in February 1943, *Time* magazine estimated that its total expenditure was $27,189,370 (approximately one-fifth of 1 percent of all WPA appropriations). This appropriation had employed approximately ten thousand writers, the vast majority off the breadlines and varying greatly in their skills, to document their own communities in state, regional, city, and local guides (K. McKinzie 23).

There was always a gap between the public perception of the American Guide Series and of the Federal Writers' Project. Whereas the American Guide Series was widely celebrated as an invaluable introduction to the cultural diversity of the United States, the project was constantly under attack in the 1930s as a boondoggle for the undeserving unemployed or as a propaganda machine for the federal government. Recent scholarly analysis has paid only cursory attention to the substance of the guidebooks, treating the Federal Writers' Project as the main event in the politics and personalities that swirled through it from 1935 to 1943. Yet the two are inextricably intertwined. All the ideological ferment ultimately devolved on the guidebooks and the mechanism by which a wide range of constituencies sought, literally, to put themselves on the map.

Working from the voluminous administrative, editorial, and personal archives left by the Writers' Project, I have reconstructed the processes of production, circulation, and reception of selected guidebooks in an effort to trace their brokering of individual, community, and national identities. Particular fault lines emerge: the tensions between federal bureaucracy and regional difference; the competing claims of "specialized" versus "local" knowledge; the effects of "official" sponsorship on the setting of cultural norms and the jostling of local groups and narratives for recognition within the national framework.

Although the issues and conflicts around the production of cultural identities were similar in all four Arts Projects, the guidebooks did not fall under the sign of "art" to the same degree as did the murals, theatrical productions, and musical performances. This difference made the guidebooks at once more modest and more persuasive as arbiters of public culture. Their documentary status allowed project publicizers to speak of them as "discovering"—rather than "creating"—American culture, thus effectively naturalizing their very selective and interested representations. The dynamics of an informational genre also facilitated considerable slippage from administrative to representational categories: federal regulation and employment practices devolved directly on the guidebooks' typologies and classifications of the American scene, their inclusions, exclusions, and positionings of socioeconomic groups. And the combination of the guidebooks' utilitarian accents with their "official" sponsorship made their plotting of gender, race, ethnicity, and class on the American landscape—indeed, their conferring of cultural ownership of particular sites, spaces, and places—authoritative to a wide range of interested constituencies.

How the politics of representation played out in particular guidebooks was intensely site-specific. This book first lays out, in Chapters 1 and 2, the cultural dynamics of the guidebooks as a genre in the context of the administrative and editorial policies established by the central project office in Washington, D.C. Then it moves to five locations—distinctly different in demographics, politics, and economies—to discover the various intrusions of federal sponsorship into state and local community building across the country.

Idaho, subject of Chapter 3, is famous for sprinting ahead of larger and richer places to publish the first state guidebook in 1937. Here, the dominant agenda was that of the state director, Vardis Fisher, who managed to defy the central office to imprint his own individualist, masculinist, and anticollectivist agenda on the form, in the process establishing certain benchmarks for the series as a whole. Chapter 4 exposes the other side of the coin. The Highway Route Series—*U.S. One* (1938), *The Ocean Highway* (1938), and *The Oregon Trail* (1939)—was almost entirely under the editorial control of Katharine Kellock, national tours editor in the central office; thus it imprints a progressive, New Deal version of America with atypically unmediated zeal. Chapter 5 covers the political turmoil of New York City, tracking the means by which the most energetic left-wing voices of the project were simultaneously represented and contained by the processes of production and textualization informing *New York Panorama* (1938) and the *Guide to New York City* (1939). In Chapter 6, the production of *North Carolina* (1939) is read for what it suggests about the complex formations and interests of local knowledge, especially regarding race, class, and gender. Chapter 7 looks at the left in Missouri—a very different configuration from radicals in New York City—and traces the turbulent and tortuous steps that led to *Missouri* (1941), the guidebook with—of these considered here—the most tenuous and fictive relationship to the area it purports to represent. The book closes with a reflection on the cultural and political uses made of the American Guide Series in the decades since the 1930s.

Then and now, the tendency has been to read the WPA guidebooks as unproblematical celebrations of American democracy and cultural diversity. Resituated within their production and circulation histories, however, the guidebooks expose the complex cultural processes set in train by federal intervention into local image-making, the cultural fallout from the New Deal mapping of public space. This study cannot definitively answer the question of *whose* landscape was inscribed on public consciousness by the American Guide Series. The stories in the following pages do suggest, however, how fiercely and variously that process mattered to a vast constituency of stakeholders in the representation of America. Remembering and analyzing these stories also matters now, as U.S. public debate mushrooms once more around the proper role of government in the cultural lives of its citizenry.

The WPA
Guides

The Cultural Work of Guidebooks

They call it the American Guide Series. But it is the states themselves, talking.
—Stephen Vincent Benét

As contributors to the shaping of a national citizenry, the WPA guidebooks carried a double authority: the truth claims of an informational genre and the official sponsorship of the federal government. This chapter considers how the first of these was yoked to the second: how the Writers' Project central office mobilized the conventions and expectations of the guidebook genre in support of New Deal aspirations, along with some of the ruses and responses that process involved. The next chapter looks at the internal imposition of a federal agenda on the project's employment policies, administrative structures, and editorial practices. Subsequent chapters move out to the states, to explore more extensively how local interests alternately collided and negotiated with these attempts—rhetorical and administrative— at centralized regulation and what versions of community were imprinted on the guidebooks out of that process.

Travel guides had a particular charge in the context of the New Deal in mapping public space and landscape. In response to the widespread social upheaval, economic collapse, and personal suffering of the 1930s, Roosevelt's administration created a social safety net of "alphabet agencies." The Works Progress Administration and the Civilian Conservation Corps organized the unemployed into huge workforces, which (among other tasks) or-

3

chestrated the scenery along the highways that more and more Americans were driving. The result was what Alexander Wilson calls "the massive conceptual reorganization of the landscape" into a nationally regulated pattern (43); Phoebe Cutler describes the New Deal landscape as "a wholesome combination of work, play, and education" (4). The American Guide Series supported this effort by teaching the public how to read this landscape-in-the-making: introducing Americans (selectively) to their histories, mapping social categories for them, and brokering cultural identities. The guidebooks were not the only educational initiatives in the public interpretation of landscape—others emerged from the National Park Service and the Department of the Interior, as well as from state and local cultural agencies that increased their efforts toward preservation, education, and display during this period—but none were so closely tied, by production and rhetoric, to the New Deal's vision of the United States as a nation of communities (Kammen 299–527).

The authority of the WPA guidebooks—and the tautology on which that authority potentially rests—is nicely underscored in a story by Harold Rosenberg. Rosenberg, who had served as both national magazine editor and national art editor in the Federal Writers' Project, was sent out to Washington State in late 1939 to bring that troubled and tardy guidebook to completion. When the state WPA administrator closed down the local project, Rosenberg and his assistant, Mary Lloyd, had to scramble to finish the volume on their own. For one incomplete section of tours, they asked an English professor from the unrecorded region up near the Canadian border to talk through the routes, making up numbers for the scattered populations as they went along. The result was reviewed by a writer from the area as the most accurate factual guide of the series. When the Census Bureau came to compile its lists soon after, it used the guidebook's figures for the remote region. "They didn't want to go up there either," said Rosenberg, "and thought, well, these fellows were just there. . . . We closed the doors both ways. I mean, what could be more accurate than a figure that's by the Census Bureau and what could be more accurate to the Census Bureau than a figure made up by some people who didn't bother to count anybody? As soon as you start counting, you make mistakes."[1]

One of the generic qualities crucial to this kind of authority is that guidebooks do not announce themselves as ideological. Clearly, an individual's or group's perceived relationship to place can be decisive in the formation of political consciousness, as the anecdote by Theodore Ward that is the epigraph to the introduction to this book suggests. Travel guides' intervention in this process is primarily taxonomic: cultural ownership and social hierarchies are played out, implicitly, in the ordering and naming of landscape and cityscape; functional ends disguise ideologically loaded means; the genre's documentary status camouflages its constructions as found landscapes and social relations. "Americans Discover America" was the oft-repeated claim of American Guide Series publicists on radio and in the periodical press, from the first spoken and published statements of Harry Hopkins as WPA administrator to the brouhaha surrounding "American Guide Week" in 1941.[2] Thus, for example, Roland Barthes analyzes the ideological charge of the *Blue Guide* to Spain, which lends implicit support to Francisco Franco's regime by "reducing geography to the description of an uninhabited world of monuments" (76). And Janet Wolff traces ways in which "travel vocabularies" both naturalize masculinist perspectives and infiltrate them into larger social and theoretical discourses (11).

The trope of use contributes to the political sleight of hand. Guidebooks bring readers into a particularly applied relationship with their ideological templates—whether users agree or quarrel with their readings of specific sites—while, at the same time, conferring the illusion of individual control over the operation: what Ivan Doig has called the genre's "see-it-yourself" quality (21). In materializing reading, travel guides shift responsibility for the production of myths of national cohesiveness onto the volumes' users; by reading sights within those framing myths—even by reading in resistance to those frameworks—the guidebook user is connecting ideologies with place. Part of this process is illuminated by W. J. T. Mitchell, who points to the relationship between management of place and of cultural identity by reconceptualizing landscape as cultural *practice*: "Landscape as a cultural medium . . . has a double role with respect to something like ideology: it naturalizes a cultural and social construction, representing an artificial world as if it were simply given and inevitable, and it also makes that representation operational by interpellating its beholder in some more or less determinate relation to its givenness as sight and site. . . . Landscape *circulates* as a medium of exchange, a site of visual appropriation, a focus for the formation of identity" (2).

5

That the purposes of the Federal Writers' Project went hand in hand with the genre's naturalized authority is shown partly by the discourses of circulation eschewed and enabled by the central office. Publicity for the project avoided the explicitly political, playing down the guidebooks' connection to the New Deal and to work relief. The perils of the association were proven not just by the considerable brouhaha in Congress and beyond about the Writers' Project as a propaganda agency but by moments of reception beyond the central office's control. For example, when a favorable *New York Times* review of the Virginia guide turns to the political, its language shifts into something approaching the alarmist: a "missionary spirit projects New Deal aims, aspirations and preferences. . . . The New Deal is not mentioned, but the right perspective of serious Virginia concerns is considerably distorted in the general assembly of the essays which precede the guide book proper. In other words, we have here not only tourist promotion, but social propaganda."

Central office press releases skirted the guidebooks' commercial imperatives almost as assiduously as they did the political. The period was on the cusp of the touristic age. The era of mass tourism had not yet begun, but travel and its more modest accessories did experience something of a boom in the Depression and New Deal years. One report assessed that "American tourists . . . spent nearly half a billion dollars abroad even in the depression depths of 1932"; expenditures for gas rose, though car sales did not, and cheap camping sites proliferated (Barkley; Belasco 142–43; Jakle). There was enough money to be made from tourism and enough sense that America was failing to exploit its touristic potential that the Senate held hearings in 1935 on a bill "to encourage travel to and within the United States," which led to the creation of the U.S. Travel Bureau (Barkley; Bustard 104). Certainly, project personnel were conscious of the growing market: in one address to a gathering of state officials, Darrel McConkey, a representative from the central office, stressed that tourism was the second biggest industry in 1936; Henry Alsberg, national director of the Federal Writers' Project signed an article in the *New York Times* stressing the commercial potential of guidebooks. And yet the language of tourism does not dominate guidebook publicity; the architects of the American Guide Series had loftier ambitions to reeducate an entire citizenry.

Part of what the WPA guides guarantee, according to the terms of their circulation, is a united nation. That unity is figured, first, in the representation of the guidebook audience as the harmonious sum of quintessential American citizens: what Jonathan Harris, talking of the Federal Art Project's contribution to the formation of New Deal citizenry, describes as "a subject bonded into legitimate economic, juridical and familial relations; a citizen among a multitude of citizens located within the social structure but unmarked by class, gender or racial antagonisms" (40). This vision of an unproblematical collective is perceptible in Henry Alsberg's claim that the American Guide Series' "publication must eventually, I am immodest enough to imagine, effect the conception of America by Americans."[3] That claim is echoed in Lewis Mumford's description of the series as "the first attempt, on a comprehensive scale, to make the country itself worthily known to Americans" (306–7) and in publishers' assumptions of a middle-class readership—they emphasized that the guidebooks had been priced "well within the average means" ("44 Publishers"; Bindas 114).

That the collective subject positions offered by the guidebooks were much more partial and conflicted than suggested by this rhetoric of circulation is demonstrated by the trajectories of project employees, from guidebook authors, to subjects, to readers. Fieldworkers, sent out to document the local scene, could well be writing about themselves or a community they identified as their own: Ralph Ellison has talked about how collecting folklore in Harlem, as a project employee, "threw me into my own history" (Banks xix). Editors in Washington, D.C., however, were prepared to substitute "expert" for local accounts when the latter diverged too far from their blueprint for the guidebook: both James Thompson of the Oklahoma Project and Jack Balch of Missouri went on record as objecting to the unrecognizable portraits by these state guides.

Exclusions were particularly stark along race lines. Sterling Brown, national Negro affairs editor, objected on several occasions that the guidebooks were addressed to white travelers. W. T. Couch, associate state director in North Carolina, worried that his state's volume amounted to "whitewash" because it failed to note (and therefore work toward the correction of) the lack of tourist facilities for blacks in the South.[4] And as the following chapters demonstrate, the guidebook gaze was often gendered male, with greater or lesser degrees of explicitness. W. J. T. Mitchell assumes an Althusserian operation for landscape, asserting that it "interpellates" its beholders. That

7

operation is distinctly partial in the guidebooks: their production of landscape "hails" certain social groups more than others, presenting traveling perspectives and personae available for identification only by selected constituencies of readers. Although there was much emphasis on the cultural diversity discovered by the guides, that multiplicity is distanced—out there, in the surrounding landscape—from a fairly homogeneous guidebook user.

These exclusions then mark the larger body politic conjured up by the rhetoric accompanying the guides' circulation. For example, Lewis Stiles Gannett's review of the series, which can be seen as part of both dissemination and reception, reads: "It is no accident of the Depression that we have today in the WPA *American Guides* our first real series of handbooks to the nation. . . . We do not know where we are or why we are so confused; and in the absence of firm counsels for present and future we go back to our roots, trying to discover how we got that way" ("Reading" 1818). The question begged by Gannett, of course, is "who are 'we'?" or "which 'we'?" Alfred Kazin talked, in similar terms, about "a literature of collective self-consciousness" (486). The record of production exposes some of the exclusions on which these claims to inclusiveness are based. Both New Deal priorities and local politics affected the differential visibility accorded social groups as well as the conceptualization of the intended reader, as later chapters in this book demonstrate. Results differed across the country: the Idaho guidebook basically privileged men, the North Carolina guidebook basically privileged whites, the Highway Route Series basically privileged types who fitted the Progressive paradigm. Structurally, however, the published guidebooks shared a common function: they worked to demarcate cultural insiders from outsiders against the American landscape and cityscape.

The guidebooks also served national unity by contributing to the growth of American cultural confidence. The most basic expectation of the genre—that the landscape was interesting enough to sustain a guidebook's attention—had particular purchase in a period whose public discourse was heavy with cultural self-consciousness. The series was lauded for shaking off European cultural imperialism, specifically giving the lie to the cultural stereotypes of Karl Baedeker, who had produced a modest one-volume guide to the United States in 1893. One project administrator, Howard Greene, wrote to the vice-president of the Association of American Railroads: "Many foreigners think of America as largely consisting of a primeval forest populated by red Indians ready to pounce upon and scalp them. The guide will have the effect of disabusing the minds of prospective foreign visitors of this illusion at any rate. . . . There is as much variety among the people of America as there is in Europe and South America."[5] The dominant tone in newspaper coverage of the guides is relief that America's cultural legitimacy has been proven. Reviewing the series in 1941—under the heading "Guides Better Than Baedeker's"—Louis Bromfeld welcomed them as a democratic necessity for America: "It is true that a good many wealthy and snobbish American travellers remained indifferent to the need so long as Europe existed as a tourist's paradise, but Europe no longer remains, and Europe, even when the war is ended, will remain a tourist's desert for at least another generation." Cultural diversity was a sign that the country had come of age on the international stage.

It was a small step from correcting the record to wiping it clean: publicity repeatedly effaced previous U.S. productions—such as the See America First series of the 1920s—by insisting on the WPA guidebooks' status as the first indigenous guidebooks to provide country-wide coverage. The resulting tabula rasa made plausible hyperbolic claims for the guidebooks' "panoramic" and "comprehensive" accounts. A typical leaflet declared, "For the native there will be a Columbian discovery of his own heath"; even the press most hostile to the Writers' Project seemed to accept this claim, admiring the guidebooks' conversion of an "unknown continent" into what Jared Putnam called the "new America," "the real America."[6] These claims that the guidebooks got to the heart of the country and confirmed its place on the world stage raised the stakes on their contents. Not only were representations mooted as unmediated discoveries, but they carried the weight of America's claims to cultural maturity.

A third mark of unity touted in the guidebooks' circulation, one again connected to cultural status, was the aesthetic. Repeatedly, project personnel claimed that the American Guide Series birthed a national populist style: what John Newsom, national director from late 1939, called in a radio talk "plain Americans anxious to make their community better known to the nation, and the nation better known to their community."[7] The focus on style and voice was useful partly because it removed the guides from the political arena to the mystificatory realm of the aesthetic. But the eagerness with which the sympathetic press repeated the aesthetic claim suggests that it had a wider efficacy for building national confidence. On 10 May 1941, the *Washington Post* praised the series as "the WPA project which raised the usual rubberneck handbook to the status of first-class literature." Lewis Mumford made the collectively composed guidebooks representative of a dominant 1930s' social realist schema when he praised them for manifesting "that ultimate purity of literary style which is free from merely individualistic mannerism" (306–7). And the London *Times* of 22 July 1939 agreed: "One is amazed at what appears to be the country-wide emergence of a contemporary American style, in exposition especially, which is lucid, subtle, and intense."

How much mystification is at work in the identification of a unified, grassroots, modern style is suggested by the stories I will tell in subsequent chapters of struggles, negotiations, and acts of cultural appropriation. For example, many states, from Massachusetts to South Carolina, sought to emphasize their historical achievements, according to local standards of distinctiveness, only to have editors in Washington, D.C., pick through and reject any representations or organizational practices or rhetorical styles that failed to conform to the central office's principles of progress and modernity. Within states, there was considerable vying of cultural interests, too: more often than not, for example, Native American voices were heard only indirectly and African Americans were underrepresented in the organization, with visible consequences for guidebook copy. The Oklahoma office's response to the central office's stylistic fiats—itemized in the next chapter—demonstrates a sense of alienation quite at odds with these claims for a singular "American tradition" expressed by a diversity of "plain American" voices: "We have wondered why we must use simple declarative sentences (and that is what they are, even when connected interminably by semicolons) when the most feeble impulse in our brains demands something else. . . . The Guide Book . . . is not ours" (qtd. in McDonald 744–45).

All the rhetoric about the guides reuniting the nation was further enhanced by the genre's management of difference. The terms in which the guide series offered place as a system of social differentiation were considerably less threatening to the status quo than the other discourses of difference currently in the ascendancy among liberal and left intellectuals, that is, discourses of class and race. According to the conventions of this genre, the disruptions of difference are contained—or at least camouflaged—by the larger scheme of orderly diversity. Although each guidebook tells a site-specific story, the series as a whole is marked by a tendency to naturalize social difference—even social dysfunction—as "local color," part of an ultimately harmonious landscape defined as "the nation." The power of that tendency is suggested by the case of the guidebooks most explicitly marked by left politics: the two guides to New York City, in which social and political criticism is contained by its incorporation into the contemporary scene (see Chapter 5).

The genre also offers an unthreatening introduction to modernity, crucial cultural work in a period of widespread social dislocation. Predominantly a series for automotive travel, the guides positioned the reader-traveler within modernity in terms that smack of control and safety. Mobility, especially when both individualistic and technologically sophisticated, has long been a central trope of American identity, propagated in frontier mythologies and other narratives of socioeconomic advance. Phil Patton has demonstrated "the special status of the road in the metaphorical landscape of the American mind," symbolizing the "American Dream" of democratic opportunity and individualistic progress in many periods (9). In the 1930s, documentary photographers, writers, artists, and filmmakers on the left challenged that received image. Looking to expose the felt reality of economic devastation, they refigured travel along America's highways as a "drift of human atoms": sign and symbol of familial, social, and national collapse (Rorty 56). In Lawrence Levine's words, Depression bewilderment was symbolized by "a good deal of movement without direction" (210). Borrowing many of the textual and visual techniques of the documentarists, the guidebooks reversed that representation. With their essays, tours, maps, and photographs, they chart orderly, purposeful movement along the main arteries and back roads of America. The genre's claims to unmediated representation also had a particular efficacy in this connection. As Alan Trachtenberg has said of the Farm Security Administration (FSA) photographic file: "A quest for 'the real' had another significance in this decade of exodus, of uprootedness and movement: it was also a quest for place, a desire for images of rooted settlements and familiar landmarks" (65).

Part of the control promised by guidebooks came from the accrual of knowledge that one commentator, in the *Pathfinder* of 17 December 1938, averred was missing from American mobility: "Americans own more than 26 million cars and have the best highways and railroads on earth. . . . They are the most travelminded people in the world but their travel is 2% education and 98% locomotion." The more closely the central office controlled a guide's publication, the more directly was this educational project linked to Progressivism. This mapped movement offers carefully demarcated travelers the opportunity to read themselves into a historically and culturally dense landscape in terms that are coherent, informed, and contained. The roads charted in the Highway Route Series (see Chapter 4), for example, take automobile drivers through scenes whose natural and architectural details demonstrate the steady rise of American civilization.

The cultural authority of all these messages was reinforced by their dissemination via other discourses of cultural citizenship: tourism, education, immigration, military training, and the transportation systems of people's daily lives. Volumes in the American Guide Series were distributed to public schools, to refugee centers, and to the libraries of military bases, as well as being prominently exhibited in bookshops, department stores, hotels, transportation depots, and advertisements throughout the subway system. By mid-1936, 431 radio stations were using Works Progress Administration radio material; guidebooks also featured in what Warren Susman calls apparatuses of "social reinforcement": game shows (162). On occasion, too, guidebook information was marketed under the "Believe It or Not!" rubric, which linked the series to the knowledge-as-entertainment industry beginning to boom with Robert Ripley's extremely popular newspaper and radio productions. Again, the conventions of an informational genre—functionality, accessibility, ordered diversity—were crucial in enabling high claims of national maturity to be inserted, without dissonance, into a wide range of cultural and institutional practices.

Accumulatively, the rhetorical maneuvers attending production, circulation, and public reception attempt to yoke the guidebooks to discourses of Americanism—that is, discourses that aspire to "fix" cultural identity and provide a natural order to social relations. This is a distinctly different function from that theorized for the vocabulary of travel post–World War II. Dean MacCannell, among others, has argued that the tourist functions as paradigmatic modern man (since the tourist is always gendered masculine) in his state of commodified nomadism. The American Guide Series uses travel to produce a landscape that reverses images of nomadism. In the

WPA guidebooks, landscapes become sites of stability and cultural reassurance: comforting in the density of their historical and contemporary sights, in their evidence of progress, in their orderliness, and in their conversion of social inequities and dislocations into a "safe space" for those travelers able to share the gaze offered by these guides.

The political utility of all the rhetorical maneuvers surrounding the floating of the guidebooks—the claims that they reveal and enable stable, unified, carefully demarcated cultural identities for America—became particularly stark when the project had to be steered through changing ideological climates. Attacks on the project were refuted in the name of the linkage among regional diversity, national unity, and patriotism. For example, publishers appealed to the regional base of project activities to defend it against charges of communism made by the Dies Committee: "America is a nation of communities, each rich in its special lore, customs and history. The Federal Writers' Project books have delved deeply into this picture of its true character." Similarly, Bernard DeVoto, editor of *Harper's Magazine* and recognized dean of American letters, defended Katharine Kellock before another congressional investigative committee: "Her work on the WPA American Guide Series is evidence of her fundamental and unshakable Americanism. . . . It is in itself a vindication of her loyalty and patriotism," an imprimatur that he also intoned in *Harper's Magazine*: "The guidebooks are an educational force and even a patriotic force, an honorable addition to our awareness of ourselves and of our country" ("Project" 222). Michael Kammen has identified this joining of populism with patriotism as a signal development of the 1930s and the WPA guidebooks as a key mechanism in the linkage (464).[8]

With the onset of World War II, the guidebooks were harnessed to the war effort. By this stage, the Writers' Project had become the Writers' Unit of the War Services Subdivision of the Work Projects Administration, producing, among other publications, a series of Servicemen's Recreational Guides. But the link between the American Guide Series and national defense had been laid earlier, in the rhetoric of their circulation: the slippage between regionalism and nationalism was facilitated by the guidebooks' evidence of national community, and their genre conventions had long been represented as natural conduits for a rich outpouring of "the people's" voices. Spokespeople of very different orders repeated the trope. Lawrence

Estavan, a former employee of the San Francisco Writers' Project, compared the comprehensiveness of the American Guide Series to the eighteenth-century French encyclopedias, calling it "perhaps the first large scale contribution toward this national awareness, which is the backbone of national defense." An anonymous commentator in the *Jacksonville Journal* (Florida) of 13 January 1941 wrote:

In this hour—when all available man-power and industry are being mobilized for the national defense program—we should remember that an American takes pride in his community, state and nation only after he has acquired a broad knowledge of their democratic character, and has seen how he, as an individual, fits into the American tradition. By providing such knowledge, the WPA Writers' Project is making a definite, though indirect, contribution to the national defense program. . . .

As long as such institutions as the Writers' Project are allowed to provide a realistic basis for patriotic feeling, we need not fear the Himmlers.

Roosevelt himself contributed to this rhetoric in November 1941, during American Guide Week, with its slogan "Take Pride in Your Country." Linking regionalism, democracy, and patriotism, he declared: "All [guidebooks] were compiled and written on the spot by men and women who knew the particular locale in all its richness, with the result that the books clearly and graphically portray not only the ideals and traditions shared by all Americans but also the diverse local patterns of thought and behaviour that distinguish our free and democratic way of life. . . . At this time of crisis, when every student needs to know what America is and what it stands for, educators everywhere should be aware of the invaluable contribution that has been made by the American Guide Series."[9]

How all these textual strategies and rhetorical claims were actualized by specific readers and travelers—whether or how the ideologically ambitious terms of the guidebooks' circulation were perceptibly matched by use—is a question beyond the available archive. Even hypothesis is difficult because the genre is multiply readable, not just for its differing interpretations but quite literally, for who read what in which order. As Katharine Kellock, national tours editor, noted, different professional and political purposes delivered different readings: "Whereas the reviewers have skipped back and forward through the books, skimming over introductory articles on subjects that appealed to them and hunting out descriptions of towns and countrysides they happened to know, the critics have read the guides from cover to cover as they would novels" (474). It is also clear that multiple audiences and various uses were anticipated by—and therefore influenced—the architects of the guide series. Kellock directed colleagues to think of state directors as typical readers because she was primarily concerned with the accuracy and practicality of tour directions. In contrast, Henry Alsberg, national director, was at least as concerned about metropolitan reviewers—whose opinions circulated via national and international media—as he was about local users. And at all levels of the project, editors and administrators were edgily conscious of their political paymasters who could use the guidebooks as evidence for or against the project's right to continued funding from the public purse.

That some readers did identify, and quarrel with, guidebook ideologies is most easily documented in the reception by the public bodies influencing fiscal appropriations. Tellingly, flash points of contestation tended to occur precisely when the fault lines of class, race, or ethnicity reasserted themselves in the guides' representations of the American scene. Members of Congress denounced the Washington, D.C., guide for documenting that George Washington's step-grandson (and son by adoption) fathered a part-African American daughter, a public furor was stage-managed in response to the Massachusetts guide's exposure of the politics of ethnicity in the Sacco-Vanzetti trial, and the local press expressed outrage at the momentary foregrounding of racial privilege in the guide to North Carolina (see Chapter 6).

The attitudes of individual travelers to guidebook representations, in the face of material sites, presumably ran a gamut beyond my itemization or the guidebooks' rhetorical control. What can be said is that the genre offers in situ users a powerful operation: simultaneous withdrawal to a more coherent, more mapped world and immersion in the felt reality of landscapes and cityscapes. Some users embraced that combination. In Frederick Gutheim's account, the tripartite structure of state guidebooks—discursive essays, city descriptions, and tours—organizes the traveler's experience so thoroughly that the slippage from the textual to the "real" goes unremarked: the traveler reads the essays at home, as an introduction to the destination, then plans the trip on the basis of city and tour descriptions, then carries the guide only for reference when necessary, without being distracted from "soaking up the real thing" (4). What is at work here is the unacknowledged establishment of norms, with results evident in the Idaho guidebook: that volume's assumption of the wilderness as the "real" West naturalizes individualism and masculinism in varied forms. For some travelers, however, the use imperative not only exposed but mitigated against the guidebooks' ideological ambitions: Bernard DeVoto complained, "When we are touring, we'd trade fifty pages of interpretation for one page of pertinent information. . . . We don't think that people do their philosophical generalizing with fifty miles more to go before dinner. It isn't a guidebook if you have to leave it in the car" ("WPA").

One difference in this range of use lies in the responses available to visitors versus residents and, in the second group, readers who self-identified as cultural insiders compared to those who felt positioned as cultural outsiders. Those who recognize themselves, individually or by social group, as having some sort of agency and significant presence in the guidebooks tend to question only the specificities of the information. By contrast, cultural outsiders—those effaced from or naturalized into the scene as passive "local color," by virtue of their racial, class, or gender affiliation—occasionally challenge a guidebook's very frame of reference. Reading against the grain of naturalized representation seems, however, an uphill job. In recognizing and resisting the constructedness of an account, those erased by it seem to get no further than reading the gap. To jump to a fictional, European example, Janice Galloway's rebellious and quarrelsome guidebook user, in *Foreign Parts*, continually chafes against the ideological templates of her tour guides but never manages to shake them off. However exasperated she becomes with the guide's failure to acknowledge her perspective as a woman or the layered and complex lives of its subjects, she continues to follow designated itineraries and routes. An analogous chafing at the American Guide Series was occasionally visible in the black press (see, for example, the *Opportunity* review of the North Carolina guide, in Chapter 6) and, more frequently, in local newspapers outraged by some oversight in the representation of their constituency.

On-site readings—whether by visitors or residents, individuals or communities—clearly heightened the intensity of interest. Cultural and geographical groups gauged how visibly a guidebook put them on the map and judged its worth accordingly. Thus, "Lancaster will be able to see what the United States government thinks of the county on October 1, the publication date set for the huge 'American Guide' designed to tell the tourist what to see wherever he goes," declared the *Lancaster* (Pennsylvania) *News*, while a headline from the *Witchita* (Kansas) *Eagle* celebrated: "The American Guide Puts Wichita on 'Crossroads of Nation.'" The intensity of investment can also be measured by the opposite response: an editorial in the *Jackson* (Michigan) *Citizen Patriot*—titled "A Misguided Guide"—noted that its state guide contained no chapter, no map, no pictures of Jackson, hence "the book, so far as factual information is concerned, belongs properly in the waste basket." The Scranton, Pennsylvania, Chamber of Commerce contemplated taking legal action against the Pennsylvania WPA because of the unflattering and erroneous description of Scranton in the Pennsylvania guide. Individual readers and travelers also seemed to read for the landscapes they knew and whose representation they felt the authority to critique: a Missouri state employee described the arrival of their guidebook off the press: "Everyone has grabbed it to look up his home town, or some special spot dear to his heart."[10]

Perhaps, ultimately, the salient point is the depth of investment in the guidebooks' representations by a wide range of interested constituencies. On the one hand, the federal office attempted a hegemonic operation with its blueprint for the series, as the language of reviews and publicity repeatedly suggests: "Uncle Sam steps out in the role of Baedeker, preparing to give his vast constituency a vivid modern picture of their own country. . . . Perhaps these guides, taken together, will enable us for the first time to hold the mirror up to all America" (Duffus). On the other hand, countermoves by objecting groups and individuals across the country, during both production and reception, challenged the casual effacements and seamless panoramic claims of the genre and the rhetoric that flourished around it. The fundamental struggle was for visibility and voice in a series which, it was claimed, would define America both at home and abroad.

In an era dense with demonstratively political genres—photo-textual documentary, reportage of domestic and international upheaval, workers' theater, party manifestos—the guidebooks can seem the least political of documents. In that impression lies at least part of their ideological power. As this chapter has itemized, travel guides have the potential—via their taxonomic representation of landscape, their documentary status, and the trope of use—to intervene in fundamental processes of cultural perception and national self-consciousness. The New Deal harnessed these generic features to particular cultural work: the guaranteeing of a united, harmoniously diverse citizenry; the demarcation of a safe, knowable (and hence controllable) space within all the changes and threats of modernity; and the demonstration of cultural maturity on the international stage. In other words, the WPA volumes were floated as guidelines to cultural citizenship in modern America, with all the appropriations and elisions that notion evokes.

The Federal Writers' Project

In 1935, the United States of America sat itself down, took its pen in hand, and started to write a book.

—*Raleigh News and Observer*, 9 November 1941

The above epigraph was widely reproduced during American Guide Week, the event organized to celebrate the completion of the American Guide Series. As I suggested in the previous chapter, the presentation of the series as an unmediated outpouring of national diversity was central to its marketing and political appeal. The employment policies, organizational structures, and editorial practices of the Writers' Project show how highly managed, and conflicted, production in fact was. In many ways, project policies and practices attempted to shape employees as proper citizens of the modern, bureaucratized nation. That regulatory process then passed into guidebook copy, along with the strains attendant on the confrontation of central management by local resistance of various political stripes.

With the Arts Projects, the New Deal offered workers a culture of collectivity much different from what Michael Denning calls the thriving "union culture" of the 1930s (68). Organizationally, the projects brought together government bureaucracy and cultural production in ways that clearly had implications for the definition of "socially useful" art. Employees' reactions differed. Anthony Velonis, an Arts Project employee, celebrated the projects for "rescu[ing] a generation of artists to become productive citizens rather than cynical revolutionaries" (qtd. in Bustard 18-19). Anzia Yezierska, writing of her time on the New York Writers' Project, recorded at least one employee's bitter resentment at capitalist quietism: "Mass bribery, that's what W.P.A. is. Government blackmail. We'd fight, we'd stage riots and revolutions if they didn't hush us up. We're all taking hush money" (162). Other autobiographical, fictional, and institutional accounts show how leftist union activity infiltrated and complicated project workings in some cities and states (see, for example, Roskolenko, MacLeod).

The Federal Writers' Project was centrally managed by a small group of East Coast intellectuals who attempted to stamp their version of cultural nationalism on a diverse and geographically dispersed body of workers. Pressure from the center took different forms and meant different things in different places: in North Carolina, for example, an unusual alliance of local interests emerged in opposition to Washington's dictates, whereas in Missouri, some local workers hoped to lever out established state interests by making common cause with East Coast Progressives. A common pattern across the heterogeneous relations was the central office's insistence that its vision of diversity represented desirable, forward-looking regionalism while local priorities amounted to retrograde provincialism.

One of the few characteristics shared by the vast proportion of project employees was that they came from the breadlines. Their qualifications as "writers" were varied and sometimes tenuous in the extreme: the project hired—in Harold Rosenberg's rather dismissive phrase—"anyone who could write English" (99). Jerre Mangione, the project's national coordinating editor, characterizes their variety: "Lawyers, teachers, librarians, doctors, architects, recent college graduates (among them Studs Terkel, Saul Bellow, Ralph Ellison) rubbed elbows with published authors such as Conrad Aiken, Edward Dahlberg, Miriam Allen de Ford, Maxwell Bodenheim, Claude McKay, Nelson Algren, Jack Conroy; and with such promising young writers as Richard Wright, Kenneth Rexroth, Loren Eiseley, Norman Macleod, Margaret Walker" ("Project" 33). Some employees went off Mangione's scale: as James McGraw, who interviewed applicants for the New York City office, tells it: "There was (and this is an actual story) a letter carrier who came in. When he was asked why he was sent they [sic] said they knew he was a man of letters. And all sorts of other strange fringe people, people who had called themselves writers because they had written letters to the newspapers protesting things and public officials, and so on."[1] These workers tended to operate at street- and highway-level, as fieldworkers, sometimes state editors, combing published records and unpublished archives, conducting interviews, logging roads for tour details, and writing up copy for editing further up the line.

What did it feel like to be plucked out of destitution and set to work writing travel guides at the lowly end of the blue-pencil chain, often worlds away from the power center of Washington, D.C.? One sketch is paraphrased from 1930s author Paul de Kruif: "The ordinary WPA employee had no travel allowance. He toured on his thumb, and sat at night in a cheap room pouring out thousands of his finest words describing the America in which he was an economic outcast. What is worse, the best-loved of his essays came out as one cryptic sentence, and someone else's sentence at that" (Horlings 502). Ralph Ellison (who served on the New York City project) offers a different impression: he agreed with Margaret Walker of the Chicago project that certain individuals and constituencies were empowered by their employment in the field: "The entire WPA system gave Negro intellectuals, clerical people and so on the first opportunity that they had ever had to exercise their skills and, as with me, to learn new skills. There's no doubt about it, that, to that extent, the economic and social disaster of the country was a freeing experience for the Negro people."[2] The project has also been credited with halting the literary evacuation of the American hinterland by sponsoring writing activity beyond the magnet of New York City ("Writers' Project: 1942" 480).

With such a heterogeneity of employee profiles, it is difficult to generalize about the imprint of these workers on the American Guide Series. Not only did they bring a wide range of political, social, and professional allegiances to the project, but employees at this level differed in their sense of how they related to their production. Because workers could be hired only in their area of residence, they were all potentially, at one and the same time, subjects, coauthors (to some degree), and readers of the guidebooks. For Paul de Kruif's anonymous worker, clearly there was paradox in writing about an America from which he was outcast. In contrast, Ralph Ellison's observation, quoted in the previous chapter, demonstrates that guidebook work gave him ownership of an African American heritage made newly visible to him. Some of the range of employees' attitudes is visible in the chapters that follow: the fiery young writers on the left, from New York City to

Missouri, who tried to enlist the guidebooks in the war against the status quo; the political appointees who understood the guidebooks as advertising for the state's established interests; the cultural custodians, for whom the guidebooks were bulwarks against change or incursion from elsewhere; the "local heroes" who claimed the guidebooks as their own mouthpieces on the basis that theirs were "representative" voices. The reactions and agendas of project employees were myriad and intensely site-specific.

More socially and ideologically homogeneous was the group of key administrators and editors in the central office in Washington, D.C., who steered the production of the American Guide Series for as long as the project was under federal sponsorship. The routes by which these officials entered the project, the editorial principles and practices they thrashed out, and their cultural and political assumptions all reflected negotiations with state workers and the guidebook copy that resulted. The template imposed on guidebook production by the central office was so strong that its influence remained even after September 1939, when the project was devolved to state sponsorship and editorial control by congressional mandate.

The project's main architects were hand-picked by Jacob Baker, a staunch New Dealer in charge of white-collar projects in the WPA (and himself hand-picked by Harry Hopkins). Working within the networks of East Coast, Ivy League intellectuals, Baker put together a group—not from the relief rolls—already bonded by ideology, class, and gender. The casual insiderism of the process is suggested by Henry Alsberg's reminiscences about his own entrance into New Deal service in 1934 as supervisor of reports and bulletins for the Federal Emergency Relief Administration, forerunner to the WPA: "Jake Baker got all his radical, liberal friends down [chuckles] and, out of a clear sky . . . I saw him; he said, 'why don't you come down, it's a lot of fun'; and, eh, so I came down." Vincent McHugh, a relief roll employee who elected not to join the Washington office, throws the class dimension into sharp relief: "One reason I never wanted to move to Washington during that time was that the Wash. HQ was middle class and since I come from a working-class family I felt much more comfortable with the NY crowd." And the Washington office was overwhelmingly male, many of them bachelors who bonded together in homosocial camaraderie fictionalized by John Cheever, briefly one of this group (Mangione, *Dream* 102-3). Region and race were common factors too: mostly East Coast by education if not birth, many of the Washington officers knew Europe better than the American hinterland, and the vast majority identified themselves as whites with Euro-American lineages. This group formed the National Office of the Writers' Project, an office with a degree of centralized, mainly editorial, power unusual within the WPA structure.[3]

Among the most visible figures in this group was Henry Alsberg, appointed national director of the Federal Writers' Project by Harry Hopkins, on the advice of Jacob Baker, in July 1935. He was a fifty-seven-year-old Jewish bachelor and self-dubbed "philosophical anarchist" (characterized by others as a "tired radical of the 20s") whose previous career had the international, freelance cast of the well-educated, economically comfortable man without responsibilities (Mangione, *Dream* 56). After some years in law, he worked in the New York press, first as an editorial writer, then as a foreign correspondent across Europe and Mexico. He had also seen foreign service in the U.S. embassy in Turkey and as director of the American Joint Distribution Committee providing emergency famine relief in Russia in 1922 and 1923, an experience that had made him highly skeptical of Soviet regimentation and led him to edit *Letters from Russian Prisoners* as a way of protesting Soviet persecution of dissidents. Back in the United States, Alsberg contributed to the fostering of independent, experimental American voices by becoming a director of the Provincetown Playhouse in New York City, as well as adapting the Yiddish play *The Dybbuk*.[4]

With all this in his past, Alsberg brought to the Writers' Project a visionary sense of its potential to join social reform with the democratic renaissance of American letters; Kellock said that Alsberg harbored "Greenwich Village dreams of sponsoring genius." He became infamous for breeding administrative chaos: in the words of his assistant director, "Henry, in addition to being a philosophical anarchist, was a sort of anarchist about the way he ran an office." Yet it was widely agreed that his missionary zeal made the project much more ambitious and exciting than it otherwise would have been, as well as giving him the patience to negotiate the endlessly conflicting demands of writers' unions, politicians, WPA administrators, and scholarly and heritage groups and to mediate between warring political factions within the project. His role as peacemaker probably also prolonged the project's life when it came under attack as a communist hotbed in 1938 by Martin Dies's Committee on Un-American Activities and Clifton A. Woodrum's subcommittee of the House Committee on Appropriations. He himself, however, was a casualty of that process, dismissed in 1939 when the project lost its federal status, to be replaced by John Newsom, a former army officer whose attitude was considerably more managerial and less fervent about national culture.[5]

To oversee editorial structures more closely, Baker appointed George Cronyn, whom he had known among the literati of Greenwich Village, as associate director. A little younger than Alsberg, Cronyn had led a roving life of a different order: he had been a cowboy in New Mexico, a rancher in Oregon, then an instructor at the University of Montana, which meant that, unlike almost everyone else in the central office, he had experience and knowledge of the West. He had also been a magazine and encyclopedia editor, author of two novels—the best-selling *Fool of Venus* (1934) and *Fortune and Men's Eyes* (1935)—and editor of an anthology of Native American songs and chants, *The Path of the Rainbow* (1918).[6] However demotic his career and however liberal his editorial priorities, Cronyn had a reputation for autocracy with project employees which, on more than one occasion, exacerbated politically awkward situations. His instructions in "The American Guide Manual" were particularly imperious; he tried to deal with tensions in the California project by a summary dismissal, an action that led to a complaint to Harry Hopkins and the eventual splitting of the state into two project offices, north and south; and his attempts to make Vardis Fisher toe the central office's line only goaded the Idaho director into more flagrant demonstrations of independence. Cronyn's administrative style also exposed a general attitude among national editors: their easy assumption of cultural leadership over the dispossessed, with whom they most certainly sympathized but were not necessarily eager to empower.

Much more the diplomat was Reed Harris, originally brought in by Baker in 1934 to assist Alsberg's editing of the *Project* (a periodical publicizing the work of the Federal Emergency Relief Administration), subsequently assistant director in charge of administrative matters on the Writers' Project. Harris was the youngest of the three. Expelled from Columbia University not many years before for his investigative journalism, he went on to publish *King Football: The Vulgarization of the American College* (1932), an exposé of the corruption around the university football team, and to work in New York City journalism. He became the administrative mainstay of the project, negotiating complex problems with the states and mediating between Cronyn and Alsberg, who frequently clashed over the implementation of policy.[7]

Beyond this three-man directorate and coming to the project by a somewhat different route was Katharine Kellock, who exerted significant editorial influence as national tours editor. Kellock's background was not dissimilar, in its mixture of social work and scholarship, to that of other central editors. She had worked for Lillian Wald's Henry Street Settlement House at home and with Quaker relief groups in western and eastern Europe and Russia; she had written entries for the *Dictionary of American Biography* and done research for her husband's study of Houdini; and she came to the Writers' Project from an editing position in the Resettlement Administration. Kellock was every bit as dedicated to the Writers' Project as Alsberg—she took a $200 pay cut (to $3,600 per annum) to join—but her vision of it was much more practical and less literary. She was also, of course, a woman outside the dominant homosocial community of the central office, and some of the resentment toward her was clearly gendered. When, thirty-five years after the event, Harold Rosenberg wrote about "the contemptuous self-assurance of the head of the 'tours' section of the Guides," then admits that this "lady . . . was to become the dominant editorial power on the Washington staff," one wonders how much of his irritation is at a woman in a position of authority (99–100). Kellock herself commented in later life, "It is unfortunate, I now think, that I had almost no social relations with people on the project. I had been in Washington since 1927, early, and my social life was mainly with people Kel [Harold Kellock] had known before we were married."[8]

All these people had worked at the nexus of government, social reform, and writing, and they clearly believed in the political possibilities of that combination. The Writers' Project forced them to answer additional imperatives. In the course of lobbying for a work program for unemployed writers, Jake Baker, Edwin Rowan, Nina Collier, Clair Laning, and other New Dealers had consulted widely on the question of an appropriate literary undertaking.[9] Recognized authors—consultants included William Carlos Williams, Theodore Dreiser, Conrad Aiken, and Dorothy Canfield Fisher—argued for the sponsorship of established and promising writers in need to allow them to pursue their own literary projects free of government censorship. Writers' unions were concerned with the maintenance of professional skills at minimum wage for a broadly defined range of writers. Politicians and employees of federal agencies, keenly conscious of the need for public accountability, proposed work that was both socially useful and manageable by a broad range of skills: in Harry Hopkins's words, "a compromise between furnishing jobs for relief workers and furnishing culture for America—with the emphasis on the relief aspect" (qtd. in Mangione, "Project" 2). Meanwhile, publishers argued for an undertaking that would not compete with private industry, and businesspeople generally sought a form of work that would provide economic stimulation.

As the guide series emerged, its characteristics finely balanced these demands, and the tensions among them—between, for example, the artistic and the economic, or the cultural and the utilitarian, or authorial autonomy and governmental accountability—continued to mark its production and reception. Planned as a collective production across the entire country involving a large range of research, editing, and writing tasks, the guidebooks provided limited opportunity for creative innovation; in defending the project, Alsberg liked to insist, "The tour form is a difficult form; it is like a sonnet; but, if you can learn it, you can be more interesting in the description of a tour than in any novel" (qtd. in McDonald 694). It was also argued repeatedly that the only guidebook to America was Baedeker's, first published in 1893 and most recently revised in 1909. The lack of competing publications and the inability of publishers to take on such a massive project during the Depression meant that the American Guide Series provided a distinct national service that would stimulate tourism as well as regional and national pride without undercutting private industry. Although the Writers' Project did develop other activities through time—life histories, slave narratives, folklore collections, and very limited provision for individual creative writing—none was able to juggle as many competing interests as the American Guide Series. This also meant, however, that these supplementary projects were less marked by the strains and compromises of trying to be all things to all constituencies.

Some structural compromises were the result of disagreements within the central office. Lawrence Morris, a WPA administrator, judged retrospectively that "not only was the project itself a compromise between social and cultural purposes, with the social ones the only lever strong enough to get money voted in Congress, but the form of each individual guide was a compromise between the two quite different conceptions of what the book should be, conceptions that were hotly argued around the long table in Alsberg's office before members of his staff were sent out to get the project going in the States. Actually, the differences were never really reconciled." Alsberg's passion was for a great literary excavation of America that would produce a cultural portrait that revised democratic representations. At his instigation, the front third of each state guidebook was dedicated to essays on local culture, history, geography, economics, and so on. George Cronyn thought guidebooks should be encyclopedic repositories of information, and he seems to have been the main impetus behind the guidebooks' middle section, itemizations of cities and towns. Katharine Kellock's vision was the most precise of all. Her experience with Baedekers abroad had convinced her of the cultural importance, indeed the patriotic contribution, of thoroughly informed, mile-by-mile tours that would introduce visitors and natives alike to the details of America's heritage. Retrospectively, she said that it was "the 1914 Baedeker to Russia, which I used when I was with the Quakers in Russia 1922–23, that gave me my dream of good guides to the U.S"; given the chaos and astonishing sea change worked on that particular landscape during the period, this comment suggests high confidence in the ability of guidebooks to effect cultural order. The final third of state guidebooks was dedicated to tours, and Kellock reigned over this task with ferocious devotion.[10]

Other Washington editors had particular mandates that cut across that tripartite structure and created additional layers of scrutiny for copy coming in from the states. Sterling Brown, for example, one of the few African Americans in the central office, was brought in from Howard University—where he was professor, poet, and literary critic—in 1936. In his position as national Negro affairs editor, he oversaw the representation of black American culture in all sections of the guidebooks, as well as initiating other African American studies. D'Arcy McNickle, who went on to the Bureau of Indian Affairs, served as Indian editor. Roderick Seidenberg, a progressive architect and old friend of Alsberg's, was art and architectural editor; later, Harold Rosenberg, "a freelance Marxist" (as Vincent McHugh later termed him) took over the art portfolio. First John A. Lomax, then Benjamin A. Botkin oversaw the handling of folklore, while the sociologist Morton W.

Royse was responsible for social-ethnic studies (Hirsch, "Portrait" 36–61). In 1937, Jerre Mangione came in as national coordinating editor to negotiate publishing arrangements and sponsorships for the major project publications, bringing with him experience of New York City publishing, strong ethnic identification, and passionate antifascist sentiments (*Ethnic*). These names represent only a portion of the central office, whose personnel numbered sixty at the height of the project, dwindling to sixteen just before its closure. They suggest the range of (sometimes irreconcilable) demands bearing down on the guidebooks and marking their structure and selection principles. For all the demographic and ideological differences, however, the central office was (and certainly was perceived as) relatively homogeneous in comparison to the great diversity of workers in the field.

The organizational structures that connected the central office to the geographically dispersed mass of project employees reinforced the impression of a unified center and attempted to secure ultimate control of production for those key officials. They established the fundamental coordinates of the guide series and retained editorial veto. With these tools, the cluster of New Dealers, progressives, and liberals in Washington, D.C., attempted to foster cultural regeneration delivered by the display of cultural diversity. From the beginning, then, there were tensions and ruses embedded in a system of centralized planning and oversight designed to flush out regional and local differences.

The central office had editorial authority over fifty state offices (one for each state, two for California, and one for New York City because of its density of literary talent). At certain periods, Washington established field supervisors, later regional directors, as intercessors between federal and state levels; for most of the project's life, however, state directors negotiated directly with the central office. State directors were chosen by Alsberg, but they had to pass political muster with the state WPA administrations. The first group included sixteen newspapermen and women, nine college professors and instructors, seven novelists, three historians, a poet, a bookseller, and a dramatist, as well as some socialite and political appointees whose claims to literary experience were unclear (Taber 41; "Mirror to America"). Annual salaries ranged from $1,800 to $3,600. Within state offices, editors processed fieldworkers' copy before sending it on to Washington, D.C. The wage scale for the bulk of project employees was based on the prevailing security wage scale set for professional and service projects by WPA, with three classifications (professional, skilled, and unskilled) and a differential for cost-of-living standards across the country. "Professionals," for example, received from $103.50 per month in New York City to $50 per month in the rural South.

Alsberg and other national editors seem initially to have read the heterogeneity of employees mimetically, expecting them to demonstrate America's rich democratic diversity by delivering their indigenous beliefs, habits, and knowledges in their localized voices. The expectation was that Washington would simply edit this spontaneous diversity, an expectation reported as achieved practice in the *Pathfinder*: "Its structure resembles a big daily newspaper. The Washington office is the city editor, the state offices are desk men, and the county field workers are the 'leg men.' Most of the actual writing is done in the state office. In Washington, where there are unlimited research facilities, each fact is checked three times. The Washington office includes a policy editor whose duty is to watch for possible libel and make sure that WPA's socially conscious writers stop at describing slums, instead of going on to theorizing about what has caused the slums." Appeals also went out to readers of popular periodicals to "join us in this effort to build up the distinctive atmosphere and background of your community." According to a piece titled "The American Guide in the Schools," these project practices had stimulated "a genuine folk movement."[11]

When the fieldworkers' copy came into the national editors via the state offices, however, it defied Washington's expectations of localized folk cultures. National editors saw the imprint of "mass culture"—which they judged homogenizing and trivializing—everywhere. They complained that the language was hackneyed and indistinguishable from one region to another: copy was full of "such sentimental and trite expressions as 'a quaint town,' 'the noble Red Man,' 'the hardy pioneers,' 'the sturdy settlers,' 'the famous so-and-so,' 'an Indian maiden,' 'the brave warrior.'" The pieces were also motivated by a competitiveness which Michael Kammen identifies as widespread in the period: "a roiling sea of inter-regional rivalries and resentments, a yearning for cultural respect or recognition" (376–77). Writers rarely concentrated on the distinctive attributes of their own locales; instead, they used Chamber of Commerce clichés to claim national (if not international) distinction: "This is the cross roads of America"; "This is the shrine of the Nation"; "This is the finest tobacco in the world"; and "This state is the playground of the Nation." According to the magazine *Pathfinder*: "Bursts of civic pride also have to be edited. To date 335 cities claimed to be the crossroads of America. One city ascribed to itself 67 'firsts' and 'bests.' Middle western prairie towns have a curious fondness for beginning their story, 'Bottsville, like Rome, was built on seven hills.' " Project editors constantly despaired of what they saw as bombast and boosterism that made every town and city sound, to their ears, like every other one.[12]

From the states' perspectives, however, the national editors' expectations were equally unrealistic and ungrounded and thoroughly uninformed about the felt experience of local cultures. Mabel Ulrich, state director in Minnesota, pointed out that "we were completely baffled by the tendency of all federal editors to regard us as inhabiting a region romantically different from any other in the country" (656). For many of the fieldworkers, the language and emphases of their copy expressed local pride, and Washington's directions, at least initially, were bewildering.

In response to this output, the central office became considerably more interventionist, tightening the reins of standardization in the interests of what Karal Ann Marling has dubbed "regionalism by fiat," a strategy which—in federal patronage of mural art—she concludes created "a chimera" (*Wall-to-Wall* 83). The national editors issued a series of manuals to state offices, eighteen in all, which dictated collection practices, filing systems, the flow of copy through the editorial office, textual organization, and style. The regimentary intent was made clear by Cronyn, who composed several of the manuals: "We will have to gradually discipline all State Directors in the precise method and literary treatment which we demand for the Federal work" (qtd. in McDonald 744). Kellock—who wrote the manuals on tours, folklore collection, and style—was equally enthusiastic about standardization and irritated that not every state director could be forced to toe the line: "Once we provided examples of work for the people in the states to use in preparing their own copy, we had much less trouble with state copy. Though we always had an occasional Vardis [Fisher] or what-was-his-name in Arizona [Ross Santee] who declined to follow orders." Telling writers that "anything in the community that is common to all or many communities in America should be given little space. Anything of interest that is peculiar to the community or its region should be treated more fully," the central office laid down "impersonal" and "impartial" usages, as well as the avoidance of specific terms (the word *tour* and the passive voice, for example, were disallowed). And the dictation of wordage allotments to specific sights and topics, under the rationale of "balance" and "proportionality," revealed how thoroughly Washington was removing fundamental decisions about self-representation from state control to privilege a centralized perspective (Cronyn's efforts in this direction in 1935 are quoted and paraphrased at length in Taber, "Project" 34–36). The engineers of the project first created evidence of regional diversity, then pulled it together into a national, unified—"balanced"—expression; thus they replayed the movement described by George L. Mosse in his work on the nationalization of the masses, producing a major icon of American national unity in these fractured years (Vaudagna 225).[13]

Essentially, the central office was reconceptualizing its role. Articles of faith brought by the national editors to the project—tenets such as regionalism, nationalism, and cultural diversity—changed from cultural characteristics which the guidebooks would record into cultural values into which project employees (and, by extension, entire communities) had to be educated: guidebook production as, in Alsberg's phrase, "a great popular university" (qtd. in Hirsch, "Portrait" 18–19). Indeed, throughout the life of the project, national and state officials pushed for colleges and schools to adopt the guides.

Regionalism is a case in point. *Regionalism* was a key word for intellectuals in the 1930s, combining a belief in the vitality of modern folk art with a conviction that landscape could be translated into culture: the diverse physical resources of the country, went the argument, inescapably gave rise to diverse forms of cultural expression. Therein lay America's true richness and its full independence from Europe.

Alsberg promoted this vision in his original design for the American Guide Series, which portioned the country into five major regions, each to represent its unique attributes in its own guidebook. Political interests mitigated against this plan—to receive support from all states, Alsberg had to promise each its own publication—but the vision of regional diversity survived as an editorial credo. The term was also in prominent use by Lewis Mumford and other supporters: "Guides like those which have been done in New England are indispensable toward creating that new sense of the regional setting and regional history, without which we cannot have an informed and participating body of citizens who will understand the problems that grow out of their intercourse with the earth and with other groups" ("Project").

In practice, this vision amounted to unselfconscious paternalism and respect for difference of the right kind, joined with a typical New Deal zeal for planning. The combination is expressed most eloquently by John Frederick, who understood it to empower local communities. Frederick was an editor at the regional rather than the national level; significantly, though, he was Alsberg's choice to replace him when Alsberg was ousted in late 1939. Frederick argued:

The guidebooks' greatest importance is in what they will do for the people of the states themselves, and what they do there it seems is to stimulate and foster a new appreciation of what the state is, what it stands for and what the cultural possibilities are. . . . If we can, in dealing with Galena or Dubuque, or any other small town, or small city of the middle west, help people who are living there, and growing up there to see that they have something in their own home town that is special and intrinsically worthy, not something to get away from, but something to foster and appreciate, I think that is a pretty good job for us to try to do. (Qtd. in Hirsch, "Portrait" 20–21)

Harold Coy, a Washington, D.C., editor, was more alive to the ironies in a federal agency educating states to appreciate their own regional distinctiveness. Retrospectively, he acknowledged the considerable interventionism practiced by the central office, as well as the limits of its efficacy:

We tried to see that labor unions were recognized as a bonafide part of the local scene, thereby frightening more than one state director, and succeeded perhaps in adding a timid mention now and then or in modifying some particularly atrocious anti-labor version of an historic strike. We also battled for the recognition of Negroes and other ethnic minorities and for the avoidance of racial stereotypes—not too successfully, I fear, when I turn to the Mississippi guide's essay on Negro Folkways and read, with a shudder, in the closing paragraph: "As for the so-called Negro Question—that, too, is just another problem he has left for the white man to cope with." We bowed to regional preferences.[14]

An equally centralized definition of local color held sway in the Washington, D.C., office. Although national editors frequently paid lip service to the value—almost the moral imperative—of local color, the dominant assumption was that this quantity could be slotted or injected into a discursive framework authorized by experts. Harris argued: "Unlike the usual commercial guide book publishers, the Federal Writers' Projects have been able to follow a method which allows definite local color and feeling to penetrate into the guides—material has actually been collected locally, on the spot, by Guide workers who are native to the location and catch its real spirit. This local material has been assembled in state editorial offices and rearranged and rewritten somewhat, but there has been constant attention to the problem of catching and keeping the local color."[15]

Harris's final clause betrays a Progressivist, preservationist ethos that reifies local culture as separate from processes of change and the passage of time. Similarly, in talking of the need for expert writers (in this case of radio dramas), Howard Greene, publicity person in the central office, represented local specificity as an additive, completely compatible with the agendas set by specialist writers: "One thing they [experts] can not do and that is give the dramas the local color and vernacular which they need to make them accurate and individualistic."[16] It was logical, then, that central editors expected Massachusetts workers, for example, to fit the details of their city descriptions into centrally mandated grids that were completely alien to the historically distinctive organization of Massachusetts towns. And, clearly, Katharine Kellock never recognized the contradiction between her insistence on local difference and her imposition of a north-to-south and east-to-west rule for tours, directions that enraged almost every state office because, in their view, they ran counter to the characteristic dynamics of their localities.

The fallout from centralized directives was often unpredictable, as the battles over the politics of style show. What the Washington, D.C., office saw as the orderly facilitation of regional and local expression, and what reviewers at home and abroad often touted as the modern American style, state offices—of all political stripes—resented as New Deal regulation, infringing on their rights to self-definition and self-representation. The standardization of style and form seems to have provoked reactionary ideologies. For example, James Thompson was an editor on the Oklahoma project, whose record very much suggests sympathies on the left and in favor of documenting the voices and social contributions of "common" working people. Thompson was so enraged by Washington's syntactical rules that—by the final lines of this quotation—he begins to sound distinctly anti–New Deal, antifederalist, and tending toward individualist, capitalist politics: "The Guide Book . . . is not ours. There is hardly a sentence in it that has not been changed from one to a dozen times. . . . We have come to know how the six hundred must have felt when they marched into the valley of death. All of our literary training may have taught us that interest and originality should never be sacrificed for brevity and simplicity, but we have learned to follow orders no matter how wrong we know them to be. We have not developed our talents; we have simply become cogs in a machine, the like of which is not to be found in private industry" (qtd. in McDonald 744–45). It was ironic, too, given the central office's complaints about the lack of spontaneous regionalism, that its stylistic directions sometimes provoked a strongly conservative regionalism. One investigator reported: "I find among the Western states a continual disposition to criticize the Washington office on the grounds that they are judged by Eastern standards and that the peculiarities of their states are not appreciated. . . . There is a certain strong pride in state individuality here in the West. . . . The very task of working on the Guide strengthens this local pride and patriotism; so that there is everywhere apparent a discontent against criticisms which they claim tend to emasculate this individuality and rob the tours and essays of color."[17] The language here, with its gendering of the polarization between West and East, not only buttressed a conservative disposition of power but also enabled Vardis Fisher's normativizing of masculinity in the Idaho guidebook, one of the most anti–New Deal volumes in structure, voice, and content in the American Guide Series.

The tension between center and periphery was exacerbated by many states' perception of the Washington, D.C., office as distant, all-powerful, and capricious. As Kellock reported to Alsberg from one of her field trips: "Each State Director feels uncertain about what the GOVERNMENT really wants . . . I've had to try to make them feel 'National Director Dr. Henry Alsberg' is not a mixture of State Archivist, Chamber of Commerce Director and Chicago city magistrate, that you want initiative and imagination. You know the Russian peasant proverb on the indifference of Moscow to all human concern—you're Moscow to the provincial governors."[18] The hierarchy of apprehension was extended into the state offices. Mabel Ulrich quoted a Minnesota fieldworker who had been a police reporter: " 'Fear stalks in our midst!' he blazed at me one day. . . . 'Fear of what?' I asked. . . .

'Fear of you! You hold our lives in your hands!' and to a degree it was true" (659).

Predictably, the hierarchy looked much less powerful and the organization much less watertight from within the central office. Far from being in monolithic agreement, the Washington editors could, on occasion, become locked in internal power struggles. Kellock was keenly aware of the chaos in the central office as editors struggled to keep up with the mass of copy flowing in from the states: "Few people realize how shockingly small our staff is. We are trying to check and edit around 12,000,000 words of copy with little over a dozen editors. The tours—my job—have about 4–5,000,000 of that and cover the whole of the US outside of 500–600 cities and villages. I have 1 1/2 assistant editors and 2 secretaries, who chiefly check routes."[19] It also seems that the one clear case of political surveillance—the hiring of Louise Lazelle to censor "subversive" material—was imposed on the central office by a WPA administrator higher up the line (Ellen Woodward, head of the Women's and Professional Division); and, in fact, Lazelle turned against Alsberg and other national editors when she gave evidence of their communist sympathies to the Dies Committee in 1938 (Mangione, *Dream* 302–3).

For all the evidence of ideological and rhetorical manipulation by Washington, D.C., I disagree with Ronald Taber's conclusion that "national regulation and editing . . . forced the state writers to produce standardized, innocuous, and non-controversial manuscripts which are of small value in understanding the 1930's" ("Project" 177); with Paul Sporn's analysis that "the unrelenting sameness of the series organization" expunged all localized difference in the guidebooks (213); and with Harold Rosenberg's judgment that the manuals from the central office "established the Guide Series as a ready-made publication package, which field workers had only to stuff with the appropriate local data" (101). Although it is clearly true that the Washington, D.C., office set the terms, the definitional agenda, and the upbeat New Deal vision for guidebook production, it is precisely in the contestations that emerged from and within states, as a broad range of voices struggled for cultural representation, that the process of cultural image-making is unpacked. Ray Allen Billington, Massachusetts state director when a public furor erupted over that guidebook's representation of the Sacco-Vanzetti case, has judged that the sensationalist uproar was not, ultimately, significant. What mattered, to his mind, were the politics of workers and fights with Washington over the drive for uniformity, which stimulated among local writers a committed regional identity.[20]

Benedict Anderson has argued that "communities are to be distinguished, not by their falsity/genuineness, but by the style in which they are imagined" (15). The making of the American Guide Series shows the depth and variety of investments in the production of a representative style: in the local scene, as on the national stage, competing ideological interests vied to map culture, class, gender, race, and ethnicity onto the landscape. In the 1930s, communities across the continent were preoccupied with consolidation and self-representation. Michael Kammen has traced the intense and competing engagements with America's cultural heritage in the period: nationalist, regionalist, and localist agendas played out in the mushrooming of tourism, collecting of Americana, public history, official monuments, historical pageants, as well as versions of documentary realism in literature, drama, art, and photography. At the same time, ideological movements—from the Popular Front to corporate capitalism—attempted to seize the definition of Americanism. Among all these players in the discursive construction of 1930s America, the Federal Writers' Project was the most prolific spawner of geocultural images that joined the local to the national and the agency that most explicitly brought the federal government into what Warren Susman calls the period's central preoccupation: the "complex effort to seek and to define America as a culture" (157).

The national office running the Writers' Project was intent on mapping out America according to a regular grid and a Progressive ideology, thus effecting cultural as well as economic recovery. Across the country, however, local groups, agencies, and individuals had their own agendas and internal conflicts: vying for national recognition of their distinctive cultural contributions; protecting or exposing the privileges of race, class, and (sometimes) gender; consolidating local knowledge, communities, and identities under the pressure of "outsiders'" attention. The WPA guidebooks were forged amid the collisions and negotiations among these various interests.

Idaho

Vardis Fisher, Local Hero

Idaho: A Guide in Word and Picture was the first of the WPA American Guide Series to see publication, in January 1937. The story of its making and circulation demonstrates the potency of landscape as a site for negotiating cultural and political interests, specifically the formation of local culture and its resistance to federal control. In the Idaho guidebook, the "local" was, essentially, seized and voiced by one man—Vardis Fisher—in the name of masculinist individualism. As state director of the Idaho Writers' Project, Fisher assumed the authority of author, guide, and traveler in the guidebook. Guidebook and author were conflated as the representative voice of Idaho, defending its distinctive identity against an effete eastern establishment.

The slippage between state and man, guidebook and author, was made possible by the cultural baggage of this particular landscape. In one sense, Idaho was an unknown state, but in another—as the West or the "frontier"—it was part of an overdetermined cultural space, already heavily coded in social and political terms and commodified for popular consumption. Part of the guidebook's announced agenda was to reverse that commodification, in the process rolling back the contemporary scene to a presocial wilderness. In turn, that emphasis made *Idaho* the most deeply dissenting guidebook in the series. It refused to conform to the New Deal's cultural vision, implicitly challenging the dominant 1930s' meanings of the frontier, authorizing rugged individualism in a presocial landscape, and thus naturalizing a version of social relations profoundly at odds with the Progressive history critical to New Dealers' faith in social improvement.

This representation had much to do with the conditions of the guide's production. Vardis Fisher was the primary architect of the Idaho guidebook: an outspoken westerner and recognized historical novelist of the West by the time he became state director of the Idaho Writers' Project, he went on to receive Harper's fiction prize for *Children of God*, one of the novels he wrote while working on the project (Attebery, Flora, Grover, Milton). More than any other state director, Fisher conflated his role in the project with his persona as author, personalizing local production, individualizing the guidebook's composition, and wresting an unusual degree of control away from the central office. One function he saw for the guidebook was to convert the local into the personal.

Fisher organized, and spoke about, the state project as a support system for his authorship of the guidebook. In the face of Washington's quota requiring him to hire thirty-five unemployed authors, Fisher repeatedly insisted to Alsberg that "Idaho is not, of course, a state of unemployed writers," and he tended to employ about fifteen to twenty workers, mainly as secretarial and clerical help, which allowed him to compose the guidebook, as he said, virtually unaided.[1]

Although Idaho did not have large numbers of published authors, and none of them may have been seeking paid employment, there are some indications that Fisher was not working in the cultural vacuum he suggested. The Historical Records Survey (a companion federal project to the Writers' Project) listed about two dozen Idaho authors publishing in the period. The record also makes it clear that project workers in the Pocatello district office, at least, felt themselves to be doing real fieldwork in compiling data. Hortense Straus, their local supervisor, put genuine efforts into drafting the results into readable prose, encouraging fieldworkers to use an amalgamation of their own knowledge and Fisher's material.

Thirty years after the event, Harold G. Merriam (who had been Fisher's mentor and Montana state director) wrote to Jerre Mangione: "Fisher's comment that there were no writers in Idaho used as standard a pretty tough set of requirements. Idaho, like other states, had a good number of at least would-be writers but none of Vardis's stature. He preferred to do the work himself. He was a prodigious worker."[2]

The point is not to undermine Fisher's claim to sole authorship of the guidebook: he wrote all published copy except the two essays on Native American peoples, which he delegated to his secretary, Ruth Lyon, and the city description of Pocatello, which he allowed the businessmen (as he said) to compose; and he personally logged thousands of miles of roads while composing tours. But his isolation as sole competent did remove local challenges to his cultural authority and allowed him to speak on behalf of entire local communities: "My opinion of what Idaho's guide should be rests upon conversations I have had with Idahoans all over the state, and is, therefore, not my own personal opinion, but a consensus of opinion of scores of persons with whom I have talked."[3]

Certainly, his investment in the project was intensely personal. Described as "a curmudgeon," a "dyed-in-the-wool individualist," he was quick to interpret tensions with local WPA officials as their personal dislike of him and to equate Idaho's beleaguered national position with his own. His first resignation threat came one week into the job—28 October 1935—and was followed at periodic intervals up to his actual resignation on 7 November 1939, in which he stated that he "had had enough of federal bureaucracy and uncooperative state officials." When local WPA officials initially refused to provide resources for the project office—the Writers' Project began with cardboard boxes for seats and pencil and paper for secretarial equipment—Fisher financed the operation out of his own pocket; later, he offered to pay for good quality negatives for guidebook illustrations if necessary.[4]

The rhetorical purchase was clearly Fisher's, too. The language of the enterprise's exhaustiveness and significance, used by the Pocatello supervisor in her approaches to local organizations and in the project's press releases, was recognizably his. Fisher also had an unusual degree of control over the guidebook's publishers, Caxton Printers, who also published his own fiction. James Gipson, owner of Caxton and a personal friend of Fisher's, came to act as an editorial resource—almost a barometer of local opinion—as the guidebook proceeded. He wrote to Fisher that his secretary read him chapters from the guidebook of an evening: "There is no question, Vardis, but that your first chapter would have greater appeal to those outside of Idaho than in Idaho. . . . For that reason, you may want to do some revising. Not in the interest of art, nor in the interest of truth, but in the interest of sales." Gipson consistently allowed Fisher the prerogative of final arbiter—"the book must be exactly as he wants it"; in the face of this policy, Fisher was much more prepared to negotiate the balance between diplomacy and honesty than he was with his official editors in Washington, D.C.[5]

All of these production strategies put the Idaho project at a greater re-move from central office control than that of any other state. Fisher was cer-tainly the most loudly combative of the state directors. Styling himself the lone individual fighting "the monstrous bureaucracy in Washington," he re-sisted both administrative and editorial directives, believing—like so many state employees across the country—that Washington's drive to centralize and standardize decisions about the guidebooks' format robbed Idaho of its distinctive strengths (Mangione, *Dream* 370n). He was incensed, for exam-ple, at the requirement that tours be written north to south in a state where the tourist traffic was so consistently in the opposite direction that forestry signs faced south only. "Are western states to be forced to defer in tour treat-ment to a pattern which may be all right for eastern states?" he asked Als-berg, mustering support for his case from the Idaho Falls Chamber of Commerce, the Idaho State Automobile Association, and the *Lewiston Morning Tribune*, among others. He also saw the central office's agenda as part of a larger politics: at one point, he objected to James Gipson about the associate director's directives: "Sinclair Lewis was wrong in the title of his last novel—it can happen here. . . . It may be that Mr. Cronyn has had enough fun playing the dictator with us."[6]

Fisher also resisted the distinction between personal and public which threatened to limit his control over the guidebook's perspective. Washing-ton officials attempted to excise all "personal opinion" or "private" judgment from the public document. In one of several letters, George Cronyn insisted to Fisher: "It must be remembered that no product of the Federal Writers' Projects is a private affair. . . . Of necessity and by implication it is as much a Federal product as an annual report by a Government division. This is un-derstood in law and accepted administratively." Alsberg worried that there would be "legal action" if "the property of the Federal Government" were not "handled according to certain established rules and regulations." As rep-resentative of Idaho, Fisher argued it was his job *to* editorialize, to stamp his strong opinions and revisionist scholarship on the state's cultural geography. Resisting Washington's injunction not to use the guidebook for "private ani-madversion," he asserted to Cronyn that "there is no detachment in a book but only in some books the impression of it."[7]

As the terms of the working relationship between Washington and Idaho were thrashed out, the conflict became explicitly gendered. In the face of

Fisher's defiance of editorial directives, some Washington editors began to shift from the language of creative artistry and challenges to the status quo toward a more establishmentarian discipline: at one point, reminding Fisher of his obligations via a letter to Gipson, Cronyn characterized both of them as "members of the Government"; Kellock called him "insubordinate." In turn, Fisher derided the eastern establishment, generally, as "effete" and accused Cronyn, specifically, of having a skin "so tender that he has cut out everything except the innocuous—and sometimes he seems even afraid of that" and thundering at him by telegram: "WHY THE DEVIL DON'T YOU SEND THAT PAGE PROOF BACK." Cronyn then attempted to flex his muscle, traveling out to Idaho in an attempt to intimidate Fisher and James Gipson into making two thousand revisions. The meeting ended up as a drinking match which Cronyn lost (thereby also ultimately losing control over the guidebook). His capitulation to Fisher's prerogative was signaled in a later project, when he apologized for light editing by the central office with the promise that it would not "emasculate" Fisher's copy. Fisher used the same bullish tactics on the national director: when Alsberg phoned Fisher to ask that he delay publication of the Idaho guide, to permit the Washington, D.C., volume to appear first, Fisher's response was so aggressive that, as Opal Laural Holmes (at that time a member of his office, later his wife) reported, his staff "worried that Fisher had queered the Project because of his profane reply to Alsberg." Significantly, it was women administrators who were conscious of the discourse bred by Fisher and poked gentle fun at it: Mary Isham, regional director of the Division of Women's and Professional Projects, wrote to Ellen S. Woodward, assistant administrator of the WPA in Washington, D.C.: "We are sorry that the misunderstanding between Mr. Vardis Fisher, State Director of the Federal Writers Project in Idaho, and Mr. Harold Pugmire, Coordinator of the Statistical Projects, has reached such an acute stage that real western cowboy language seems to apply. We are taking this matter up with the combatants, and will soon have them harmonious again I am sure." This comment may have been evoked by Fisher's threat in a letter to Reed Harris: "One of these days I will go over and pop Mr. Pugmire right in his eye and you will be looking for another director out here in Idaho!"[8]

Although a degree of compromise was forced on Fisher as copy went back and forth between Boise and Washington, D.C., he managed to thwart many of Washington's directives. He retained considerable control over both written text and illustrations mainly by having such a clear vision and by working so independently that he was too fast for the national editors. According to the judgment of one former project worker, the Idaho project was "almost a one-man job. . . . The real goals of accomplishment were established by Fisher himself and not by the Federal Government" (qtd. in Taber, "Project" 129). By the time Washington had refined its editorial directions, Fisher's manuscript was in press; much to Washington's chagrin, and against the central office's repeated stalling, the Idaho guidebook appeared first in the series, beating the Washington, D.C., guide by several months.

One of the stakes in these prohibitions and confrontations was the meaning of place. *Landscape* emerged as a key term, a repository for a great variety of opinion, energy, and knowledge for both sides of the editorial negotiations. For Fisher, the West explained much both about his own manhood—he liked to emphasize his upbringing on Idaho's last "real frontier"—and about his small team, whom he characterized in rugged terms: F. M. Tarr, his mapmaker, for example, "is typical of the old adventurous spirit of the West."[9] But Fisher also connected self to place with a more ambitious scheme: the true source of his being, as he saw it, lay in a vast explanatory framework of philosophical, psychological, sociological, and historical inquiry, all played out over the evolutionary development of nature and culture which marked the land around him. This was the vision that fueled his autobiographical tetralogy (*In Tragic Life* 1932; *Passions Spin the Plot* 1934; *We Are Betrayed* 1935; *No Villain Need Be* 1936), which centered "Vridar Hunter" as the pseudonymous protagonist. Dissatisfied with that effort, he embarked on a twelve-volume *Testament of Man* series (1943–60), which narrativized the development of Neanderthal, then Cro-Magnon man, and onward through a massive chronological sweep up to *Orphans in Gethsemane* (which includes an account of Fisher's project experiences), each evolutionary figure a prototype of Vridar Hunter–Vardis Fisher.

For the Washington office, the western landscape came to function as a kind of discursive safety valve. Washington drew the line between acceptable and unacceptable commentary as follows: "The readers will not quarrel over opinions about landscapes and natural objects; only a few of them will take issue with critical expressions concerned with the fine arts and literature, but a much larger number will be thrown into turmoil by strong personal remarks concerning economic questions, civic and State matters, religious issues, and the like." Thus editors blue-penciled Fisher's manifestly political comments on, for example, the assassination of former governor Frank Steunenberg as well as derogatory remarks about the ugliness of small towns and about a resort charging "extortionate rates for what look like abandoned hen coops." Fisher countered by driving his opinions down more deeply into the presentational structure of the guidebook and displacing them onto landscape description.[10]

The guidebook's opening essays—on Idaho's history, Native Americans, natural and industrial resources—serve, as much as anything, to establish the authority of the narrative voice. This rhetoric seems a continuation of Fisher's seizing of authority over production. As well as battling Washington directives, he trusted only himself to drive the tours and tended to prefer his own knowledge over that of the locals: he wrote to Cronyn that "going to opinionated old-timers for information on origins, etc., has proved only that old-timers don't know half as much as they think they do."[11]

Although the essays' voice is neither first person nor explicitly identified, it is positioned as single and singular in its refutation of all other versions of the West. First debunked are "the gaudy imbecilities of newsstand pulp magazines and . . . cheap novels . . . [which] appease the hunger of human beings for drama and spectacle" (17). Then critical historians are dismissed as personally inadequate: "Those who argue, as some have, that the frontiers were settled largely by vagrant shysters must be overwhelmed by distaste for their own anemic and stultified lives; and doubtless seek through perversity a restoration of their self-esteem" (18). Finally, "pious historians" are lambasted for sentimentalizing and glorifying pioneers (26). Attacking one stereotype and legend after another, the author ultimately delivers an alternative version of Frederick Jackson Turner's historiographical procession. The stream of explorers, trappers, missionaries, miners, and sheep and cattlemen who explore and settle Idaho is a familiar historical pattern, but the insistence on the primitive instincts, unscrupulous motives, and "white brutality" (24) driving the process is provocative. That the provocativeness is somewhat staged, more about authorial pose than revisionist knowledge, is suggested by Bernard DeVoto's response: "One doubts that tourists are so simple-minded as Mr. Fisher seems to believe—they hardly need to be told at this late date that the pioneers were not supermen or that the Indians were much sinned against. . . . [And] they are likely to resent the curiously adolescent irony in which Mr. Fisher chooses to phrase his remarks" ("First Guide").

The counterdiscursive status of the authorial voice is most explicit when it rewrites a famous battle between the Nez Percés and federal troops from the perspective of an apocryphal Indian historian (30–31). This account emphasizes the heroism of the outnumbered Natives, records the ineptitude of the white soldiers, and challenges the ideological interestedness of the traditional versions. One could read this account as destabilizing historical authority: by recoding historical narrative, Fisher exposes the codification or fictiveness of *any* "factual" account. That, however, is not the claim within the rhetorical economy of the guidebook: all revisionist moments, including the apocryphal passage, are presented under the banner of "plain fact" and "matter of fact." Indeed, scholarship generally was defined by Fisher as knowing that "a thing is either right or wrong and that there can be no argument about it" (Taber, "Project" 130). From this stance the narrative voice gains moral authority and the superiority of authentic knowledge to support its general demarcation of the "real" and its specific intervention in frontier mythmaking.

This intervention is mobilized most vigorously in the second half of the guidebook, the eleven tours that crisscross the state. As quoted in my introduction, W. J. T. Mitchell talks about landscape as cultural practice, a key site of identity formation, which is the more ideologically powerful because it naturalizes its own constructedness. The link between landscape and identity (cultural, political, personal, or all three) is most visible in the tours section, where the relationship between the implied author and the implied reader takes its most applied form, the authoritative narrative voice directing the traveler to material sights along selected routes. The framing of the reader/traveler is made more coherent by the photographs, whose placing— by Fisher and Gipson—is literally illustrative of the written text and thus reinforces the illusion of unmediated representation. And in some of the *Idaho* tours, Fisher usurps the traveler's perspective with such elaboration that the tour description can function as a substitute for (not just an aid to) actual travel, a substitution that attempts to shape and contain the armchair traveler's responses more thoroughly than any actual use of the guidebook would allow. This process was obliquely recognized in at least one review of the guidebook: "It is not just a book. It is an adventure," declared Albert

Charles Norton in *Social Studies* (qtd. in *Vardis Fisher* 15). Whatever the responses of particular readers to this narrative strategy, the key point is which landscapes the reader is most vigorously enjoined to enter and how, rhetorically, an identity is constituted for the traveler in the process.

In the Idaho tours, the directions systematically—image by image, comment by comment, and place by place—strip the landscape of its urban accretions. A typical comment, on St. Anthony in tour 1, reads: "There is nothing of unusual interest in the town itself, but west of it are two of the most remarkable natural phenomena in the State" (202). Similarly, "Far out in the west on Birch Creek (but not worth a visit) is the ghost town of Viola" (216). Having been thwarted by Washington from describing Pocatello in graphically derogatory terms—"all of Pocatello would rise in fury if we called it the 'ugliest of the larger Idaho cities,'" remonstrated Kellock—Fisher then cared so little about the piece that he allowed the businessmen of Pocatello to write their own brief and rather formulaic city copy.[12] The town of Twin Falls is characterized almost exclusively in terms of geology, paleontology, and topography; its sites worthy of mention are a museum, taxidermist, and botanical garden—all instances of the natural world preserved institutionally. And the illustrations of Boise turn away from the city toward "A Boise Sky" and "A View in Boise," all lake and trees which mask the distant, barely perceptible buildings. Indeed, in place of the city descriptions that appear in all the other guidebooks in the series, *Idaho* has "The Primitive Area" and "Ghost Towns": sites that prove the survival of nature over civilization, not the opposite.

What gets privileged in the tours are three categories of natural landscape which shade into each other while situating the reader rather differently. The most manifestly humanized landscape is the agricultural one. Intermittently, though rarely at any length, fields of potatoes, beans, peas, and alfalfa and apple and cherry orchards are noted, often—atypically for this guidebook—announced by giving their quantitative or qualitative preeminence in national or international comparisons. Closely related is the controlled environment of "Hunting and Fishing," which records plans for managing natural resources—stocking lakes, exterminating predators—to exploit "Idaho's opportunity to become one of the great playgrounds of the Nation" (153). The effect of this activity on the land becomes evident in photographs that emphasize the regular patterns of "A row of onions" and "A lettuce patch." Although these illustrations implicitly celebrate human productivity, their placing of human figures is more ambiguous. In "Idaho's big potatoes" (Ill. 1), the people are so small, so visually indistinct, and so statically posed (as opposed to vigorously working) that they are barely perceptible. And the reader is given no particular access to the agricultural process or any particular presence with which to identify. Only twice in two hundred pages of tours is the reader invited into the details of a working environment, reported entirely in impersonal passive constructions. Of the Potlatch Forests plant, "the second largest sawmill in the world," it is said: "Visitors are welcomed to this mill. At the gate a card of admission is given, together with a map of the plant and directions. Most impressive is the fetching of logs out of the pond, the huge band saws with their miraculous precision of machinery, and the box factory and planing mills. Sawdust here is now converted under enormous pressure into logs for fireplaces" (308–9).

The elision of human agents in these descriptions conforms to the structures of tourism analyzed by Dean MacCannell: "the work display" deflects attention from workers, thus removing the specificities of their situation from the significant social landscape on view (67–68). In Fisher's case, the gap where we might expect celebration of human workers seems doubly suggestive when read against his 1928 novel, *Toiler of the Hills*, which challenges the agrarian myth by graphically detailing the dehumanizing conditions of the "agricultural poor," an emphasis which one reviewer, at least, saw as comparable to Erskine Caldwell's and William Faulkner's representations of poor white southerners (Bishop 355).

Within the rhetorical economy of the guidebook, which celebrates Idaho's natural and agricultural abundance, Fisher does not quite know what to do with human workers. Any attempt to foreground the combination of human agent and worked-over landscape produces an awkward fit. The illustration "Hunting Is Good in Idaho" (Ill. 2), for example, seems heavily imprinted with uneasy self-consciousness, ascribable to the hunters, the photographer, the illustration's selectors, or all three. This photograph, posed against a suburban picket fence, can be read as either playing up or simply betraying the odd staginess, the comic disjunctions that result when humans try to harness natural abundance to their own designs.

It is a short step to the next category of landscape floated by the tours: the most familiar and heavily coded landscape of the "frontier." The fundamen-

1. Idaho's Big Potatoes

2. Hunting Is Good in Idaho

tal formula for converting western landscape into a "frontier" is the opposition of wilderness and civilization, finely balanced and heroically mediated by men. By this scheme, it is integral to the condition of the frontier that it be constantly disappearing. Indeed, the guidebook is one sustained rehearsal of that process. The guide's opening sentence—"After three centuries of adventurous seeking, the American continent has been explored and settled, and the last frontier is gone" ([17])—is repeatedly contradicted and qualified in the rest of volume. "Idaho," we are told later, "is no longer a frontier, but the frontier still lives in countless ways within its borders"(36); "the last of the frontiersmen" can still be encountered around Big Creek Hot Springs (276);and Boise's small cabarets and clubs are "still invested with much of the spirit of the Old West"(257). The essay title, "Emerging from the Frontier" (183), explicitly articulates the trope as an ongoing process. The heroizing of this frontier is legible in the difference between "Hunting Is Good in Idaho" and "Journey's End" (Ill. 3). The marks of "civilization" are still present in the latter illustration—in the technology of the gun, the social implications of the mirror, and the portrait's composition, looser but still symmetrical—but the final equation seems significantly different. These men exist at greater distance from civilization's comforts: they have lived rough in the woods in their pursuit of bigger game and look the hardier for it.

The reader is explicitly invited into the vicarious frontier experience only very occasionally, but then with a vivid approximation of presence not evident in the descriptions of agricultural landscape. In describing Massacre Rocks, Fisher goes into full novelistic mode, creating for the reader a perspective that strips away the technological accretions from the landscape and returns the traveler to 1862, sharing the point of view of a wagon driver in the pioneer caravan that was attacked by Indians and is commemorated now by a monument at this site (233–35). The reader is encouraged to experience the finely balanced tension of the frontier, the hardship and danger as lived by white settlers—the Native Americans' lived perspective is not represented—at a particular historical moment. Thus Fisher positions the reader within his revisionist perspective, tacitly supporting his campaign against manifestly commercialized versions of the frontier, the "shoddy sawdust counterfeits" (17).

Of all the landscapes selected for tour descriptions, the most attention is lavished on a vision of primitive wilderness. Thirty years later, in the prefa-

3. Journey's End

tory note to his novel *Mountain Man* (1965), Fisher stressed the presocial West as the brief moment in which the myth of the West was reality. Given the particular rhetorical power of "'the real' . . . in this decade of exodus, of uprootedness and movement," Fisher's handling of the wilderness powerfully normalizes values of nature and individualism quite at odds with the central office's emphasis on the cultural and the social (Trachtenberg 65).

More copy is devoted to, and the reader's participation is more emphatically channeled toward, the state's myriad caves, lava fields, hot springs, and other natural wonders than to any other sights, even though this topography is concentrated in the southeastern corner of the state. Unspoiled nature is here sufficient to play the role of culture, an entity which the Washington editors repeatedly enjoined Fisher to include through conventional attention to the arts and architecture. Refusing that directive on the grounds that Idaho had no significant aesthetic achievements, Fisher displaced cultural signs onto the landscape: a natural cave formation, for example, demonstrates the "Gothic majesty of its sculpturing" (220); and the Silent City of Rocks "is a weird congregation of eroded cathedrals and towers and shattered walls . . . mosques and monoliths and turrets . . . bathtubs and hollow cones and shells and strange little pockets and caverns . . . [which] suggest from some distance the famous sky line of New York City" (236–37).

As in Fisher's novels, nature that exceeds human control is also the ultimate measure of human existence. The tour of the Craters of the Moon National Monument reads in part: "Few spots on earth have such power to impress the human mind with the awful inner nature of the huge rock-planet upon which the human race moves at incredible speed through the universe" (267). The passage proceeds by reveling in the ancient cataclysms and "stupendous eruptions" (268) that produced this "desolate waste" (269), in terms that anticipate the *Testament of Man* series. The accompanying illustrations suggest, in their near abstraction, the magnification of the natural perspective and the erasure of human agents from the scene in a way that the frontier landscapes, with their recognizably picturesque conventions, do not: see, for example, "A Lava Field Near the Craters of the Moon" and "Lava Flow—Craters of the Moon" (Ill. 4), which defy easy assessments of human scale and perspective. (Again, DeVoto was skeptical: "photographic stunts," he called them.) Fisher's tendency to dismiss people from the scene was noted and critiqued in the production stage by Ruth Crawford: of Fisher's history essay, she objected: "There is no feeling for people in the essay. In fact, throughout the copy they need to be treated a little more sympathetically. They may be dumb, but they're the best we have." Thirty years later, Fisher made explicit his vision of humans as dispensable, primitive beings. In an interview, he said: "After infinite labor there is race with conscience enough to know that it is vile and intelligence enough to know that it is insignificant. We survey the past and see that its history is a blood-and-tears of helpless blundering, of stupid acquiescence, of empty aspirations." In much more utilitarian, less dramatic, and therefore more persuasive accents, this is the vision which the Idaho guidebook undergirds.[13]

That erasure of human presence had particular implications for certain segments of Idaho's population. Only by reading the tours in *The Oregon Trail*—the WPA guidebook put together by Katharine Kellock—can we situate Basque, Greek, African American, and Chinese communities in particular Idaho cities and towns. The tours in the Idaho guide virtually efface these residents from the scene; only in the "Racial Elements" section of the essay "Emerging from the Frontier" do they receive passing mention. Fisher consistently resisted Washington's pressure to pay significant attention to ethnic and racial difference in the guidebook and, subsequently, the state encyclopedia. He was happy enough, however, to contribute a story on

4. Lava Flow—Craters of the Moon

Basque settlers to "Pockets in America," a national project whose very title announced its contents as peripheral to mainstream America.[14]

Equally lacking in the guidebook is attention to women as social and political agents. Again Ruth Crawford, as reader of the draft guidebook copy, noted and challenged the lacuna: in response to an essay titled "Growth and Development," she commented, "Women are not mentioned"; of "Government," she asked, "What rights do women have in Idaho?"[15] Other sources suggest a particular cast to female politics in Idaho, given that it was the fourth state in the Union to grant women suffrage. In the guidebook, women function only as oddities (and rare ones). There is the single woman to climb Mount Borah: "Old-timers here say that only one woman has ever reached the top and they are dubious of her, surmising that her husband recorded her name there" (272), a name which the guidebook chooses not to reproduce. And there is Lydia Trueblood Southard, "Idaho's notorious female Bluebeard," in the Boise penitentiary (290). Only two illustrations fore-

5. Surf-riding on Lake Coeur d'Alene

ground white female presence. The one photograph features prepubescent girls, triumphantly held aloft in a paternalistic Charles Atlas stance: "Surf-riding on Lake Coeur d'Alene" (Ill. 5). Rather more curvaceous symbols of women posed like fashion models in two-piece bathing suits appear on the Map of Recreation, marking resorts. Predictably, within the conventional terms of frontier discourse as well as Fisher's masculinist production, female qualities appear most extensively and most lavishly as they are displaced passively onto the landscape: a massive stalagmite is named "The Bride . . . her creamy trousseau draped virginally around her" (221); "virginal wilderness" (323 and elsewhere) is everywhere in the tours section.

The containment of the Native American population is somewhat more complex. Clearly, one revisionist thrust of the guidebook was about restitution of an American Indian perspective on the frontier story, as witness Fisher's apocryphal passage in his "History" essay, as well as the essays

6. Jim Marshall of Fort Hall

"History of Idaho Indians" and "Anthropology of Idaho Indians," which he handed over to Ruth Lyon to compose while taking some pains to secure "a qualified Indian to work getting information on matters relating to Indian life not covered by published materials" (he managed to requisition Minnie Y. LeSieur as a nonrelief worker, as well as two unnamed Native American people).[16] Even that description, with its easy assumption that the director was the appropriate judge of such qualifications, hints at the limits of Fisher's tolerance of difference. The illustrations (like the Massacre Rocks account) suggest the consequences of that attitude. While one Native American portrait is individualized with an anglicized personal name—"Jim Marshall of Fort Hall"—they all adopt stereotypical poses and they are the only studio photographs in the book, taken indoors, separated from the landscape on which Fisher put such store (Ill. 6). The method of representation contains Native American agency in other ways: of the Nez Percés, Fisher says unequivocally: "They were children" (29); of the Kutenai farming around Desmet, he speaks in glowing terms, approving of progress as an unreservedly good quality in a way that he never would for his white subjects: "Comparing favorably with those of white men in both their manner of operation and in living conditions, these farms suggest the progress that these Indians have made" (306). Though heroic and admirable, the Native American population is ultimately figured as childlike and powerless, its access to the social realm entirely dependent on assimilation to white ways.

The repeopling of this prehistoric scene with fully human agents happens only via the relationship between authorial voice and reader. The reader is most vigorously invited into the primitive, prefrontier landscape but in terms that style both reader/traveler and author/guide as ruggedly male. In the tours, the personal, knowledgeable voice of the guidebook author becomes the voice of experience: it has fished the lakes, hiked the trails, explored the caves, hunted the mountains, talked to the old-timers, and knows the extremities of this landscape as few others do. Of Minnetonka Cave, for example, it is said: "Nobody knows how much of it remains undiscovered and unexplored. Only a few persons have entered it" (219); as the knowledgeable source, the author is clearly one of those few, and he takes the reader down into caves, along tunnels, through inner chambers with a visualization of detail and advice about dangers that far surpass attention to other sights. In the process, these passages characterize the reader as "the hardy adventurer" (249, 291, 341, and elsewhere) and "the explorer" (203, 204, 220, and elsewhere), thus challenging him (the pronoun is always male) to rise to the adventure of this wilderness landscape, to follow these minimally mapped routes into caves, up mountains, along little-known trails.

The acceptance of travel as masculine genders the relationship with the landscape: "Once a person has penetrated this huge central Idaho terrain he can vanish into utter wilderness over several forest roads or by innumerable trails" (298). What is penetrated is "virginal wilderness" (323 and elsewhere) and mountain ranges with "soft flanks voluptuously mounded" (273). Contextualized by these descriptions, the extended directions for entering caves begin to read like the description of Glenn's Falls and its hidden caves in *The Last of the Mohicans*, glossed by Annette Kolodny as narrow passages and womb-like caverns which Natty and Chingachgook penetrate in terms alternately phallic and fetal (96–98). This confirmation of the landscape as

7. A Monument on Monumental Creek

men's preserve occurs most explicitly and extensively in "The Primitive Area" and "A Trip into the Area" (titled "An Essay for Men" when a version of it appeared in *Esquire*, September 1936), in which the imagined details of such a trip and its effects on the explorer climax in the declaration: "There will be much that any man, once he has known it, will wish to return to, or that any man, never having known it before, will take to his heart" (359). The ultimate symbol is the reclusive, self-reliant Cougar Dave: "Dave was not something that hunted adventure: he was adventure itself" (357). It is no accident that the most explicitly phallic symbol of the book appears in this section: "A Monument on Monumental Creek" (Ill. 7).

One awkwardness in the reproduction of the wilderness condition is, of course, the automobile, the very technology which the guidebook must introduce into the scene so as to function as a genre. The text works hard not only to stress that driving in this terrain is risky—"only the most adventurous" and the most skilled should attempt certain roads (278 and elsewhere)—but to mask roads, technological inventions, as part of the wilderness: one trip "is so adventurous that it demands tolerance of fair or poor roadbed and the fortitude necessary in exploring a vast wilderness" (294). In the final count, however, fulfillment of the adventure requires leaving the car behind: real explorers get out of the car and hike "over rugged trails" (244) to climb a mountain, peer down a gorge, or penetrate a subterranean cave. That sense of the automobile on the periphery is suggested, too, by the illustration "South Fork of Payette River." On a narrow, winding mountain road the car is perched precariously by the edge of a cliff that drops sheerly to the foaming river; barely visible in the photograph, the automobile is an insubstantial presence, overwhelmed by the scale of the wilderness and threatened by natural hazards on all sides. The author's fundamentally derisory attitude to motorists comes to the surface again in "The Primitive Area": "Signs have been and will continue to be placed until even the most terrified dude will be able to retrace his path and find his way back to his automobile" (347).

Also masked in the primitivization of landscape is the commercial function of the guidebook. Tourism was a distinct consideration in the guidebook's production, especially given the public debate in the late 1930s about opening an Idaho tourist bureau. Fisher himself calculated, in a letter to Alsberg, that "beauty of country is the chief thing we have to offer tourists"; and his resistance to social analysis was justified on these grounds: he wrote to Cronyn that "I do not think myself that expanded statements on such matters as the growth of a state are going to be of much interest to tourists." The dust jacket "hoped that the book will serve the double purpose of increasing Idahoans' appreciation of their state, and of inducing tourists to share in the rich recreational bounty Idaho has to offer." And Caxton and Fisher planned both the "library edition" (selling for $3) and a "tourist edition" (for $1.50; the latter project died with the March 1937 fire at Caxton that destroyed the guidebook plates). Yet the word *tourist* does not figure in the guidebook's text; indeed, with Fisher's investment in combating the commodification of the West and his concomitant representation of travel as rugged, individualist, masculine exploration, he could not afford to acknowledge the guidebook as an act of recommodification—an early example of the cultural simulacra analyzed by Daniel Boorstin and Dean MacCannell. At least one review did come close to that realization; Don Russell, in the *Chicago Daily News*, noted wryly: "The Craters of the Moon, the Salmon river gorges, 1,000 feet deeper than the Grand Canyon, the caves where one gets dust in the ears, are probably less known to tourists than they will be now that this guide is published." This was the bind in which Fisher was perennially caught, lobbying for the preservation of Idaho's natural wonders by converting them into recreation areas and for the guidebook as an enabling part of that process. In a 1936 article, for example, Fisher is quoted: "Phosphate beds and recreational resources are practically all Idaho has left, Vardis Fisher, author and WPA historian, told the junior chamber of commerce Thursday noon at Hotel Boise. He advocated immediate capitalization on Idaho's natural facilities to provide the nation with a playground. . . . To bring the nation to that playground, Fisher advocated wide circulation of an Idaho guide which he is compiling in conjunction with his 75-page digest of Idaho for the American guide. He solicited chamber backing of a drive for funds to advertise his book in New York."[17]

When Hayden White explicates the process by which historical narrative is received as naturalized fact, he argues that it is crucial that the account take the form of "a plot structure with which [the reader] is familiar as a part of his [sic] cultural endowment" (86). In the case of this guidebook, the touring reader is positioned within the most familiar of American cultural narratives: the competitive individualism of western melodrama, naturalized and authenticated into a confrontation with an untamed landscape. Idaho becomes an arena of natural phenomena that challenge men—by implication, white men, as the only beings with agency in this scene—to demonstrate their ruggedness and stamina. In other words, both in the production process and in the textual details, Fisher conceived the volume in terms of a competitive individualism and braggadocio thoroughly appropriate to the kind of pulp western showdown he so evidently despised.

These terms reappear in the guidebook's circulation and published reception, again a process over which Fisher attempted to exercise close control, naturalizing the fit between the guidebook and the community's interest. Locally, he made distribution into almost a cottage industry, offering commissions to Idahoans—including schoolchildren, his own sons, and Ruth Lyon's mother—who solicited orders for the guidebook. Again, the sales pitch that was passed down the line of solicitation was recognizably

Fisher's; this system meant that he was not only in direct communication with door-to-door salespeople but also recorded every customer's name. For example, in a letter to Sophronia Lathen of Moscow, Fisher advised: "If Idahoans whom you approach object to the price of the book, please explain that the price is the actual cost of production and that this undertaking was not a commercial one with the Caxton Printers. Explain that the Caxton Printers undertook this book at their own risk and that Idaho ought to be grateful to them on that account. Explain also that in the commercial market a book like this would sell from $5 to $10. Add, if necessary, that Idahoans are not being urged to buy this book. Say that the book is being called to their attention at the lowest price at which it will ever sell; and if they want one, all right, and if they don't, all right."[18]

In wider circulation, Fisher and Gipson again conspired against Washington's explicit instructions by including in press review copies promotional material that articulated the guidebook's production as a heroic narrative of individualism triumphant. The publicity statement itemized the extent of the guidebook written by Fisher, explained that government rules forbade his acknowledgment as author, and detailed the low cost of the project, the meager salaries, and the lack of human resources: in other words, all the disadvantages against which Fisher struggled in producing such a magnificent work. A typical circular was drafted by Richard Lake of the Caxton Publishing Department: "By a ruling of the Washington office, Vardis Fisher's name as Director of the work in Idaho may not appear on the title page. We think it important, however, that you know that the materials for the book were gathered under his supervision and that most of the copy was written by his hand . . . the book is Fisher's work and bears the stamp of his personality and his style. . . . We wish to present the book to you primarily as the first extended essay of a nationally known creative artist in factual characterization and objective description."[19]

This narrative was reproduced in whole or in part across a range of newspapers, from the *Boise News* to the *New York Herald-Tribune*. One result was that, though all reviews acknowledged the hand of the WPA—and judged the product evidence of federal money well spent—they placed more emphasis on Fisher. George Snell, a writer from Idaho reviewing the guidebook in the *Salt Lake City Tribune*, was typical in celebrating the work as "a monument to the patience and determination of Vardis Fisher"; "The strongly individual vigor of his style is everywhere apparent in the book." It was a short step from Fisher's masculine style to the masculinization of truthful knowledge. The *Boise News* praised "the virile hand of Fisher, realistic, uncompromising, yet treating historical authority with the respect of a scholar"; Thomas D. Clark in the *Lexington* (Kentucky) *Leader* judged: "Throughout this federal guidebook the reader is conscious that he is being told the truth, sometimes he senses that he is being told the bare truth. . . . It is written from a sane point of view and with a frankness which perhaps will shock every service club in Idaho." From Lewis Gannett to William T. Couch to Bernard DeVoto, reviewers praised the guidebook's "candidness," "frankness," and "proud honesty." These qualities—the product of particular interests, maneuvers, and responses—were ultimately conflated with "a contemporary American style" (in the London *Times* review, for example).

If this equation privileges a masculinist style as the sign of unadorned truth, it also naturalizes this very partial representation as inclusive. The words of the *Salt Lake City Tribune* review demonstrate a common slippage: from the guidebook's "strongly individual vigor," to its "candidness," to its value as a "comprehensive survey." In an important review in the *Saturday Review of Literature*, Bernard DeVoto, the editor and well-known authority on the frontier, praised the Idaho guide for "facilitat[ing] our knowledge of ourselves," without interrogation of the inclusions and exclusions marked by that "we" ("First Guide"). The ideological interestedness of this characterization of the guidebook is exposed by a review at the other end of the political spectrum. In the *New Republic*, Jack Balch, proletarian novelist and member of the Missouri Writers' Project, stressed the lacunae produced by the guidebook's ignoring of labor conditions and contemporary society generally: "Too many things are left out or only hinted at. One such omission is the Coeur d'Alene strike and massacre, inseparable from the state's history. Because of a neglect of the contemporary scene and whatever is vital in the state's business, political and social background . . . the conclusion is inescapable that this is only a half-visit to Idaho."

The terms of this public reception were the more important because they framed what was conceived as Idaho's introduction onto the national map. "The Traveler's Notebook" in the *Washington Sunday Star* announced that, hitherto, Idaho had been one of the "so-called dead spaces on the travel map." An Associated Press release to Idaho newspapers called it "a state less known east of the Mississippi than any other in the west." And Fisher him-self claimed that "this young state has almost no standard sources of refer-ence in regard to itself." Local jubilation was at least partly prompted by regional competitiveness. When the *Boise News* reviewed the "Brilliant Idaho Encyclopedia" in January 1938, it was still chortling over the speed of the guide's appearance: "Novelist Fisher and his WPA writers put one over on the nation a few months ago when they turned out the commendable Idaho Guide ahead of the other 47 states." Local pride also affected more general attitudes toward the WPA, according to Fisher: "Inasmuch as Idaho has an inferiority complex these statements by national critics on the volume are doing much to whoop Idahoans up in regard to the worthwhileness of this project and the work of the Works Progress Administration in gen-eral."[20]

The guidebook continued to shape Idaho's self-image, at least at the offi-cial level: thirty years after its publication, the executive secretary of the Idaho State Department of Commerce and Development said that the Idaho guide was of the "utmost importance" to the department and the main source for its centennial *Idaho Almanac*" (qtd. in Taber, "Fisher" 76); ten years after that, the state archivist judged the WPA guide "still the best thing for us to start a visitor out with" (qtd. in Doig 21). The guidebook also increased Fisher's cultural capital. He became increasingly visible as a pub-lic figure, often positioned as the voice of the state, the "Idaho literary titan" (in the words of the *Pittsburgh* [Pennsylvania] *Press* of 20 February 1938). Within the Writers' Project, the enthusiastic reception of the guidebook won him virtual autonomy with his next two projects, the state encyclopedia and atlas; his help was solicited with the Utah guidebook; and in March 1939 he was invited to become regional director for the mountain states (Idaho, Montana, Colorado, Wyoming, Utah, and New Mexico). In 1936, Caxton produced the *Vardis Fisher News*, which organized review excerpts by re-gional affiliation and attitude in an attempt to sell a particular image of the novelist. In 1939, the same press produced a more elaborate publicity book-let, titled *Vardis Fisher: A Critical Summary with Notes on His Life and Per-sonality*. By 1941, a dozen state newspapers carried his syndicated column, "Vardis Fisher Says" (Grover 9). And over the years, state honors to him ac-crued.

If the guidebook played a part in constructing a national image for Idaho and Fisher, as the first state publication in the American Guide Series, it also contributed to the consolidation of the genre contract. Reviewers chose to accept Fisher's claims about the noncommercial nature of the Idaho guide at face value. Repeatedly, reviews value the volume's rugged honesty in contradistinction to previous (unnamed) guidebooks, which, as a genre, are linked to the tawdry commercialism of the tourist trade. W. T. Couch declared in the *Raleigh News and Observer*: "The volume is filled with an honesty and directness the opposite of what might be expected in a guide book, and it is the best possible kind of advertising for Idaho, because it is not advertising," unlike "the ballyhoo which has characterized tourist trade in the past." Clark, in the *Lexington* (Kentucky) *Leader* judged: "Tourist and other travelers should no longer find themselves victimized by overzealous localities which scrape up catch-penny wonders to ensnare the tourists' cash." The equation of masculinity, honesty, and anticommercialism became increasingly explicit in the reception of Fisher's work: at the time of his death, for example, Van Allen Bradley judged that "the late Vardis Fisher shared with James T. Farrell and a handful of other writers of his time a single-minded devotion to truth in literature and a gallant disdain for the commercial side of publishing."

Aligned with admiration for the guide's anticommercialism is the valorizing of it as a truly aesthetic work. In a letter to Fisher, Alsberg expressed delight that the guidebook copy was "real literature."[21] George Cronyn said of the history essay: "Mr. Alsberg and I both agree that you have succeeded in raising Guide writing to the plane of permanent literature" (qtd. in Taber, "Project" 135). Reviews repeatedly use similar language, sometimes lifting it from the dust jacket: Jay du Von, in the *Des Moines* (Iowa) *Register*, declared: "It is no ordinary guidebook but a handbook of the state, giving the dignity and beauty of living literature to a factual characterization of the state"; Bruce Catton wrote, "It is actually a bit of literature, worth reading for its own sake." This praise seems to proceed from traditional aesthetic measures, assuming that the volume gains value via an individualistic style that transcends the genre's functionality and commercialism. The reviews also promote the Idaho guide as a benchmark to which the rest of the series should aspire. DeVoto called the publication of *Idaho* "momentous, since inevitably the first will be judged as typical of the whole enterprise"; Horace

Chadbourne proclaimed it "definitely the high water mark for guide books in this country or any other."

The Washington editors took a rather different view. Although they were delighted to have a substantial publication to brandish before Congress, they did not want *Idaho* instated as a model. They emphasized the discursive constructedness of the volume as evidence of aberration, not truthtelling. Henry Alsberg offered this characterization to his superior: "This State Guide Book will be unique, since it bears throughout the stamp of Vardis Fisher's unusual personality" (qtd. in Taber, "Project" 144). Katharine Kellock refused *Idaho* entrance even into the category "guidebook"; she called it "an old-fashioned kind of travel book that wandered from subject to subject that interested the author" (qtd. in Mangione, *Dream* 208).

The larger point, of course, was that Fisher's version of the frontier narrative was inimical to the New Deal. Federal cultural agencies in the 1930s promoted an image of the frontier as a site of human cooperation, triumph over nature, and promise of continuing progress: visions of healthy, determined pioneers working together peppered the walls of post offices across the country. The guidebook also implicitly opposes the Progressive view of history—symbolized particularly in its attitude to the automobile—which was a strong part of the Washington, D.C., agenda in shaping the American Guide Series. Washington tried repeatedly to make Fisher attend enthusiastically to architecture and to towns in his tour descriptions—at one point, Kellock protested, "It is impossible to give Lava Springs more space than you give to Pocatello, the second city in size in the State"; she directed him to pay attention to Progressive developments and contemporary industry in the history essay and to add an essay on social growth and development. That Fisher never capitulated to Washington's priorities is evident in one of the project's last productions, the "Idaho Digest for Travelers," which carries the following statement by him: "In the following list only those points of interest are given which it is felt are worthy of attention. If such items as the universities and other institutions or public buildings such as the State Capitol, are omitted, it is because they are unimpressive in comparison with corresponding features in many other states."[22]

The spin the central office put on the Idaho guide after publication suggests the distance between Washington's agenda and Fisher's. For example, it was the photographs of Arrow Rock Dam and Salmon Dam—that is, of technological triumph over nature—which the publicity director in the central office solicited for official exhibits of American Guide Series works.[23] The guidebook shows Fisher to be at least ambiguous about the hydroelectric schemes. Although he records the impressive statistics attendant on these structures, he also emphasizes the cost in "Idaho's scenic losses" (243): Bear Lake, for example, had been ruined by the Utah Power Company; it "can never recover its former glory as long as its water is at the mercy of capricious interests" (221). In the classic progress-versus-nature dilemma that informed discourses of the West from the beginning of white settlement, the tour commentary firmly favors unspoiled nature as the locus of the "real" West. The larger WPA project was dedicated to notions of American progress, demonstrated by the rhetorically and visually contained landscapes of the guidebooks.

Of course, the Idaho guidebook contains its landscapes, too, but in different terms. Fisher returned Idaho to a presocial landscape whose primitive, wilderness features challenged travelers to act like real men. In positioning the reader in this coded landscape, Fisher was also producing himself as rugged individual and cultural authority. What gets played out in the production process and the textual representation is individual identity, not the social formations that predominate in other guidebooks in the series. By revivifying clichés of masculine individualism and the West, the Idaho version of the genre emphatically genders both travel and knowledge as male. Yet because Fisher articulated his politics in the authoritative voice of the guide and displaced them onto a presocial landscape, reviewers were able to represent the work as an apolitical account of unmediated honesty. The public reception converted Fisher's very partial representations into the defining qualities of a comprehensive guidebook: coordinates not just for Idaho but for the American Guide Series as a whole.

Katharine Kellock's Highway Route Series

The View from the Road

If Vardis Fisher was the maverick on the project, rebelling from the western periphery against eastern regulation, Katharine Kellock was the figure in the central office whose practices most epitomized all that he resisted. Their attitudes to the automobile demonstrate their difference: for Fisher, the car was an awkward technology to be set aside in his pursuit of the wilderness; for Kellock, the car was front and center, symbol of everything modern and enabling to which the guidebook provided democratic access. As national tours editor, Kellock set about implementing a clear Progressivist agenda nationwide with a fearsome energy, attention to detail, and close adherence to central office policies. Early in the project, she dedicated a mini-series—the Highway Route Series—to America's roads. Because this was an aside to the main American Guide Series, she could control its editorial process and accelerate its production in the interests of demonstrating the project's productivity to Congress. Ultimately, three volumes of tour descriptions cutting across state lines were published: *U.S. One: Maine to Florida* (1938), *The Ocean Highway: New Brunswick, New Jersey, to Jacksonville, Florida* (1938), and *The Oregon Trail: The Missouri River to the Pacific Ocean* (1939). The production and circulation of this series suggest how guidebooks could orchestrate a unifying, uplifting story of the nation in the practical minutiae of their directions and in the categories with which they framed the cultural landscape.[1]

One way of assessing Kellock's vision—thoroughly concentrated in the detailing of routes and roads and tours—is to measure it against dominant representations of the American highway in the 1930s. Whereas in earlier periods, the American road had crystallized the democratic opportunities of America's westward movement, during the Depression writers and photo-journalists converted it into a symbol of human displacement and suffering. When Nathan Asch and James Rorty felt impelled to learn about the crisis in their country in the early 1930s, they took to the road. What they discovered was the futile wandering of a generation. For Asch, the road led nowhere: "I began to see the entire country, with its maze of road, twining, twisting, entering everywhere. I saw the million automobiles, and trains, and buses, and people walking on the road, all trying to get somewhere. I suddenly saw the map of America . . . with scarlet road extending through the states, across mountains, by the sides of the rivers, through the cities, and never getting back anywhere but into itself" (140).

Struck by the numbers of destitute hitchhikers by the highway, Rorty wondered: "What profound failure of American life did this drift of human atoms signify and embody, and to what would it lead?" (56) In 1936, John Dos Passos focused on the same phenomenon when he ended *U.S.A.* with the passive hitchhiker without purpose or goals, who simply "waits on the side of the road" to be carried "a hundred miles down the road" (1183, 1184). By the end of the decade, John Steinbeck was suggesting that down the road lay merely illusion. In *Grapes of Wrath* (1939), he described Highway 66 during the worst of the drought: "People in flight along 66. And the concrete road shone like a mirror under the sun and in the distance the heat made it seem that there were pools of water in the road" (165).

These visions were corroborated, perhaps most famously of all, by the Farm Security Administration photographers. Roy Stryker, head of the Historical Section of the FSA, protested several times that his photographers recorded "positive pictures" of America as well as destitute migrants (14); nevertheless, from 1935 until the outbreak of World War II, the most widely reproduced and remembered photographs were those of bewilderment and fortitude in the face of extreme poverty. In this photographic "memorial of the Depression era," the road served repeatedly as focal point (Keller 25). Dorothea Lange's famous *Westward to the Pacific Coast on U.S. 80, New Mexico, 1938* uses the image of the straight, empty highway to hint at an unending disillusionment: stretching far into the distance, the road offers the possibility of direction, movement, perhaps progress; but that suggestion is undercut by the absolute barrenness of the scene which shows that the road is, in William Stott's words, simply "traveling from emptiness to emptiness toward a receding goal" (62). When Lange peopled the road, she did so with dejected wanderers and straggling, homeless families, as did Walker Evans, Margaret Bourke-White, Russell Lee, and others. Even for the working traveler, the road threatened insecurity: Ben Shahn's *Farmer Carrying His Wheat to the Silo, Ohio, July 1938* (Ill. 8), shot from behind the driver's right shoulder, epitomizes the perspective of Depression documentarists. They were attempting to represent the road and all it signified from the viewpoint of those who were stuck in the horse-and-buggy era, those who were vulnerable to the environment around them, those whose journey along the road was fraught with the possibility of failure.

The American Guide Series generally and Kellock's Highway Route Series particularly challenged this symbolism. In this representational climate, emphasizing the positive potential of the road could easily read as a more general reversal of social breakdown. Various public figures exploited this political mileage: Huey Long won popularity with his road repair measures in Louisiana, while Franklin Roosevelt made highway beautification a prominent New Deal project (Patton 52–53, 73–77; Jakle 126-27). Kellock's contribution operated at the level of image production. She used the guidebooks' rhetoric of fact to reverse the crisis symbolism and their structure to regulate mobility to Progressive ends. In her editorial directives to project workers, roads reveal purposeful movement by linking the nation's past and present:

Roads have not developed by accident; the general course of all routes of importance has been worn by the movements of large numbers of people who wanted to go from one place to another. Many routes were developed by migrating hordes. Thus the tour route is often a thread on which a narrative can be built, with history from the days of Indian occupation of the country to the present, told in geographical rather than topical or chronological sequence. The *social, economic, cultural,* and *political* histories of towns along routes are related to the history of the route itself and most points of interest are closely related to the main theme.

Tours make history coherent by following significant roads and detailing "the rise of civilization in the States at the places where the events occurred." By this vision, geographical mobility served national mythologies of progress once more.[2]

8. Ben Shahn, *Farmer Carrying His Wheat to the Silo, Ohio, July 1938* (Courtesy of the Library of Congress)

Kellock's conviction about the ideological potential of the tour form seems to have derived from her own travels in Eastern Europe and the Soviet Union. She visited that turbulent zone in 1923 in connection with relief work; in 1928, with her husband, when he was exploring trade possibilities; and in 1929, when she conducted a group study tour arranged by the Open Road. Traveling herself and leading others, she realized how thoroughly tour descriptions shaped perceptions of a country and how guide literature could confer international status on a location, all at a level of applied detail that was both useful and rhetorically persuasive. She determined that the United States should have an appropriately elaborate guide series, describing not pleasure excursions but the industrial and social activity bordering on the country's most heavily traveled routes and designed to reach not just the expanding number of motorists at home but the American public at large: in the early days of the project, she emphasized in her letters to state editors "how entertaining . . . [tours] can be, even for the fireside traveler."[3]

That faith in the tour genre was yoked to a larger faith in the Progressive view of history. Kellock was educated in history (along with other social science subjects and journalism) at Columbia University after World War I, a period when Charles Beard, newly departed from the university, was still a major influence (Hofstadter 285–317). Progressivism taught Kellock that the history of America was the sum of its individual citizens' achievements, with due democratic attention to the ordinary worker's role; economic and industrial developments were prime movers in the historical story; and a generally optimistic picture of the nation's course resulted from the panoramic view. With this vision, Kellock became part of the distinctively New Deal impetus described by Alfred Haworth Jones as the use of past history to shore up present national confidence (716–17). She contributed to *The Dictionary of American Biography*, a cornerstone of 1930s' preoccupations with the achievements of individual Americans, and she applied those principles of selection to the Highway Route Series. In a confidential memo to national director Henry Alsberg, she recommended that all project employees read, or at the very least consult, Charles Beard and Mary Beard's *Rise of American Civilization*:

The Beard *Rise* is chiefly valuable for giving workers perspective on what is important and what unimportant. The introduction to the latest edition could very well serve as an explanation of the purposes of the guide; the real purpose is, of course, to educate Americans to an evaluation of their own civilization. "The history of civilization, if intelligently conceived, may be an instrument of civilization. Surveying life as a whole, as distinguished from a microscopic analysis by departments, it ought to come nearer than any partial history to the requirements of illumination."[4]

For Kellock, guidebooks—successful guidebooks—produced civilization, and tours were key to the realization of that project. Her editorial directives sought to systematize this understanding across the country; all state offices were subject to the same directional grid (with tour directions running north to south and east to west despite the local topography and traffic flow), stylistic rules, and ideological framework: "A well-written tour provides a guide to the rise of civilization in the country through which it passes." She repeatedly instructed project workers to shift their attention from the nostalgic and the picturesque to the contemporary and the industrial. Writing under

Alsberg's name, she admonished the New York state director, Bertrand Wainger, that his workers were guilty of "over-writing the scenic features at the expense of the towns"; she wanted "more visual description of people at work—what part human beings play in the industrial process." South Carolina workers were directed to reduce descriptions of antebellum life and say "more about the present day life in the state—descriptions of life in the mill villages, of people at work in canning factories, and cotton mills." One yardstick was the 1909 Baedeker, the most recent guidebook to America as a nation: "We are trying to get away from the Baedeker type of guide that reveals little about the average citizen of the country today, about his interests—homely and otherwise—and about the way he makes his living . . . we endeavor to avoid the antiquarian viewpoint, with its emphasis on old-time events to the exclusion of the less romantic periods of development. We consider the story of the development and the description of a large factory of more importance than the details of settlement of a village." In the "mini-Depression" of 1937 and 1938, Kellock was sending workers out on the roads to look for evidence of vigor, self-sufficiency, and achievement, in other words, evidence of American progress.[5]

This understanding both of the guidebook genre and of American history flew in the face of many local agendas. Not only was Kellock's civilizing mission completely at odds with Fisher's recuperation of the presocial wilderness, but her priorities were counter to many localities' aesthetic, political, and cultural aspirations (as is detailed in the later chapters of this book). Her near-blanket refusal to negotiate with these local knowledges exposes the limits of her democratic inclusiveness: her democratic sympathy for workers extends only to those clearly contributing to a Progressive story of the nation. The tension between respecting and reforming the working poor was typical of New Dealers generally; as with so many Writers' Project administrators, the tension in Kellock is traceable to one additional, relevant strand of her biography: her training in social work.

Born into an Anglo-American, middle-class, Baptist family in Pittsburgh in 1892, Kellock began voluntary service through the Baptist Society and trained with the Red Cross. She then undertook relief work abroad and at home: from 1921 to 1924, she served as a relief supervisor for the American Friends Committee in Poland, Austria, and Russia; she also did public health work with the Taos pueblo and the Henry Street Settlement in New York. In

1935, Lillian Wald was one of the people who recommended her for a position in the Resettlement Administration, which Kellock left in 1936 for the Writers' Project. Kellock's response to this relief work seems typical of the "second generation" of women to enter the central New Deal administration. She was not part of what Susan Ware calls the "women's network" (the top-level appointees such as Frances Perkins and Ellen Woodward, who came to Washington in 1933), whose members' Progressivism was a mixture of reformist zeal and feminism (37–38). Kellock, ten years younger than these women, seems to evince the attitudes of those who arrived in Washington around 1936, as part of the Second New Deal. Ware explains that changes in social work training produced new ideological priorities: "The old reformers, with their concern for the dispossessed and the downtrodden, especially the female dispossessed, were now being replaced by younger, professionally trained women whose visions were considerably narrower" (130). Certainly, Kellock's correspondence with project administrators and directives to workers give little sense of a relief operation; she repeatedly stressed competence and professional standards over rehabilitation. Moreover, though she recognized individual cases of hardship, she did not advocate general reform to the social and economic environment, and she certainly did not intend to hand over the guidebook to the voices of the dispossessed.

What a reading of the Highway Route Series provides, then, is an awareness of Kellock's intersecting ideological commitments (to a Progressive interpretation of history, to professionalized relief, to the ideological purchase of the guidebook genre), all devolving on her crafting and large-scale editorial imposition of the tour form. In later years, she characterized the series' production as hurried: "*U.S. One* and *The Ocean Highway* were slung together because Henry had trouble meeting the charges that we had nothing to show for the money that had been spent on us. It was all I had available that I could link together in a known route. I did *The Oregon Trail* to make up for it, working in the Library of Congress on Saturdays and Sundays and getting some books out of them on loan."[6] That speed may well have led to the inscription of Kellock's ideological agenda at its most unadorned. Certainly, to read from the earliest to the latest guidebook in the series is to move into increasingly coherent narrative and increasingly large claims that the guidebooks provide access to an orderly history and a secure future. Kellock chose U.S. 1 as her first highway project because the route was one of the busiest and oldest in the country (linking twelve of the thirteen original colonies as well as North to South). She devoted most space and detail to the smaller communities and isolated sights along the way, partly because the larger cities were allotted to the state guidebooks but also because, as she told Alsberg, she believed that in the smaller communities lay the true, "undiscovered" America.[7] In 1938—the year of the guidebook's publication—U.S. 1 apparently had some currency as a central route to documenting the nation. Muriel Rukeyser's *U.S. 1* is a volume of poetry whose first, documentary section explores the silicosis scandal of a West Virginia mine. "Road Signs," in *Life* magazine, features Margaret Bourke-White's photographs of U.S. 1 to make its case against the ugly jumble of "hot-dog stands, signs, shacks, dumps and shoddy gas stations" cluttering the entire U.S. auto highway system. Kellock's agenda for U.S. 1 was very different: she coached project writers to look along this route for evidence of progress of various kinds, as expressed through individual activities and industrial achievements.

The effect of these instructions shows up in the selection and description of sights bordering the highway. While references to Revolutionary War battles, colonial architecture, and southern plantations by no means disappear, they jostle side by side with descriptions of steel bridges, cement plants, and asbestos quarries. Ridgefield, New Jersey, is described as an "unpretentious shopping center," with a bank, railroad tracks, and "drab homes and factories"; one mile down the road, Fairview "is announced by the acrid smell from a bleachery" and by the plant of the International Fireworks Company (126). Such industrial constructions are marked much more frequently than the "mile-by-mile" rate promised by Kellock in the book's preface (ix) and attain a stature at least equivalent to that of the more traditional sights.

There is also partial democratization of the historical record. Plenty of sights continue to be associated with Paul Revere, George Washington, Robert E. Lee, and living artists and statesmen. But minor, forgotten players are also recovered for the record, as points of access to visible history: Mason House, Calais, was the home of Noah Smith, "said to have been one of the last people who had official business with President Lincoln before his assassination" (3); the witch-hunt craze was played out in the pond in Fairfield, Connecticut, with the "trial by water" of Mercy Disbrow and Elizabeth Clawson (190); and there is itemized a whole raft of women called Judith, after whom Point Judith, Rhode Island, might (or might not) have been named (81). This profusion of hitherto unremarked buildings and people, with the implication that all are worth attention, gave the lie to Henry James's famous complaint that the American landscape lacks associations.

As well as being crowded, the scene is invested with vigor through its descriptive language. Kellock's editorial reach extended to the minutiae of style: she forbade not just clichéd adjectives and superlatives but personal pronouns and passive or subjunctive verbs in tour write-ups.[8] As a result, the text is dense with inanimate objects linked with active verbs: the road "runs," "connects," "swings," "swoops," and "plunges"; the sea "attacks with a roar, retreats, and returns to attack again" (1); and buildings "border," "look out," "rise," "recall" and "guide." When human figures appear, the sense of energetic activity is reinforced by the manner in which anecdotes about them rush upon each other without comment or conclusion. The impression is one of unflagging activity.

The thread that runs through all these descriptions and details and activities is the emphasis on sights linked, one way or another, with social activity. *U.S. One* pays little attention to natural scenery, concentrating instead on detailed portrayals of architecture and long explanations of industrial processes (such as the cotton gin and the turpentine still in the Georgia chapter). Much space is given over to metaphorical manufactures: despite Kellock's insistence on factual accuracy, she admitted huge numbers of narratives based on legend, tradition, or even gossip. The logic seems to be that the stories, like the buildings and the industrial plants, are evidence of human ingenuity, elaborations heaped up on the American landscape. And this logic seems to determine which people and events the guidebook rescues from oblivion: the text pays attention not necessarily to the famous but to those who have left their mark on the landscape.

This orientation is most marked in the photographs in the volume. Kellock selected thirty illustrations from the states' submissions by many photographic hands; though she rarely participated in the initial selection and framing of subject matter, her control over inclusion does seem to have produced more focus and consistency than was possible in the dense, crowded (and hurriedly compiled) written copy. These illustrations also had the potential to frame the expectations and impressions of both actual and fireside

9. U.S. 1, Stretch of New Jersey

travelers with a pointedness and impact less obvious in the more diffuse text. When Fox Talbot began photographing monuments in the 1830s, his priority was to record "the injuries of time," to preserve historic ruins visually (Sontag 69). A hundred years later, the photography (like the text) of *U.S. One* has the opposite thrust. It is intent on recording what individuals have accumulated through time, via technological achievement, legend-building, or simply by making their mark on the landscape.

First and most obviously, the visual representations suggest the perspective adopted by the architect of *U.S. One*. "Stretch of U.S. 1, New Jersey" (Ill. 9) shows that the viewpoint is no longer that of the Depression documentarist: the road is seen not by the horse-and-buggy farmer, open and vulnerable to whatever the road delivers, but by the motorist, enclosed in a vehicle and limited in vision by the narrow rectangle of the windscreen. This traveler represents what Rexford Tugwell called the "comfort group": that class of people who lacked the ostentatious luxuries of the rich but who were protected by their employment from the vicissitudes of the poor (124). (In 1922, a much richer year for Americans in the aggregate than 1938, Tugwell estimated that only one-eleventh of the total incomes in the United States were at the comfort level.) Not only is the motorist protected from the landscape by modern technology, but the scene into which she or he drives is not unadorned: along the clipped borders of this highway, unlike Dorothea Lange's, appear human constructions in the shapes of billboards and buildings.

The bulk of the illustrations sustains this emphasis on construction by focusing on architectural subjects, most of them distinctively ornate. In *The Culture of Cities* (1938), Lewis Mumford distinguishes between two categories of architecture: on the one hand, buildings, whose appearance is determined by their functional purpose; and on the other hand, monuments, whose facades declare their interest in glorification, remembrance, or decoration (357). In this guidebook's thirty photographs, there is only one image of a building, and it is specifically linked with New Deal resourcefulness: a rectangular, plain house from the Resettlement Administration's Greenbelt experiment in Maryland. All the other subjects are emphatic monuments photographed in an emphatically monumental style: neoclassical churches and capitols and, in particular, the majestic City Hall in Philadelphia, which was photographed especially for this guidebook lighted by a battery of spotlights so as to emphasize the grandeur of the sight while blacking out any life surrounding it. Very often photographs show ordinary Americans' attempts to monumentalize their buildings. "Wedding Cake House," Maine (Ill. 10) superimposes upon a square, conventional house the decorative, nonutilitarian qualities of a monument: wooden pinnacles, trellised canopy, elaborate tracery, Gothic peaks, and large wooden arches (all detailed in the textual description). The text makes explicit the human agency implied in this site: "A local legend is that the decorations were added by a sea captain whose bride had been deprived of her large wedding cake when he was ordered hastily to sea in an emergency" (43).

When that process of monumentalization is linked to modern technology, the spirit of progress lurking within all the illustrations becomes explicit. One photograph portrays Bayonne Bridge in New Jersey (Ill. 11), which, the text reports, was opened to traffic in 1932 and was "the longest steel-arch bridge in the world" (129). The angle of the photograph, chosen from several differently configured shots (which survive in the New York City Archives), was the only one to strike an emphatic contrast between past and progress. In the foreground, at the bottom of the picture, are the old, decaying remains of either a ferry landing or a pier. Rising in an arc away from these

74

10. *Wedding Cake House*, Maine

11. Bayonne Bridge, New Jersey

ruins is the steel bridge, majestic and modern, extending the road across barriers to new distances. Another photograph shows Hutchinson River Parkway in New York State, one of several 1930s' beautification projects that were associated with federal funds and job creation (Patton 71). This nature parkway is gently curving and well kept, bordered by the blossoming foliage of planted trees. Again, it is a world away from Dorothea Lange's and Ben Shahn's roads: a highway whose artificially pastoral appearance "instruct[s] drivers about how best to appreciate the scenery out the window," a road for the motorized who have the resources for pleasant, purposeful travel (Wilson 29). It is also a moment when the New Deal–funded guidebook serves the New Deal–created landscape, a nice tautology that goes entirely unacknowledged.

That there is cost to this celebration of progress is indicated by one final illustration which superimposes the present on the past. "Old Slave Market, Louisville, Georgia" (Ill. 12) introduces an odd category of photograph to the guidebook. More a holiday snapshot than an informational illustration, the sign of progress seems to be the achievement of holiday leisure in a site previously dedicated to the exploitation of human labor. Tellingly, it is white women—simultaneously objects and agents in southern history—who literally block out the market's interior while returning and deflecting the reader's gaze; the focus is on the modern, progressive South at the expense of any textured representation of its costs or oppressions. The written text helps little here, its emphasis all on architectural detail and anecdotal narrative with no mention of the African Americans whose bodies gave the market its meaning.

That Kellock selected this illustration with this caption suggests, simultaneously, her attempt and her failure to include the oppressed in her ostensibly inclusive, democratic gaze. The access to history provided by *U.S. One*, for all its revelations and recoveries of those whom national memory forgot, ultimately seems a structural impediment to any histories that refuse the Progressive narrative.

The logical consequence of the tension in *U.S. One* is played out in *The Ocean Highway: New Brunswick, New Jersey, to Jacksonville, Florida* (1938), when anecdote becomes teleological narrative and African Americans become discordant presences rather than awkward absences. In the

12. Old Slave Market, Louisville, Georgia

first guidebook, the shaping force of Kellock's interpretation of American society is limited to the selection of anecdotes and sights in the locality of the highway. The range of the next volume is more ambitious: very similar material becomes synecdochic of an entire region. *The Ocean Highway* traces four segments—parts of U.S. 130, 40, 30, and 17—from New Jersey to Florida. Much of this route parallels U.S. 1, but a much greater proportion runs through the South, which becomes the framing history for the tours. Kellock explains in the guidebook's introduction: "An outline of that history is a necessary adjunct to a description of the towns and points of interest along the route; but much of the story of the Ocean Highway country is necessarily the story of the whole South" (xv). The historical account that follows shows, again, the influence of the Beards' *Rise*: conflict between North and South is explained predominantly in economic terms, with slavery presented more as an economic than a racial issue. Indeed, African Americans figure remarkably little in this essay, which ends on an optimistic note: the prospect of newfound prosperity, with "the Old South . . . entering a new cycle in its long history" (xv).

The tours carry the same note of optimism and historical continuity as the introduction. There are fewer sights listed than in *U.S. One*, each more extensively treated in a narrative that links origin to contemporary appearance. For example, the history of Brunswick, Georgia, is detailed, from its beginnings as a Spanish port in 1566, through its development as a plantation in the eighteenth century, to its downfall in the Civil War. The description ends on a typically optimistic note by pointing to the recent construction of a pulp wood factory that "provides opportunity for a major industrial development" (155–56). Instead of dashing from one anecdote to another, the traveler here is guided through a series of ostensibly complete local histories that purport to link past events to present progress in a chronological flow. The guidebook ends with a final demonstration of continuity. Having led the motorist down the southern coast, the text ends with a 1584 travelogue, "Barlow's Description of the North Carolina Coast." The implication is that, in following the road by this guide's directions, the contemporary traveler is put in direct touch with the country's past and all that has been achieved in the interim.

Against all these aspirations to completeness, the limitations on the guidebook's access to history become particularly noticeable. The most obvious gap in the record is the disproportionate attention to African Americans, a problem noted by Kellock herself. Evidence indicates that she chided workers in the southern states to give her more material on blacks, but she never managed to solicit an appropriate quantity: mentions are never proportionate to the acknowledged African American presence in society. The description of New Bern, North Carolina, for example, reveals that African Americans "constitute 52 percent of the population" (111), then, after a hasty remark about their workplace and residence, the text turns to a very long, detailed paragraph about the town's German settlers. Similarly, the South Carolina chapter gestures to the high proportion of blacks in the state, then provides very little description of them. Project workers' failure to document black culture is, of course, evidence not just of local racism but of the imbalance in project employment patterns across race lines as well as the structural limitations of the Progressive narrative which workers were being directed to compose.

The photographs, again, dramatize the interestedness of the guidebook's view. By and large, the illustrations in *The Ocean Highway* are the familiar mixture of monuments, dressed-up buildings, and industrial sites. But five

13. A Tangier Island Scooter

photographs depict single human figures—never the case in *U.S. One*—and their placing of the human in the landscape exposes some of the social consequences of the guidebook's frame of reference, especially when yoked to a Progressive agenda. Essentially, the guidebook defines social contribution in entrepreneurial terms, thereby limiting the types who can qualify for national recognition and instantiating human worth as material productivity.

The two photographs of whites stress ingenuity and visible achievement in mildly humorous accents. "A Tangier Island Scooter" (Ill. 13) documents a member of a remote, upstanding community in Chesapeake Bay, Virginia. The details of the photograph suggest that a potential victim of poverty has been transformed into an ingenious inventor. Children were a frequent subject for Depression photographers, but the image of this child contrasts markedly with the compositions of Evans, Lange, and Lee in the same way that the guidebook's roads contrast with theirs. Like any of Walker Evans's southern children, the figure here is grubby and the clothing tattered. But in

Evans's photographs, such children invariably appear clutching at parents or physically hemmed in by their environment, passive and trapped. In this illustration, however, the child's ingenious invention—the "primitive sailboat"(72)—provides mobility and some measure of control; like the motorist photographed in *U.S. One*, the child is "in the driver's seat," steering her or himself, metaphorically at least, out of the Depression.

The second photograph of a white figure—the final human portrait in the book—shows a man surrounded by gigantic fish, one of which he has apparently caught. This illustration mobilizes another discordant category of representation: the "Believe It or Not!" view of the world. In the outsize fish, we see an example of what Karal Ann Marling calls "the colossus," versions of which dotted the roadside in 1930s' America and shown in Ripley's newspaper features and radio travelogues, newly produced and vastly popular in the period; the 1930s have been called Ripley's "Golden Age" of syndicated newspaper features, books, radio shows, movie shorts, lectures, vaudeville, "Odditoriums," and the yoking of bizarre facts to travel (Considine). There is a logic in Florida's gigantic natural resources appearing as the end of, and reward for, American progress; but the Ripleyesque representation seems more appropriate to the kind of booster, Chamber of Commerce pamphlet which Kellock (and the central office generally) abhorred. The photograph can be read to betray the mythological urge of the Progressivist agenda: in displaying the ordinary man with the extraordinary fish, the tour offers what Marling argues the colossus always promises: "a stopping place in time, where the everyday rules of reality are suspended and an idyllic dream commences" (*Colossus* 101).

The lack of fit between the human and the guidebook's landscape increases exponentially when the subject is African American. If the portraits of white Americans express discordancy through a measure of humor, for a black constituency the discordancy is in the social consequences of valorizing monumental achievement. These three photographs are the only illustrations of blacks in the Highway Route Series, and the figures' positioning—via what Susan Sontag calls "the un-innocent nature of a photograph's framing, angle, focus"—demonstrates their exclusion from the world in which they are framed (108). The two male figures are subsumed beneath images of monumental, entrepreneurial America. In "St. Michael's, Charles-

14. St. Michaels, Charleston, South Carolina

ton, South Carolina" (Ill. 14), the man is excentric to the focus created by the caption and the picture's composition; walking into the shadows with which his skin blends, he is clearly heading for the margins of this world. That displacement takes on additional ideological charge in the case of "Wetter House (1840), Savannah, Georgia" (Ill. 15). Again, the caption takes the reader's eye away from the human up to the decorated architecture; the man trying to make his living with the barrow—entrepreneurial a pose as that is—becomes a nearly invisible figure, set against the wall that cuts him off from the monumental architecture central to the guidebook's social imaginary.

This process of reification is confirmed in "Tenant Cabin, South Carolina" (Ill. 16). Like the white women before the slave market, the black woman is a posed, knowing subject. The difference in her positioning, however, makes it difficult to ascribe any agency to the scene: sitting in the door of the cabin, not foregrounded but part of the building, she is defined by the structure

15. Wetter House (1840), Savannah, Georgia

with which her figure blends and for which the illustration is captioned. This is a different relationship to history and society than the white women's: while their presence converts the slave market from political marker to local color, the black tenant woman is part of the local color in the making via the guidebook's priorities of representation.

The claims to completeness that frame *The Ocean Highway*'s tours, then, heighten our awareness of the guidebook's several forms of partiality. Especially in the visual material, representation comes to be about its own exclusions, heavily demarcated by the lines of race, gender, and class.

The Oregon Trail: The Missouri River to the Pacific Ocean (1939) was Kellock's favorite volume in the Highway Route Series and the most seamless. First, this guidebook traced a route—"the frontier"—that reverberated with nationalistic symbolism. Second, its historical orientation enabled a more harmonious—because more temporally and geographically distanced—representation of racial and cultural difference. And, third, this work's tours folded the reader into their triumphant narrative of nation-building more se-

16. Tenant Cabin, South Carolina

curely than ever. There was a distinct preservationist motive to *The Oregon Trail*, signaled in its sponsorship by the Oregon Trail Memorial Association (whose lineage and emphasis on education and resistance to commercialization are documented in Kammen 397–98). Kellock aimed at enshrining a certain version of the frontier past; making the Progressive link to the present was the reader's or traveler's job. The tours are constructed in such a way that their readers are well positioned to do that job on the guidebook's terms.

Kellock's introduction squarely fits the guidebook to the project of nation-building: "The history of the Oregon Trail is the history of how two million square miles of land . . . came under the control of a weak new nation and made it one of the mighty powers of all time" (1). The succeeding essays directly challenge the negative frontier rhetoric of the 1930s. In the Depression years, Turner's famous thesis about the significance of the frontier to American development was under considerable attack. On the one hand, certain historians disputed his entire argument on the grounds that he had ignored complex industrial and economic forces that were much more influential than the frontier on modern American society (see Nettels, Alexander, Billington). On the other hand, those who accepted Turner's thesis now stressed its negative connotations: to them, the Depression proved that the closing of the frontier had ended the economic opportunities that accounted for America's distinctive nationalism, democracy, and individualism. Roosevelt's use of the frontier image in his 1932 presidential campaign exploited the second interpretation to justify increased federal intervention in the economic and social fabric: "A glance at the situation today only too clearly indicates that equality of opportunity as we have known it no longer exists. . . . Our last frontier has long since been reached and there is practically no more free land"; the only solution was "enlightened administration" by the government (qtd. in Alexander 4).

The introductory remarks to *The Oregon Trail* challenge both these assumptions, asserting the frontier's formative role in American development and its continuing presence in the spirit of the American people. The foreword by Alsberg insists that "the Oregon Trail . . . presents a story particularly pertinent to our times" (v). Comparing the depression of the 1830s, which stimulated western migration, with the Depression of the 1930s, Alsberg underscores Roosevelt's point: "The great difference between then and now is to be found in the fact that today there are no longer western frontiers. Since we cannot migrate to undeveloped land as a solution for our troubles, we are now cultivating our neglected human and material resources." But Alsberg also argues for the frontier's continued relevance, declaring that "without a knowledge of the period between 1800 and 1870 it is impossible to understand the trends of our times. The American spirit of independence that carried thousands of emigrants from the East to the Pacific Coast is still alive." Kellock, who had a zeal for western history, asserted her belief in the survival of the frontier spirit even more strongly than her director. Her introduction ends: "The biological genes . . . that . . . made the United States an empire extending from coast to coast have not been bred out" (33).

The guidebook leads readers, as travelers, to a vicarious experience of the past. Kellock told Vardis Fisher that this guidebook was "an advance . . . a new type of narrative" and Alsberg that it was "the first tour-book in which American history is told in . . . geographical rather than topical or chronological sequence." The same point is made by a more recent commentator, Arthur Scharf: "Where the eastern books emphasize what you see as you drive along, 'The Oregon Trail' is a history book in geographic sequence." No longer cajoling contemporary material from her writers, Kellock concentrated on the stuff of history, requiring the traveler to effect the link between past and present. *The Oregon Trail* traces the westering movement back to the Middle Ages, tells stories about the nineteenth century, and extracts accounts from diaries and letters of the period, most of them previously unpublished. Kellock also fashioned the guidebook into a quasi-historical artifact: the photographs and reproductions are primarily from the nineteenth century, but even the modern illustrations are sepia tinted; and, as Kellock explained to Agnes Wright Spring, Wyoming state director, the cloth covers were fashioned to resemble "coarse, unbleached homespun," in imitation of the pioneers' cloth.[9]

As well as reading about and touching a facsimile of the past, modern travelers were reenacting pioneer history by following the same routes. In the book's preface, Kellock insisted on the link via transportation: "The pioneering forefathers were not different from their descendants. . . . No motorist today is more interested in his speedometer records than were the pioneers in those of their ox-cart 'roadometers' " (xi). In one tour, travelers are presented to themselves as the most recent wave of frontiersmen, succeeding previous types in a Turnerian scheme. Jackson Hole, Wyoming, is described: "Here for many years the fur trader held rendezvous with the Indian . . . here the Indians fought and failed to halt the whites as they pushed westward; here the cowman made his own law and rid the country of the outlaw, the cattle rustler, and the horse thief; and here today come thousands of visitors in search of recreation" (209). This is a considerably more genteel parade than Vardis Fisher's in the Idaho guidebook. Whether readers self-identify as visitors or as citizens of the frontier zone, they are positioned within a triumphant procession of progress.

In many ways, the past that is portrayed in *The Oregon Trail* resembles that described in the other two Kellock guidebooks. The dominant force is provided by individuals: "The history of the West is filled with the names of those whose ideas and activities, at decisive moments, determined the course of events" (1). As before, these individuals include famous names— John C. Frémont, Meriwether Lewis and William Clark, Hugh Glass—but considerable attention is also given to hitherto unknown pioneers and their unheroic problems, which come alive in private diaries and letters. For example, at different stages of the journey we learn about the adventures of a Mormon pioneer, William Clayton—everything from the extracting of his tooth to his jealous obsession with his mile-counting "roadometer." Indeed, we learn much more about Clayton than about Bill Cody and Jesse James, who are mentioned dismissively in passing. Kellock deliberately advanced the ordinary over the stereotypically heroic, telling Vardis Fisher that she wanted "good tough-minded, unsentimental stuff" and reminding the Oregon director of "the realistic slant we gave to material on pioneers that had been presented somewhat sentimentally." The guidebook also opposed the tragic view of settlement: "The story of the western migration has usually been told in terms of those who made mistakes. . . . But for every person who became a symbol of pioneer tragedy there were thousands who thoroughly enjoyed the overland journey. . . . A Utah woman who had crossed the country about 1850 remembered the trip as a picnic from beginning to end" (73).[10]

In inviting readers to identify with the "average," previously anonymous, flesh-and-blood pioneer, this guidebook crosses racial lines unbroached in the previous two volumes to adopt what had become among liberals (at least those outside areas with large Native American populations) a fairly typical cultural relativism toward Native peoples. Descriptions encourage readers to appreciate the Native as well as the white perspective. Tales of attacks on whites are always prefaced with an explanation: "By 1862 the western Indians had reached a point of desperation. They had been misled and coerced into signing agreements that confined them to lands far too small and quite unsuitable for the ways of life to which they had been accustomed. Promised payments in goods were either not being made, or were inadequate to support them. Game on which they depended for food was being destroyed recklessly by the invaders" (109). Sometimes the criticisms of a contemporary white are quoted: "No pen can describe the misery and despair of a Pawnee village . . . while the white tribe was killing, or scaring their game off into the mountains, and I say that our Government here caused as much misery by negligence as the Turks have by savagery" (74). The impetus to expose the humanity disguised by the savage stereotype clearly came from Kellock. She exhorted J. Harris Gable, the Nebraska state director, to train his workers to avoid the word *massacre* in describing Indian attacks, itemizing all the justifications for their reprisals; and she criticized Wyoming's copy: "In treating encounters between whites and Indians, the copy puts great stress on the terrors of Indian attacks, and does not give the Indian side of the story which is that the natives were being deprived of their homes by white invaders. . . . Please try to get in some material from the Indian point of view." Kellock was no longer asking for material about ethnic minorities; she was encouraging writers (thereby readers and travelers) to cross periods and racial perspectives. And by displacing difference to the past, she was able to insist on a much more explicit acknowledgment of the human cost of progress than in the previous volumes.[11]

This shift of emphasis is also indicated in a more symbiotic relationship between human and monumental landscape, industrial and natural. More than half the illustrations focus on human beings and caption their presence directly. To present industrial achievement, Kellock had requested of writers at the inception of the series "what part human beings play in the industrial process." Various illustrations of wagon trains and railroad lines center on the human beings who are bringing their inventions to the prairies: for example, the engraving "Union Pacific Workers (1867)" foregrounds men working vigorously with spades and picks and slaking the thirst caused by their energetic endeavors. In photographs of the landscape, we are reminded not just of human accumulations heaped up on the land but of the ways in which human and land affect each other. Natural formations such as Scottsbluff and Devil's Tower appear beyond human scale in the photographs of them, but the captions and written text reveal that they are ineradicably labeled for and distinguished by the human efforts applied to them. Yet the text also explains how people's attempts to monumentalize the land can come to nothing: in Nebraska, travelers past and present inscribe their names on rock face only to have storms erase their markings from the soft stone. This symbiosis is expressed most poignantly in the final photograph of the book, "Along the Trail" (Ill. 17). In a sense, the land has defeated the occupants of these graves, but, in making their journey, these travelers have equally left their mark on the landscape, as is shown by this photograph and by the profusion of grave markers noted throughout the text.

Revisionism, of course, always has its limits. When it came to the West, Kellock's limits were remarkably close to Vardis Fisher's, even though she celebrated settlement while he recuperated the wilderness. Restitution is affordable only to those constituencies that can be contained by the past: according to Kellock's introduction, the nineteenth-century West progressed from "a few hundred thousand aborigines, most of whom still had a late Stone Age culture" to "more than 11 million citizens of the United States . . .

17. Along the Trail

divided into political subdivisions with stable governments" (1). The individuation of Native American peoples in the guidebook occurs only via taxonomic portraits by George Catlin, which evacuate them from any living landscape, and legends associated with topographical features—the Native American, again, as local color.

Gender is similarly contained. Although the narrative of *The Oregon Trail* did acknowledge women's contributions to settlement, their perspective did not shape the guidebook's structure. As with the democratization of history in *U.S. One*, the access point has broadened, but the fundamental categories of historical significance—a version of the "Great Men" view of history— have not shifted. The accounts here are predominantly those of wagon train leaders, missionaries, politicians, and traders. The photographs situate women consistently in supportive roles within family groups; any agency attempted by individual women—Sacajawea guiding Lewis and Clark, Mrs. Donner opposing her husband's gullibility about a shortcut—does not shift the fundamental coordinates established by the guidebook.

Ultimately, the sacrifices and achievements are balanced into a nationalist equation that universalizes the dominant interest as everyone's. By their selection of historical details, the tours guide readers along a road of progress that extends continent-wide: "Those who write of the Lewis and Clark expedition are apt to stress the discomforts and dangers the party experienced, forgetting that these were the price, fully anticipated and gladly paid, of fulfilling a dream centuries old—that of finding a central route across North America" (161).

Countering the desolation imagery of the documentarists, the doubters of American cultural maturation, and the social implications of the Depression, Katharine Kellock's guidebooks made the nation appear crowded with monuments to the efforts of ordinary Americans, contributors to their country's progress. In the process, they also established some principles of exclusion. Right from the preliminary section, "Special Foods from Maine to Florida" in *U.S. One*, women are positioned uneasily: here, the decline in regional culinary standards is ascribed partly to the professionalization of women beyond the home. African Americans never figured comfortably in the series, though the lack of fit is most visible in *The Ocean Highway*. And Native Americans appear in the equation as the lamentable, unjust, but inevitable loss that underwrites the progress documented in *The Oregon Trail*.

The extent to which the agendas traceable in the editorial process carry over into reviews of the Highway Route Series says something about the framing power of guidebooks and the effectiveness of the national office's editorial regulation. Reviews were numerous and enthusiastic, and, by and large, they accepted the guidebooks' terms: the volumes were appreciated for their comprehensiveness (Howard Rushmore, of New York City, in the Sunday *Worker* went so far as to say that "nothing has been overlooked" in *The Oregon Trail*); the variety of their roadside discoveries, so much livelier in presentation than the dull Baedeker ("Me. to Fla." in the *New York Herald-Tribune* praised *U.S. One* as "a guide to interest and history and beauty and progress"); and their education of U.S. travelers, armchair and actual (the latter who, according to "Mirror to America" in *Time*, tend to "whizz over the surface of their country").

Most significantly, reviewers do treat guidebooks as access to history. Bernard DeVoto, dean of western history and eastern editorials, singled out Kellock's production for its use value: "'U.S. One' is the most workmanlike product, so far, of the Writers' Project. It is more purely and more consistently a guidebook than any of its predecessors. It can be carried in the pocket and, more important, it can be used in the car" ("U.S. One"). He lauded these volumes—unlike some of the bulkier guidebooks—for answering the requirements of tourists, not researchers. However lightheartedly, he also recognized that there was an ideological charge to use: the section on regional foods "makes excellent reading, should reinforce anyone's patriotism and make tourists out of the most sedentary."

Although reviews are not equivalent to actual use of guidebooks, they can be read as a form of implementation in that reviewers mobilize selected information. It is telling that, despite some noting of factual errors by local reviewers, most reproduce the guidebooks' emphases and elisions. When Katherine McClure Anderson reviewed *U.S. One* in the *Macon* (Georgia) *Telegraph*, for example, she followed the guidebook in treating the Louisville slave market simply as the occasion for an anecdote about the market bell, and she reproduced the dominant gendering of the guidebooks, putting the man in the driver's seat: when " 'time is too short' (so your husband says) to stop and read the Historical society marker . . . I recommend this guide as an indispensable and delightfully enlightening traveling companion." Similarly, Edmond S. Meany Jr. felt authorized, in his *Washington Post* review, to tease women: the guidebook brings "assurance that the Principal Passenger will henceforth confine her back-seat driving to the absorbing problems of navigation which this volume provides." The same assumption informs James Marron's review, "Going My Way?," which casually identifies a male "family breadwinner" as driver and guidebook user.

Even reviewers who emphasize cultural difference and minority figures do so predominantly in terms of visible progress. One anonymous review, "'U.S. One: Maine to Florida' Tells Tourists Where to Go, What to See and What to Eat," feminizes the process of travel specifically to document contemporary improvements: "When in 1704 Madam Knight rode on horseback from Boston to New York she found the roads 'incumbered with Rocks and mountainous passages, which were very disagreeable to my tired carcass.' Today the route she traveled is part of U.S. Route No. 1." When Lewis Gannett, in his column "Books and Things" in the *New York Herald Tribune*, foregrounded women and African Americans, he selected exceptional individuals who proved the universality of social advancement. He linked the value of *U.S. One* to stories about Margaret Brent's demand for "voyce and vote" in 1648 and the slave John Chavis's education at Princeton and subsequent teaching of North Carolina statesmen.

The one review that did not read the guidebooks simply as evidence of progress was Harry Hansen's, in his column, "The First Reader" in the *New York World Telegram*. He paused over the *U.S. One* description of Rockingham, North Carolina, noticing its exposure of the unequal labor conditions and poor living standards of local African Americans. When this passage reappeared in the North Carolina guide a few years later, it caused a local furor because, critics charged, it misrepresented the region's social and economic advances (as is detailed in Chapter 6). The ideological framework of *U.S. One*—its myth of progress—seems to have been so secure that even Hansen's quotation of this passage caused not a ripple in the celebratory reception of the guidebook.

What remains largely unchallenged, then, is the Highway Route Series' implicit claim that the history of the American landscape, in the long term, spells progress. Robert Nisbet has argued that, in all ages, "the past . . . is vital to the idea of progress. . . . It was only when men [sic] became conscious of a long past, one held in common through ritual and then history and literature, that a consciousness of progressive movement from past to present became possible, a consciousness easily extrapolated to the future" (323). With immediate application to the American citizen of the 1930s, Malcolm Cowley said: "By that past he is reassured of his present importance; in it he finds strength to face the dangers that lie in front of him" (qtd. in Alexander 36). Inasmuch as reviews suggest cultural impact, the guidebook genre seems to have facilitated Kellock's efforts at consciousness-building and reassurance. Reviewers of the Highway Route Series seem as confident as she that, by guiding readers and travelers down roads leading to a vigorous past, she was also pointing the way toward a vigorous and credible future.

New York City

The View from Rockefeller Center versus the View from the Sidewalk

Doubtless, both Vardis Fisher and Katharine Kellock would have bristled at the application of the label "political" to their vision of America. On the New York City project, however, many of the writers brandished their politics, especially those who occupied differing but equally vociferous positions on the left. Their radicalism tested the limits of both the New Deal project and the guidebook genre, ultimately helping to bring down the first but being tamed and contained by the second. The most telling dynamic in *New York Panorama* (1938) and *The WPA Guide to New York City* (1939) is their management of oppositional politics via their structures of display. *New York Panorama* is driven by a futurological perspective and a bird's-eye view, which, together, attempt to reorder the city's socioeconomic inequities into a larger pattern of balance. The organization of the *Guide to New York City* is political in a different way: it takes the user down to street level and the present, engendering faith in the city by detailing it as a series of distinctive communities.

The New York City Writers' Project occupied a privileged position, as a "49th State," within the WPA: the five hundred-plus employees on its Writers' Project included such a unusually high proportion of proven and promising writers that national director Henry Alsberg, always keen to nurture creative potential, initially gave the unit relative autonomy. This policy had unforeseen political consequences because so many of the young New York writers were active on the left. Orrick Johns, the first New York City director, was a former editor of the *New Masses*.[1] Marxists Philip Rahv, William Phillips, and Harold Rosenberg were project employees during the editing of and hiatus in *Partisan Review*. Lionel Abel and Harry Roskolenko were heavily influenced by Leon Trotsky. Kenneth Fearing was identified with the Stalinist faction; Richard Wright became perhaps the best-known Communist Party member; and Maxwell Bodenheim, of an older generation, was "Greenwich Village Bohemian turned Communist" (Mangione, *Dream* 160). Although the dominant voices within the unit were radical, the New York City project drew in a wide spectrum of employees, including zealots on the right who came to form watchdog bodies—such as the Federal Writers Association and the Civilian WPA Control—against leftist debate, in addition to traditional cultural nationalists who put themselves on record (often directly to Roosevelt) as unsympathetic toward any political activity on the project.

The unit became a cockpit for the ideological fights then holding sway across the New York intellectual scene, exacerbated by what one investigator called the "psychological insecurity" inculcated by uncertain project conditions.[2] In the fight for ever-dwindling jobs, about 75 percent of project workers came to be unionized into both ethnic and political groups: the most powerful of the former were the Jewish coalitions; the two main trade unions were the Writers' Union and the Workers' Alliance. The left mounted dramatic strikes against the limited initiatives of the New Deal—hunger strikes, sit-in strikes, work stoppages, picket lines, placard demonstrations, occupations of administrative offices, occasionally even the imprisonment of an administrator in his office—as well as bitter fights among anti-Stalinist, socialist, and Popular Front factions. Meanwhile, right wingers made the press the mouthpiece for their complaints against the project's politicization.

None of this frenetic activity made for steady output. Up to 1937, the project's main publications were mimeographed pro-Soviet newsletters—most infamously, the vituperative *Red Pen*—and Trotskyite leaflets, which provided ammunition for attacks by Martin Dies's House Un-American Activities Committee, Clifton Woodrum's subcommittee of the House Appropriations Committee, and the Republican National Committee. In response, the central office became more interventionist, replacing the New

York City director and upper echelon of editors with employees more committed to the New Deal and the guidebook project; in the four years of the project's existence, six directors came and went, as Alsberg struggled to find the right combination of administrative skill, political savvy, and editorial flair.[3] The national director also came to insist on scrutinizing all copy for the guidebooks and publicity releases. In 1938, the flood of project publications began. Ultimately, New York City published about twenty volumes—almanacs, ethnic and racial studies, natural history, maritime history, and, of course, the guidebooks—but these works came too late to change the dominant impression of the project as, in the words of the Republican National Committee, "a festering sore of Communism" (Mangione, *Dream* 290).

The turmoil within which the guidebooks were produced was not limited to the Writers' Project. According to Peter Conrad, 1929–39 is the decade "when New York most irrevocably transforms itself. The raising of the Chrysler Building (1930), the Empire State (1931), and Rockefeller Center (completed in 1940) demanded that the city conceive of itself anew" (248). During this period the metropolis became the nexus of passionate debates, fueled by the Depression at home and frightening political and military developments abroad: anti-Stalinist radicals celebrated the cosmopolitan city, progressive and conservative regionalists damned the inhuman "megalopolis," and critics of many political stripes disdained its commercialized mass culture.[4] Although individual project employees shared some of these positions, as collective productions the guidebooks did something quite different. They promoted versions of the city which attempted to reassure readers about the stability of New York, the politics of its authors, and the value of the Federal Writers' Project.

The first WPA guidebook to New York City is, in several respects, reminiscent of other promotional materials of the period such as *Advancing New York* or publicity for the New York World's Fair: *New York Panorama* exhibits the same confidence in New York City as the epicenter of American culture, the same faith in the future, and the same assurance of harmony—ultimately intact despite several essays' avowals of the city's complexities, their nice distinctions, and their refusal of easy optimism (Gelernter). What is more legible in *Panorama*, however, is the cost of that upbeat rhetoric in the suppression of alternative narratives. Although many of the specific editorial choices are no longer recoverable from this project's archive, the broader brush strokes of project processes as well as more wide-reaching ideological debates of the period can contextualize a reading of the published copy. From this perspective, certain images—the famous Rockefeller Center, the anonymous pretzel vendor—read like textual stress points, moments that come close to exposing the containment and suppression necessary to *Panorama*'s veneer of stable representation.

Several of the collaborators in the guide's production wrote very critically of the city in their off-project writings. In "I Went into the Country," Harry Roskolenko wrote, "the City creates, but is unkind, another doom"; his *Sequence on Violence* (1938)—poetry he described as "my version of hell"— won him the accolade "the very voice of the modern city" from Lewis Mumford (qtd. in Roskolenko, *Cherry Street* 155). Vincent McHugh fictionalized the collapse of New York into a maelstrom of irrationality in his novel *I Am Thinking of My Darling* (1943). Richard Wright first wrote of urban savagery on the project, winning the *Story* magazine prize for Federal Writers' Project employees and later a Guggenheim award with *Uncle Tom's Children* (1938; enlarged 1940); his novel *Native Son* (1940), among other works, displays the viciousness of the city, especially to young blacks mired in poverty. And Ralph Ellison, Wright's younger colleague on the project, later wrote some of the violence (both inter and intraracial) in and beyond Harlem in *Invisible Man* (1952).

In one textual strain in *Panorama* the imprint of the guidebook genre and the government-sponsored project bear down on these critical tendencies. Another level of suppression operated in the handling of gender. It is no accident that the novelists most frequently named to the project were men. Women were employed on the project as writers—New York had, among others, Anzia Yezierska and Charlotte Wilder, typically identified as "a sister of Thornton Wilder"—but they clustered more numerously in the secretarial and clerical divisions (Roskolenko, *Cherry Street* 154). The category of gender was not on the agenda of the Writers' Project, nor of the left in general, in the way that race was (a struggle long fought and hard won by African Americans themselves).[5] Again, the guidebook manages the representation of women by converting them from a potential generic rupture into a less threatening anomaly.

The opening essay is symptomatic of the volume's rhetorical thrust. In both its production and its textual dynamics, "Metropolis and Her Children" converted political turmoil and urban chaos into symmetrical order, partly by projecting future stability. Although the essay—like all guidebook pieces—is unsigned, Vincent McHugh is on record as its primary author. McHugh, a novelist promoted first to technical director, then to editor in chief in the reshuffle initiated by the D.C. office, was also the main architect of the volume as a whole. He anatomized the city into cultural components—history, architecture, the arts, labor, city planning, ethnic and racial groups—then persuaded politically polarized writers to cooperate on the collective composition of essays (ultimately twenty-six essays and one hundred illustrations). McHugh spoke for apoliticism, compromise, and, above all, order. As Robert Bruere wrote in his report on the New York City project commissioned by Harry Hopkins: "Almost from the start, the Guide Book has careened down through the total Project enterprise like a ten-ton truck run wild. . . . The most effective step taken by the Washington office in saving the Guide Book from the confusion into which it had fallen was the appointment of Mr. McHugh as Technical Director." An August 1938 publicity release for the work of the New York City project, titled "How It Was Done," stressed the scientific precision with which the vast confusion of the city had been subjected to techniques of fact-gathering, filing, and condensation instituted by McHugh.[6]

Textually, McHugh's essay restructures the topical, multifaceted debate about the ideological implications of the city into two competing—but by this account compatible—discourses. The essay opens in a breathless, rhapsodic style that mimics "Whitman's concept of New York as a symbol of the democratic maelstrom" (16). Having invoked what Peter Conrad names the standard genius loci of the time (21), McHugh exposes the tendency toward anarchy and commercial trivialization in Walt Whitman's "neo-romantic" concept of the city's "noble disorder" (16). In search of an antidote, the essay shifts to a more orderly expository style, expressing a 1930s' enthusiasm for city planning, a struggling profession elevated to national policy by the New Deal (Boyer 203, Tafuri, "Regional Plan" 431–47). Again, the essay conflates antithetical discourses: it cites, approvingly, the published plans of Thomas Adams and Lewis Mumford without acknowledging that Mumford had publicly denounced Adams's capitalist methods. The conclusion prophesies an "organizing principle, deeper than civic pride and more basic than the domination of mass or power," a "wise geolatry," by which "New York will emerge in greatness from the paradox of its confusions" (19). Although the political dimensions of this principle are left ambiguous, the implication is that the guidebook's textual organization will help to produce civic order.

The commitment to the symmetrical organization of diversity is sustained in the guidebook's overall composition: written text and illustration consistently bring opposites together. The architecture essay, for example, declares, "More than any other American city, New York pitches high against low, rich against poor, the elegant against the squalid" (203). Paired photographs, mostly taken by New York City Writers' Project staff photographers, repeatedly emphasize the coexistence of rich and poor: "Upper Fifth Avenue—Luxury Street" versus "An East Side Housewife Chooses Her Lingerie" (Ill. 18); "Dwellers on Central Park West Look out upon Bridle Paths and Landscaped Gardens" versus "Pushcarts at the Front Door, Clothes-Lines at the Back, for East Side Tenants" (a view supplied by the New York City Housing Authority); and "Wealthy New Yorkers May Live in Residence Hotels Overlooking Central Park" versus "The Less Fortunate May Live in Shacks in Barren Island, Brooklyn." This is the rhythm established in the guidebook, structuring the text and the reader's expectations.

The representation of social contrast can be read in at least two ways. From one perspective, the text ruptures the "generic contract," the functional emphases expected from an informational form (Jameson 106). The guidebook moves well beyond the genre's conventional attention to sights, names, and dates to expose the inequities and fissures in the social fabric of quotidian life. In such a reading, *New York Panorama* is a radical document, disturbing to anyone implicated in the privileges of Rexford Tugwell's "comfort group"—the most likely audience able to afford the $2.50 price tag on the hefty guidebook. (The *Guide to New York City* was even bigger and cost $3.)

This is not the reading produced by newspaper reviews of the time. The publication was very favorably received, named one of the best books of 1938 by *Time*, the *New Yorker*, the *New York Herald-Tribune*, the *Nation*, and the *New Republic*. Consistently, newspapers of left and right lauded *New York Panorama* as an unproblematic celebration of cosmopolitan diversity. Lewis Gannett, in the *Herald-Tribune* of September 14, 1938, epitomizes this reception in a newspaper that routinely vilified the Writers' Project:

18. Upper Fifth Avenue—Luxury Street

An East Side Housewife Chooses Her Lingerie

19. View of Mid-Manhattan from the 67th
Floor of Rockefeller Center

They were unemployed, these authors who, under the Federal Writers' Project
of the W.P.A., found work in the preparation of this book. But unemployment did
not warp their vision. They saw New York clearly, and they saw it whole. . . .

The city and the country can be proud that, putting men to work in crisis, they
produced such books as this. Proud that the men did the work, proud that the city
inspired them. . . . Sometimes it is hard to understand how so many hundreds of
millions of human beings are content to live anywhere but in this, our New York.

The left-liberal *New Republic* (26 October 1938) converted political rhetoric
into aesthetic effect: "One of the charms of the book is the constant play of
its really graceful commentary." The only readers on record as identifying
"class angling" in the publication were the witnesses who appeared before
the Dies Committee to decry the project as a communist hotbed, witnesses
generally held, now as then, to be crackpots and malcontents with a grudge

against the project. The dominant public reading of *New York Panorama* discovers reassurance that the city thrives in an all-inclusive and aesthetically pleasing economy of balance.

That the claim to symmetry or balance is at least as much about the repression of unmanageable or uncomfortable observations as it is about representing diversity is suggested by *New York Panorama*'s handling of Rockefeller Center. Despite attention to workers' tenements and urban slums, Rockefeller Center emerges as the most insistent trope of the guidebook. "View of Mid-Manhattan from the 67th Floor of Rockefeller Center" (Ill.19), shot by a project staff photographer, appears on the dust jacket and as the opening illustration in the guide, and it declares a literal perspective: as in Roland Barthes's view of Paris from the Eiffel Tower, New York becomes systematically legible from Rockefeller Center (Barthes 3–18; Duncan and Duncan 18–37). Like *New York Panorama*, Rockefeller Center contains diversity by resolving oppositional impulses:

> Every city has some outstanding monument that characterizes it in the eyes of the world. For New York, perhaps the most appropriate expression is found in Rockefeller Center. . . .
>
> In its way, the Center is an effort to reduce New York to order, still keeping it New York. The Center retains the gigantism, the ruthless preying of the large upon the small, the close packing, the impersonality of the whole; and yet attempts to secure sunlight and air (at least for itself), pleasant promenades, gardens . . . art, a sense of scale and drama, and such other pleasures as the metropolis can afford. (229–30)

Visually, too, the message is that the complex offers a meeting point—and, by implication, equilibrium—for socioeconomic extremes. Rockefeller Center caters to social privilege in "Rockefeller Center's Sunken Plaza—For Those Who Can Afford It" (Ill. 20) and mass spectatorship in "Rockefeller Center's Sunken Plaza Turned Skating Rink for the Winter"; democratic, affordable entertainment in "The Early Bird Catches the Best Seat in Radio City's Movie Palace" and the more elite exhibition of New York's polyglot culture in "Shan Kar Presents the Dances of India in the Rainbow Room Atop the R.C.A. Building." Finally, it is both business empire and pastoral oasis in a pair of the center's promotional photographs which juxtapose a close-up of a roof garden with a panoramic street scene: "Busy Executives in Rockefeller Center Can Enjoy the Quiet Beauty of Roof Gardens, High Above 5th Avenue Traffic."

20. Rockefeller Center's Sunken Plaza—For Those Who Can Afford It

Fresh Fruits and Vegetables Are Less Expensive in the Pushcart Markets

By coordinating what can look like all the aspects of the city in one rational structure, Rockefeller Center was welcomed in the 1930s—in some quarters—as a precursor of the organized, efficient city of the future. In one radio broadcast of the period, for example, Rockefeller was heralded in Rooseveltian terms for "his challenge to the depression, his gallant defiance of the dark spirit of hard times, his expression of faith in the future of America" (Tafuri, "Rockefeller" 472). Celebratory iconography informs the guidebook to a degree: not only does the text stress the innovations of the center, but written text and illustrations together camouflage the incomplete state of the complex in 1938. In positioning Rockefeller Center as an achieved point of balance, *New York Panorama*'s perspective is doubly futuristic.

The icon appears even less stable when contextualized by the political sympathies of many of the guidebook's authors. The skyscraper complex was an unabashedly capitalist project that had become embroiled in several highly publicized scandals by 1938. In particular, when Diego Rivera brought his vision of an internationalized future to the center—by painting V. I. Lenin into his mural in Radio City—Rockefeller had the work destroyed. The Rockefeller renting office also went "to the very limits of legality" when it ejected small businesses from the surrounding property, seriously unbalancing the district's real estate and drawing the ire of Lewis Mumford, Frederick Lewis Allen, and others (Tafuri, "Rockefeller" 465). These scandals are acknowledged briefly and obliquely in *New York Panorama*—buried, for example, in the passage quoted above; they are minor discordances in a major achievement, and they had no effect on reviews. The guidebook's rhythm of mutually compensating opposites, harnessed to its drive toward an orderly future, here issues in a replay of the suppression of alternative ideologies by sheer corporate force.

A key figure who exposes the limits on the view from Rockefeller Center is "Pretzel Vendor, Union Square" (Ill. 21). The anonymous pretzel vendor threatens the economy of balance twice over. First, her textual positioning reads uneasily, as if she has been incompletely "resocialized" into the guidebook's categories and classifications (P. Fisher 5). Hers is the only full-length portrait in the volume, photographed from something close to eye level, a perspective that delivers a ratio of human figure to urban context very different from the panoramic views that predominate throughout the volume. She is also the sole representation of a woman as worker. Otherwise, wom-

21. Pretzel Vendor, Union Square

anhood is associated, conventionally enough, with consumption, sexuality, and symbolic motherhood: the East Side housewife chooses her lingerie, various female figures take their leisure in cafés and on dance floors, the city scene is styled "Metropolis and *Her* Children" (my emphasis). In the photographic gathering immediately following the pretzel vendor, the potential for gender disruption is closed down when women once more appear in conventional social spaces: "A Parisian Custom Transferred to Chatham Walk," with its beam of sunlight illuminating fashionable women chatting in a sidewalk café; and the old ale house, "McSorley's, Where Men Are Men and Women Are Not Allowed." An uneasy management of this category of difference is decipherable, too, in the labeling of the gathering: "Where New Yorkers Eat and Shop"—it is unclear whether the pretzel vendor is positioned as place or subject—and the archival classification of the photograph which reifies her once more: "People—Local Color—Scenes about Town."

This image challenges not just the managed politics of the guidebook but the more deeply embedded gender politics of left liberals: what Barbara Melosh calls the dominant 1930s' "vocabulary of gender," in her exploration of another cultural wing of the New Deal (2). The original photograph was cropped for guidebook reproduction; what has been cropped out is a relation and a meaning unrecognizable within the guidebook's frame of reference: the intersection of gender with class.

In the uncropped version (in the New York City Archives), a woman in fashionable belted wool coat, dress hat, and high heels stands to the right of the vendor (from the viewer's perspective), her face turned away, possibly to a store window. This figure shifts the balance of the photograph so that it can offer the same order of political contrast as the guidebook's dominant rhetoric. I read the woman on the right as a member of the comfort group, gazing away from the working woman in the center on the edge of dereliction. On the left is the litter-can sign, assailed by the "Ashcan School" not many years earlier as "a totem of authoritarian restriction and a vehicle of anarchist revolt" (Conrad 95). Here is a composition akin in its ironic juxtapositions to the politically charged works of Margaret Bourke-White and other FSA photographers, though the project staff photographer was obviously much less technically expert. It is a scene ripe for sturdy political captioning. Situated within the world of women, however, it is a scene that can be contained by the guidebook only by its partial exclusion. Despite the presence of women on the project, gender was not foregrounded in employees' debates over social inequality, preoccupied as those were with class, race, and ethnicity.[7] In this reading, the pretzel vendor is paradigmatic of the suppression worked by the guidebook and the project: at once recognized and contained, too complex a figure for the guidebook's easy symbolism, but without explicit political commentary potentially reduced to and certainly filed as "local color."

Perhaps because of the unease inherent in rhetorically reworking the functioning city, *New York Panorama* seizes the future repeatedly. Most essays offer linear, positivist narratives of New York's progress, locating the city at the culmination of its past achievements and on the threshold of a new era. The final essay, by project employee Bip Hanson, makes the future tense explicit by celebrating the World's Fair of 1939: detail is lavished on a fair that has not yet been built; its theme, trumpeted as a major innovation, is "The World of Tomorrow"; and the social vision is unreservedly utopian. Hanson's essay opens with Grover Whalen, president of the New York World's Fair Corporation, predicting world peace in 1937. History also secures the future: the fair honors the 150th anniversary of Washington's inauguration as "a dedication of America to its future."[8] The essay particularly lauds the fair's agenda for rational, planned communities offering "individual and collective security" and "show[ing] the average man how he may live under 'the more nearly perfect flowering of democracy' in the American small town of the future" (489, 494). The end of the essay, which is also the end of the guidebook, repositions New York within the "ideologically coherent 'symbolic universes'" offered by fairs (according to Rydell 2), reaching for a utopian resolution one final time: "One thing is certain: the City of New York itself will be the smash hit of its own exposition" (500).

Writing the WPA into America's future had a particular political charge at the moment of the guidebook's publication, and the text visibly works to insert itself into the larger political discourse. Guidebook essays on current social conditions regularly characterize the WPA as an essential bridge to a better future: in Harlem, for example, the WPA checks are said to end the neighborhood's long decline into destitution and begin the tentative relief of its racial tensions. In the literature, art, theater, radio, and music essays, the Federal Arts Projects facilitate important innovations in art and entertainment. In 1938, when this material was published, Congressman William I. Sirovich of New York City was championing a bill to transform the cultural wing of the WPA into a permanent Department of Science, Art, and Literature; in the same year, the Coffee-Pepper bill in the Senate called for a permanent version of the Federal Arts Projects in a new Bureau of Fine Arts. Hearings on these bills were under way when the guidebook appeared, and the text refers to them (201). It is perhaps the clearest example of the guidebook's attempt to shape public policy discursively.[9]

New York Panorama was circulated widely in ways and places that encouraged various kinds of use. Alsberg enjoined the New York City director—at that point Harry Shaw—that "radio dramatization of our material is of the highest importance"; one such initiative was a series titled "New York Panorama," planned for Mutual network WOR in 1938. Exhibitions were mounted in bookstores, book fairs, and conferences. The guidebook was floated for adoption by public libraries, refugee education services, and school curricula: *New York Panorama* posters were mounted on the bulletin boards of every New York City public school, while the Board of Education was asked to give information about the volume to all teachers in the city. These measures led to brisk sales and generally positive responses, some of them documented in reports on attendance at book fairs and in letters from individual readers. Some clearly took pleasure in reading themselves into the scene: talking of New York infantry, the commanding officer of an Overseas Recruit Depot requested both guidebooks "to increase the contentment and enjoyment of recruits while stationed at this post awaiting shipment to our foreign possessions." The impact on a recently arrived refugee or on a schoolchild could only have been more formative.[10]

Project officials were determined, moreover, to confer definitive status on the guidebook. That they had ambitions for the volume well beyond the functional is suggested by their vigorous opposition to Berenice Abbott's *Changing New York*, a book of photographs produced on the New York City Art Project and due to appear simultaneously with *New York Panorama*. Abbott's orientation was profoundly different from that of the Writers' Project. She asserted that "through [the photographer's] eyes the now becomes past," and she represented a city in transition and under threat by the forces of bureaucratic order (qtd. in Sontag 67). Her Rockefeller Center is an unfinished structure, skeletal and impermanent against the stone mass of the nineteenth-century church that partially obscures it ("Rockefeller Center with Collegiate Church of St. Nicholas in Foreground"). Her peddlers are vanishing types, described by Elizabeth McCausland—whose captions Peter Conrad characterizes as "sepulchral prognosis" (169)—as "banished from the streets of New York in 1938 by order of the Commissioner of Markets . . . corralled into modern enclosed markets, municipally operated" (caption to ill. 24). Alsberg accused Abbott of "seriously invading the territory we are covering in our New York City guide" and fought, successfully, to delay the publication of her book for a year. In turn, Federal Art Project officers accused the Writers' Project of plagiarizing Abbott's photographs in *New York Panorama*. Seizing the space of New York City was clearly a matter of power politics and vested interests at the institutional as well as the textual level.[11]

New York Panorama can be read, then, at several levels, as a highly constructed exercise in what Karal Ann Marling calls "New Deal futurology" ("Note" 421). Produced by an ideologically splintered group under political pressure and public attack, the guidebook brings discursive order to the city through a series of representational ruses. The textual politics of the volume are double-edged: the confrontational rhetoric of what Alfred Kazin calls "old-fashioned left-wing populism" both exposes systemic inequities and reorders them into symmetrical balance ("Introduction" xv). Ultimately, it serves as a structural device for managing and containing social difference, as in a somewhat parallel case, Nicholas Natanson has argued that institutional pressures and ideological climate caused even the most radical FSA photographers to shy away from representing the deepest injustices of race and class. Perhaps more radicalism resides in the futuristic predictions, masquerading as documented facts, which distance the city from current conditions and function as an instrument of WPA survival. That this was an opinion-making exercise of some significance is suggested by the determination of project executives to establish a monopoly of the genre.

New York Panorama's stake in the future is suggested, ironically, by the widening gap between discursive and material conditions. The future gave the guidebook a spectacularly bad review, collapsing the economy of balance under the weight of its own contradictions. Grover Whalen's prediction of world peace proved to be wrong a year later. Bip Hanson's celebration of a secure future was wrong: he was subsequently dismissed from the project as a communist.[12] Vincent McHugh decided that his prophecy of urban unity was wrong; he left the project before *New York Panorama*'s publication, eventually to write a fantasy in which the commissioner of the New York Department of City Planning witnesses the city disintegrate into total chaos. And the guidebook as a whole was wrong in its predictions about the WPA's future. Congress first condemned the WPA for insinuating itself into "The World of Tomorrow" at the taxpayers' expense; then it voted down the Bureau of Fine Arts bills; and finally, in 1939, it listened to the accusations of Martin Dies's House Committee on Un-American Activities and disbanded the Federal Writers' Project.

Before this final denouement, but heavily conditioned by its unwinding, the second guidebook was produced. The politics of both its production and its form are significantly different from *New York Panorama*'s. In the course of composing *The WPA Guide to New York City*, the New York City employees merged into a much more effective solidarity, partly brought on by the precariousness of the project in the face of mounting congressional attacks. The *Guide* itself is much less ambitious in its interpretive claims than *Panorama*. Given the delicacy of the political moment, the project's publicity release stresses functional value: the second volume is "a practical point-by-point guide to the city," whereas the first was "a large-scale interpretation of various phases of metropolitan life."[13] Yet the *Guide*'s functionality also makes it more interventionist. This guidebook's gaze comes down to the street, shaping the user's eye-level encounter with details of the surrounding social scene. Its opening photograph suggests the difference: "Lower Manhattan Seen Beneath Brooklyn Bridge" delivers a view from below quite different from the bird's-eye panorama from Rockefeller Center.

The second guidebook was the first work mapped out by Vincent McHugh when he inherited the eight-million-word "hodgepodge of endless miscellanea" as technical director in late 1936 (Mangione, *Dream* 172). Seeking an orderly method for the production of detailed information, McHugh divided the city into boroughs, which he subdivided into neighborhoods and streets. Editorial desks were established for each city unit. Once this sectioning was approved by the central office, it became the procedural and textual structure for *The WPA Guide to New York City*: Manhattan divided into thirty-five districts, the other boroughs into two to five each,

each area documented into tours and points of interest, seven hundred pages in which the urban scene is itemized into a throng of details. This design constructed the city as an accumulation of communities: an act of some faith and ideological weight in a climate in which the city was routinely vilified as the site of passive, spectatorial herds or masses.

Although McHugh indelibly stamped the volume's design, he did not remain to oversee its completion, nor did he contribute an essay. The second guidebook was produced by a shifting cast of writers. Among the editors who contributed to the final shaping were Harold Rosenberg and John Cheever; Alsberg himself participated extensively, telling Harold Strauss, the New York City director at that point, "I want to read personally every word of the NY city material before it is paged," and reiterating ten days later, "Since the NY book is a very important one and will attract nationwide attention, I want to give it the once-over myself." Both Alsberg's position and the project as a whole were increasingly insecure during the last stages of the *Guide's* production. On the one hand, employees had learned to work together, and production was no longer rent by political factions. Joseph Gaer reported to Alsberg in January 1939 that the New York City project was in the best shape ever. On the other hand, the political environment was more hostile than ever, and Roosevelt's entire relief program was under threat. Bearing down immediately on the Writers' Project were investigations by the Dies Committee—whose hearings began late in 1938—and the Woodrum Committee—the body created by the House Subcommittee on Appropriations in March 1939. Further cuts in funding had occurred, and calls for the liquidation of all four arts projects were mounting.[14]

Moreover, to select community as a structural principle was to take on a political football. As early as June 1937, Robert Bruere's report had advised the project to "appeal to the local pride and interest of the New York City community which the Project has not sufficiently cultivated." But Alsberg and his executives knew that tangling with a community's identity was full of pitfalls. The free pamphlet *Your New York*, produced somewhat independently by the New York City Project in August 1936 under Orrick Johns, had caused a storm of protest. Described in the publicity release as "a foretaste of the New York City Guide" and a "chatty impressionistic picture of a locality," the pamphlet had first drawn the wrath of the Tan Omega Chapter of the Alpha Kappa Alpha Sorority, a Harlem women's group, who were outraged at the pamphlet's paragraph on Harlem. By early 1937, the property owners of Greenwich Village had gone public with their outrage at the pamphlet's whimsical depiction of their neighborhood as artistic and bohemian; as James J. Kirk, the commander of the local American Legion Post put it in a letter to Harry Hopkins, "Why does a Community such as ours have to be slandered to keep these incompetents off the bread lines?" Their case received extensive coverage in the *Villager*, resulted in a petition to Roosevelt, and eventually won an apology from Hopkins. Again, this local brouhaha existed within a larger climate of contestation: the very topic of American community was ideologically riven by the competing definitions of Communist Party members and fellow travelers, Young Americans, liberals, proletarians, progressive regionalists, conservative regionalists, independent radicals, New Dealers, and stalwart Republicans.[15]

How the principle of community is applied in the *Guide*—how it shapes the guidebook user's gaze and folds in potentially discordant voices—can be traced in the opening essays to the longest section, "Manhattan." The introductory essay, mainly the work of John Cheever, according to the editorial archive, owes much to the style of John Dos Passos, allying itself stylistically with a modernist aesthetic. Alsberg reported to Strauss that Cheever's avowed aim in his revision was to condense the material and make its expression less conventional.[16] Whereas McHugh's opening essay to *New York Panorama* established principles of order, Cheever's proceeds by the confusion and fragmentation of metropolitan bustle. Like *Manhattan Transfer* (1925), the essay brings together streams of immigrants and travelers to New York City:

The liner steams through the Narrows (the Normandie, Queen Mary, Bremen; the dozen greatest ships of the world, sailing from Liverpool, Southampton, Hamburg, Rotterdam, Havre, Genoa, head for that narrow strip of water and steam dexterously through it, turn precisely toward the slender island toward the north) . . . A dark blotch appears, takes form—an anchored tramp: *coffee from Brazil, rubber from Sumatra, bananas from Costa Rica*—and slowly disappears; another liner is suddenly moving alongside, also steaming northward, and then dissolves into the white nothing. Invisible ferries scuttle, tooting, across the harbor.

The Limited, bearing a sight-seeing family (there are 115,000 of them daily—from Waco, Mobile, Los Angeles, Kansas City), the literary genius of Aurora High School, the prettiest actress in the Burlington dramatic club, a farm boy hoping to start for Wall Street, and a mechanic with an idea, pounds across the state of New Jersey. They cross the meadows, see far off the great wall of the city and dive into the darkness beneath Jersey City and the Hudson River. Or perhaps the train comes from Winnipeg, Gary, Erie, and follows the Hudson toward its mouth or crosses the Hell Gate from New England. (49)

The essay pursues these immigrants as they atomize into a jumble of voices through a twenty-four-hour cycle, communicating the internal dynamics of the city through more Dos Passosian fragments: snatches of unidentified, individual voices alternate with snapshots of group activity by Jewish, Italian, Irish, and black populations, all interspersed among the material debris left by communal activities, quotidian and festive.

A distinctly un-Dos Passosian turn occurs in the transition from this essay to the next, "Facts about Manhattan." In *Manhattan Transfer*, what issues from the magnetic, fragmented core of New York is spiritual desiccation, human isolation, despair, and death. The *Guide to New York City* translates atomization, first, into material plenitude. "Facts about Manhattan" is essentially a list of impressively large numbers regarding geography, visitors, resident population by "principal race and language groups" (465,000 Jews, 224,670 Negroes, 117,740 Italians, 86,548 Irish, 69,685 Russians, 69,111 Germans, 59,120 Poles), transportation, real estate, economics, crime, public services, and places of amusement and education. The throng of figures ends with a quotation from the past: "'It is as beautiful a land as one can hope to tread upon,' said Henry Hudson" (56). If read unironically, the comment lends legitimacy to the preceding documentation, evoking what Michel Foucault calls the "power of enchantment" of "the mere act of enumeration" (xvi); in David Gelernter's words, "The thirties are mesmerized by numbers" (18, 40).

As the guidebook proceeds, it harnesses this spill of plenty into section-by-section coverage: Lower Manhattan to Middle West Side to Middle and Upper East Side to the Harlems and so on northward and outward to the boroughs, each district internally anatomized into south-to-north areas (another balking of Kellock's scheme, though one to which she did not object), this verbal mapping liberally sprinkled with visual maps, diagrams, photographs, and prints. What drives this methodical anatomization is the search for material evidence of communal identity. For example, in the essay on Hell's Kitchen and vicinity, which tracks the area street by street, almost building by building, this characterization appears: "Although every block in this neighborhood contains a broad mixture of nationalities, in the West Forties and Fifties there is a French population large enough to form a true FRENCH QUARTER" (159). At times the urge seems defensive: "Although to the outsider, the Bronx signifies little more than a cocktail, a jeer, or a zoo, the New Yorker knows it as a community of apartment houses peopled by families of average means" (510).

It is easy to understand why this guidebook would appeal to Lewis Mumford: it could facilitate his vision of "cultural citizenship" by offering readers a form for "locating the self in a participatory culture" through emphasis on "small-scale, comprehensible environment" (Blake 291, 292). Indeed, Mumford's vision infused Alsberg's and others' sense of what the guidebooks could give the city. Mumford was the cultural critic most strenuously, though unsuccessfully, wooed by Alsberg for the New York City directorship, and both "The American Guide Manual"—the directive circulated from the central office to the state offices—and Alsberg's letters use language reminiscent of Mumford's in advising guidebook writers to think of architecture in terms of social tendencies and the future metropolis. While the *Guide to New York City* acknowledges that socioeconomic problems exist, it textualizes the city as organic community rather than a swirl of unlocated atoms or a technologically driven megalopolis.[17]

To document community in this way was to verify, and therefore encourage, the survival of cultural difference. Whereas, for example, *New York Panorama* was nervous that rich immigrant customs were being overridden by "the poverty-stricken culture of industrial society" (82)—"No longer does a foreign colony in New York have the status of a genuine 'foreign quarter' " (83)—the *Guide* demonstrates strong ethnic presence. Although it does, like *New York Panorama*, acknowledge the complexities of ethnic difference, there is no postmodern anxiety about typification or cultural simulacra: East European Jews exhibit "native gaiety and hope" (60), entire communities are represented by individuals, and there is a fundamental confidence in the persistence of European culture: in the Sunset Park Neighborhood of West Brooklyn, for example, "the homeland's culture is kept alive by Finnish societies" (468).

One mechanism by which the guidebook affirms ongoing ethnic character is by attending to distinctive foods, evidence of thriving community that can be set against somber housing conditions or criminal hazards, as in this passage apparently contributed by the fledgling short story writer Ruth Widen:

The old Mulberry Bend—on Mulberry Street between Bayard and Park, two blocks west of the Bowery—one of the worst slums in the city, was torn down in 1892 and replaced by Columbus Park, after drawing the fiery criticism of the reformer, Jacob Riis. However, many five-story tenements remain decked with cluttered fire escapes, washlines, and crowded stoops. The pushcarts on Mott Street from Canal to Broome, a block east of Mulberry Street, are relics of a thriving market that once embraced the four streets west of the Bowery. They sell ripe and green olives, artichokes, goats' cheeses, finochio (sweet fennel), and ready-to-eat *pizza*, an unsweetened pastry filled with tomatoes and cheese, meat, or fish. (118)

One press release—"Dining Abroad in New York"—makes the politics of food manifest: "Because of world interest in the changing map of central Europe, visitors to New York may find a particular interest in the city's Austrian, Hungarian, Roumanian, and Polish cafes—virtually little outposts of these troubled nations, where compatriots and enthusiasts come to enjoy the familiar dishes of their homeland." Eating is a cultural practice, evidence of distinctive, lived community, and part of the concrete information by which the guidebook offers the city's visitors and inhabitants images of themselves as participants in a democracy enriched by their ethnic identities.[18]

Within this fundamentally affirmative representation of community identity, the guidebook can live with considerably more texture, complexity, and internal contradictions than were offered by the neat dichotomies of *New York Panorama*. Racial difference, for example, is not monolithic. "Negro Harlem," an essay to which both Richard Wright and Claude McKay contributed, shows the geography of that community to be heavily marked by class stratification and gender division:

Those who live in Harlem know it as a number of little worlds, represented by such titles as the "Valley," the "Golden Edge," "Sugar Hill," and the "Market." Each is descriptive of a different stratum of the community. The Valley is the slum area, extending from 130th to 140th Street, east of Seventh Avenue. Apartments along the Golden Edge, the part of the neighborhood facing Central Park, house the professional class. On Sugar Hill, the affluent live in dignity and comparative splendor.

The Market is the name given with ironic accuracy to the stretch from 110th to 115th Street on Seventh Avenue, which is frequented by streetwalkers. Sharp divisions exist between the dwellers in these various sections. (258–59)

The visual correlative to this description is an opening of three photographs by members of the New York City Federal Art Project. At top left is "Sugar Hill, Harlem," identified in the accompanying essay as "Harlem's finest residential section" (265): a row of apartment buildings at the top of a landscaped hill, placed at a considerable distance from the viewer. The perspective zooms in on the lower left, to confront the viewer much more closely with "Harlem Slum" (Ill. 22)—Harlem's "dreadful slums are among the most notorious in New York" (258). These images are juxtaposed, on the right, with a full-page street scene of storefronts, strollers, and shoeshiners at work: "Lenox Avenue, Harlem," described in the text as "Harlem's principal boulevard" (259). The three compositions offer comparisons of architecture, perspective, human presence, and class difference (suggested both between photographs and within them) much more complicated than the regulatory contrasts of *New York Panorama*.

The politics of composition in "Harlem Slum" contrast instructively with "Pretzel Vendor, Union Square." "Harlem Slum" more explicitly invites interpretation, with the boy at attention, apparently aware of his role as photographic subject. The title provides a sense of a way of life being offered to view: the dilapidated buildings, the displaced person, the out-of-place furniture make up the condition of a Harlem slum, where even the boundary between inside and out, or shelter and exposure, is unstable. Surrounding the child's figure is a mass of legible (because in-focus) text that offers the familiar ironic commentary of 1930s' documentary: the posters for "Free Cash" and the Renaissance theater announce precisely what are not available to this child (as well, perhaps, as gesturing to the many "experiments in renaissance" currently claimed by cultural bodies from the WPA to the Communist Party to Harlem intelligentsia). The title "Reformatory" on the Renaissance poster seems more grimly appropriate; the "Danger in the Air" played out by Robert Taylor is worlds away from the dangers of exposure facing this waif. The portrait has a much more explicit, and confrontational, politics than "Pretzel Vendor" in its exposure of disturbing social conditions. The *Waco Messenger* review may well have had this representation in mind

22. Harlem Slum

when it judged that "scores" of "Negro communities in New York" were not just "comprehensively" but "dramatically" described (June 17, 1939).

That sense of the *Guide* as facilitating not just analysis but multiple, competing interpretations—and this in a work that sold itself as factual and taxonomic—is extended by the range of illustrations. There is, first, a large number of lithographs: all works in the broad social realist style and therefore committed to the documentary project, but nevertheless representations that make manifest the mediation of artist and point of view to a degree the photographs do not. Many of these prints extend the reach of the verbal and photographic attention to unemployment and dereliction, a focus encouraged by the central office. Alsberg wrote to Harry Shaw: "To me the people who haunt the Battery at night, the derelicts, etc., are more interesting than the people who frequent it during the daytime"; the guide manual had also recommended slums as points of interest. What administrators intended by this focus, of course, was not necessarily the same cluster of meanings as guidebook contributors produced.[19]

For example, the description of South Street piers in Lower Manhattan includes the following scene: "On mild sunny days the drifters sit along the

23. Derelicts *(East River Water Front)*

docks with their 'junk bags,' share cigarette butts, and stare endlessly into the water. In winter they cluster in little groups about small bonfires; many sleep at night in doorways with newspapers for covering" (81). Near-literal illustration of this scene is provided by the photograph "South Street Pier and Wall Street Towers"—which shows men huddled in groups on makeshift stools, many nursing cigarettes—one of the first cluster of illustrations that introduces unusual angles and behind-the-facade perspectives (by contrast, no one in a *New York Panorama* photograph loiters or loafs or goes begging). Mabel Dwight's lithograph "Derelicts *(East River Water Front)*" (Ill. 23) represents the same subject matter in more grotesque yet more intimate light: her men touch and lean on each other with a degree of dependency not indicated by the more public photograph. Dwight—an elderly, partly deaf employee of the New York City Art Project—generally makes graphic the quotidian camaraderie of the working classes and the destitute, humanizing some of the guidebook's stark information. Her prints outnumber those of all other artists in the guidebook, though a similar atmosphere is communicated by the companionship of shoeshine boys in Raphael Soyer's "A Nickel a Shine" and the relaxed community of dancers in Kyra Markham's "Burlycue."

Other pieces, however, unsettle this equation. It is at least ambiguous whether any community coheres the group of derelict men in Reginald Marsh's "George Washington, Union Square," with every head (including Washington's) turned in a different direction away from every other; or Hugh Bott's human atoms struggling against the elements in "Columbus Circle"; or Eli Jacobi's indistinguishable mass of men vying for work in "Chelsea Shape-Up," a form of hiring displayed in critical light elsewhere in the volume. The spare, cubistic shapes of Louis Lozowick represent a de-populated, antiseptically modern site markedly at odds with the colorful congestion reported in guidebook copy (in, for example, "Hanover Square," Ill. 24). According to Peter Conrad, Lozowick's socialism was very different from Dwight's: he "saw in the city . . . an 'icon of the socialist future,' and his cubism imitates the social engineering which, by the enforcement of 'order and organization,' will bring that future to pass" (130). Interestingly, Lozow-ick was the other artist to dominate the print selection, and he was particu-larly courted by the New York City Writers' Project. The New York City director invited Lozowick to take over from Harold Rosenberg as project art critic; in refusing, Lozowick gave the project carte blanche with his work, and he designed the jacket for the second volume.[20] Given the cultural poli-tics of the city in the 1930s—especially debates over modernist versus pop-ular aesthetics—the range of images can provide access to those differing viewpoints without resolving them into the formal closure of *New York Panorama*.

All in all, the *Guide* delivers a city with a different tempo and dimensions than *Panorama*, closer to the organic, communitarian thinking of Lewis Mumford than to the international cosmopolitanism of the *Partisan Review* circle. In some respects, it almost reads like a different city. For one thing, this is a place much more marked by the historical than the futurological. The past is imprinted in vestiges, relics, plaques, tablets, sites of past events and personalities, and, overwhelmingly, architecture. By this account, New York is flooded with European imitations: Fifth Avenue has "the flavor of a South European boulevard" (135); two department stores are "joined by a bridge similar in design to the Bridge of Sighs in Venice" (137); "Patchin

24. Hanover Square

Place resembles a bystreet in Old London" (139); St. Luke's Chapel has architectural details "reminiscent of old England" (142); one McKim, Mead, and White building is a "reproduction of an Italian palace" (165), another is "inspired by Roman Classical architecture"(166), and yet another is "in the style of the Palazzo Vendramini in Venice"(166). Only occasionally—and never in the boroughs beyond Manhattan—does a distinctively New World design come into focus: skyscrapers such as the "modernistic" Chrysler building (224) and functionalist American inventions such as an automatic garage (281).

The *Guide*'s scale and perspective also put Rockefellers and women workers on the same spatial plane: John D. Rockefeller's bust in the Standard Oil Building is subject to the curious gazes of passersby; in the garment center, "Few women workers appear in the noonday crowd, for most of them bring food from home and eat in the workrooms" (161). With icons being, implicitly, cut down to size, the interests in the Diego Rivera scandal can be exposed more extensively, and more explicitly, than in *Panorama*: "A mural, painted by Diego Rivera and originally in this lobby, caused an international controversy when the management first screened it and finally destroyed it, contending that the artist had departed from the approved preliminary sketch. Others held that the mural was destroyed because it included a likeness of Lenin. The case became a classic conflict between the artistic rights of a creator and the property rights of a purchaser. The space is now occupied by a Sert mural depicting the triumph of man's accomplishments through the union of physical and mental labor" (336–37). The description can claim to be balanced—both perspectives are represented—but the potential irony of the final sentence and the exposure of that which Rockefeller sought to conceal speak volumes. Working women, homeless men, slums, architects, philanthropists are all resocialized not into the economy of balance but into a throng of ethnic communities.

How these differences played out in reception is heavily affected by the guidebook's publication date. By late June 1939, the bill to liquidate the arts projects as federal concerns had already been passed, overwhelmingly, by the House of Representatives. Reviews of *The WPA Guide to New York City* tended to become defenses of the project as a whole; there was more motive to celebrate the work as an act of cultural preservation than to notice its challenges to the status quo. In the *New York World Telegram* of 21 June

1939, Harry Hansen—who had criticized the scanty treatment of Jews and Italians in *New York Panorama*—argued the merits of this guidebook against the Woodrum bill to cut the Federal Writers' Project: "An awareness of social responsibility and civic alertness runs through the text; partisanship is buried." Similarly, the *Washington* (D.C.) *Daily News* of 1 July 1939 reported the Manhattan Borough president as declaring: "The style of writing, so different from the heavy-handed Baedeker, seems to catch the tempo of the city. It is my conviction that the Federal Writers' Project is a great contribution to our national culture, and must be saved from destruction." The fight to preserve the project became particularly conflated with the guidebook's own preservationist work in the assessments by representatives of various racial and ethnic groups. One black reviewer in the *Boston Chronicle* of 1 July 1939 wrote: "Through the Federal Writers' Project folk history and lore of the race has been saved for posterity where in another few years we would have lost forever our hope of knowing the true contributions of our people."

Publicity extended the motif of community from the guidebook's pages to its potential purchasers and readers, emphasizing its connections to the community it documented. Working New Yorkers—a bus driver, an information clerk—were photographed reading *The WPA Guide to New York City* for publicity stills. And New York's educational radio mounted a game show—"Know Your New York"—in which questions, answers, and prizes all derived from the city's guidebooks. Yet this localized community spirit could be marketed for international consumption: Alistair Cooke requested the guidebooks for his BBC talks, "Mainly about Manhattan," and pieces in the *London Times*; the sense that this was one of America's best faces was symbolized when Eleanor Roosevelt presented the guidebook to the king and queen of England in 1939.[21]

The distance traveled from the volatile beginnings and furious demonstrations of the New York City project to one head of state presenting the guidebook to another is a story of the institutionalization of dissent. Critical and oppositional voices were never completely effaced in the production process. They remain legible—especially when contextualized by some of the ideological debates of the period—and therefore always potentially disruptive of the status quo but contained by the generic conventions and structures of guidebooks in combination with the editorial practices of a government-sponsored project with one eye always on Congress. These guidebooks favor New Deal metropolitan agencies specifically and support the federal administration more broadly, not by whitewashing New York's uglier features—attention to slums, strikes, and political corruption is extensive—but by discovering principles of order by which the city can be reimagined.

Those principles differ distinctly in the two volumes. *New York Panorama* mounts a futurological version of the city that displaces and thereby resolves warring ideologies. Although the result is less obviously or literally futuristic than "Democracity" of the 1939 New York World's Fair, the architects of this volume could have said of their task what the fair designers said of theirs: "By producing a Fair of the Future, New York will help to create the America of the future." *The WPA Guide to New York City* articulates a more organic vision: it reimagines the city into a human scale rooted in the present, reengendering faith in the survival of ethnically diverse communities.

What impact either volume had on community formation seems impossible to assess with any specificity. Certainly, employees on the Writers' Project discovered an artistic community through their collaborative work, and individual writers have attested to the ways in which their project research increased their sense of connectivity to a larger public and a particular place (Mangione, *Dream* 186). Eduard C. Lindeman argued at the time that the Federal Arts Projects were effecting a new level of community among artists and with the public at large (207–8). Vincent McHugh later told Jerre Mangione that he refused to leave the New York City project for the central office because he preferred the working-class camaraderie of the former site. And Ralph Ellison has also gone on record several times in appreciation of the community nurtured by the project: it "threw me into my own history. Once you touched the history of blacks in New York . . . you were deep into American history" (qtd. in Banks xix–xx).

The guidebooks also appear to have retained their vigor and attractiveness long past the point at which their information was functionally useful; both of them remain in print. At least part of their popularity is predicated on their construction of a city that makes sense. As Alfred Kazin says in his introduction to the 1984 edition of *New York Panorama*, this is New York "in its last age of innocence" (xiii). This record is read as the last moment before the city's decline, in Patrick Geddes's terms, from *metropolis* to *megalopolis*, *parasitopolis* and, finally, *pathopolis*, "the city that ceases effectively to function" (*Panorama* 399).

North Carolina

Local Knowledge, Local Color

To begin at the end, in 1939, William T. Couch—director of the University of North Carolina Press and regional director for the Federal Writers' Project in the South—produced *These Are Our Lives: As Told by the People and Written by Members of the Federal Writers' Project of the Works Progress Administration in North Carolina, Tennessee, and Georgia.* This volume of interviews was explicitly aimed at introducing the voices of the dispossessed into contemporary debates over the identity and material conditions of the South. Couch's preface stated: "In writing the life histories the first principle has been to let the people tell their own stories. With all our talk about democracy it seems not inappropriate to let the people speak for themselves" (x–xi). However our postmodern sensibilities might qualify Couch's claims for the volume's freedom of voice, there is no doubt that the book brought public attention to the overlooked deprivation of tenant farmers, sharecroppers, and mill workers, black and white.

Also in 1939, Couch oversaw the publication of *North Carolina: A Guide to the Old North State,* one volume in the WPA American Guide Series. In that book, underprivileged social groups barely and intermittently come into focus against a landscape thick with other presences, and racial difference becomes a measure for separating cultural agents from reified sights. In the difference between the two publications lies the story of this chapter.

North Carolina shows most clearly, of the cases considered in this book, how the American Guide Series brokered cultural identities. The South had long been subject to tensions between centralized power and states' rights, tensions sharpened by New Deal interventions and what Daniel Joseph Singal calls "an immense cultural change" in the South between the two world wars (xi). In the Writers' Project, federal authority converged with genre expectations—that the guidebook would deliver a definitive inventory of the state—to raise the stakes on editorial negotiations. Competing interest groups in North Carolina jostled for national visibility and access to what they saw as official cultural status. Part of the politics arose from liberals in Washington, D.C., attempting to cut across the state's vested interests to empower racial minorities, in the process provoking resistance from those who considered themselves North Carolina's cultural elites. The hammering out of guidebook copy produced a triangular configuration of national agenda, "local knowledge," and the distinctive academic discourse of the state, each term in the triangle visibly forming and hardening in relation to the others. This is a particular, historical instance of the relationality of local knowledge argued by Clifford Geertz and Vincent Pecora; in David Simpson's words, "Localist rhetoric is, then, a complicated thing, and always asks to be assessed in relation to its specific applications and association" (4).

This debate was quite different from that between Chapel Hill liberal sociology and Vanderbilt aesthetic Agrarianism, another 1930s' argument crucial to the redefinition of southern identity and one that has received much more scholarly attention (by, for example, Gray, King, and O'Brien). Although the terms of the Writers' Project's debates were more bureaucratic and less ideologically developed than the academic polemics, they had a much greater vernacular reach. Project debates over authority and the right to representation also reached well beyond the regional image of southern culture into local fissures and alliances. *North Carolina* maps out guidelines to cultural belonging and exclusion, according to the large political categories of race, gender, and class, as they play out in some particular highways and byways of the South.

The North Carolina project was shaped by and against the central office's agenda. As the Washington editors shifted from assuming cultural diversity and fully articulated regional distinctiveness to attempting to produce these qualities in the image of their own political commitments, they tried to reorient the North Carolina office accordingly. Their interventions produced a triangle of ideologies: New Deal pluralists in Washington, bent on social reform, confronted an entrenched localism that saw its first duty as protecting the state's reputation. Poised between these two poles was a liberal, academic discourse that walked such a fine line on race that federal pressure inadvertently nudged it into resistant and reactionary positions. The key figures setting the terms of this uneasy triangle were Henry Alsberg, national director of the Federal Writers' Project, in Washington D.C.; Edwin Bjorkman, state director of the North Carolina Writers' Project in Asheville; and William T. Couch, first associate state director, then regional director for the Southeast, in Chapel Hill.

When the project began in 1935, Edwin Bjorkman was an obvious choice for state director. Although he was not a native southerner—having immigrated from Sweden first to Minnesota then to New York City and finally to North Carolina just ten years before the project's inception—he was one of the few state residents with a national literary profile. He had had a long career as newspaperman, critic, translator, and creative writer. The Sunday book page which he edited for the *Asheville Citizen-Times* from 1926 to 1929 attracted praise from prominent literary figures across the country, and William S. Powell's *Dictionary of North Carolina Biography* credits him as an advocate of civil rights (in 1947, after his tenure on the Writers' Project, he was president of the Asheville chapter of the Southern Conference for Human Welfare). Bjorkman also needed the job: although he had not registered on the relief rolls, he was impecunious enough to be selling off volumes from his library and receiving loans from the Authors' League of America. The conservative league recommended him for the state directorship, as did North Carolina's Democratic senators, Josiah William Bailey (an anti–New Dealer) and Robert Rice Reynolds, support that made his candidacy acceptable to the state WPA administrator (Hirsch, "Culture" 9–11).

About all that Bjorkman and Alsberg agreed on was the commercial motive: both were keen to stimulate and profit from "tourist traffic," which meant that, from the beginning, both were sensitive to the state's external image. In almost all other respects, Bjorkman's sympathies were contrary to Alsberg's. As state director (and recent incomer, by traditional southern standards), Bjorkman clearly felt himself enmeshed in a network of local politics, local pride, and local knowledge. This was a forcefield stratified by class and race: Bjorkman felt his obligations to particular "leading citizens" (invariably white professionals), and his liberal tendencies were consistently tempered by their vision of the state's (which was to say their own) reputation. His loyalty to those interests brought him into conflict with the central office within the first few months. He established the state project office in Asheville, in the extreme western end of the state, choosing his own home—where he had a grasp of local politics and social relations—rather than the capital or geographical center preferred by Washington.

Conscious of the "75 to 100" needy writers who were not on the relief rolls—who therefore could not be employed by the project and were highly resentful of the unqualified workers on relief receiving positions—he also moved very slowly to fill his quota of 130 employees (in September 1936, 114 were employed; by December 1937, employment was down to 43), and he never felt satisfied with the quality of the fieldworkers culled from relief rolls (Hirsch, "Culture" 15). They did not belong to the stratum of local voices qualified, in his view, to speak for the state. The Asheville office was later remembered by Marguerite Yancey, one of its writers, as "the usual mixed bag": "A skilled city editor, victim of retrenchment—and a newsroom hanger-on to be described only as a moderate drunk. A man who had been good at his craft, in his day, but was simply too old to adapt. And housewives, some college women, some widows with only high school, or less. There were former teachers set adrift by cuts in staff. We had a few boys and girls who had really had no jobs at all." With the little flexibility allowed by the 10 percent exemption rule, Bjorkman hand-picked a few nonrelief writers for key positions: notably William C. Hendricks, who had edited local papers, as state guide supervisor (later, state editor); and George L. Andrews, a former teacher and freelance writer, as district supervisor in Raleigh (later, assistant state director).[1]

Bjorkman directed his assistants to a geographically limited focus. They oversaw the production of city guides dedicated to the minutiae of sites with local significance. Bjorkman argued that only this orientation would attract public support in a state so geographically attentuated and so driven by local—as opposed to regional or state—loyalties. (This analysis has been recently confirmed by the scholarship of Michael Kammen, who argues that localism was a stronger force than regionalism, generally, in the 1930s; 375–406). Citing "the intense localism of our papers," Bjorkman insisted to Washington: "A local appeal is the only way of obtaining publicity. Anything sent out on a state-wide basis goes into the waste paper basket." He also warned the central office about the touchiness of certain communities: for example, he described Charlotte as "a very sensitive city." And he insisted on the need to meet local sponsors halfway, an opinion seconded by the Department of Conservation and Development—sponsors of the state guide— whose assistant director, Paul Kelly, identified "offended local pride" as the greatest peril.[2]

Consistent with his sense of his primary constituency, Bjorkman relied on determinedly local authorities as consultants. He sought to have tours and city descriptions read by what he called "representative citizens," that is, longtime community figures such as local newspaper editors and members of the State Historical Commission. He consistently preferred local notables, members of patriotic societies, librarians, church archivists, and the like over academics from the University of North Carolina and Duke University. For a contribution on literature, for example, he approached William Polk, mayor of Warrenton; and he objected to Professor W. K. Boyd of Duke writing the history essay.[3]

In promoting a form of nativism, Bjorkman was responding to a palpable strain in the cultural environment. He himself was denounced in local letters to New Deal officials as "Bjorkman the Swede," this "alien," "this tactless ill-humoured foreigner." Another disgruntled worker—Arnold McKay, who had been named by Bjorkman as one of the project's best workers—made the connection between nativism and authentic knowledge when he attacked the entire Asheville office: "Persons—that is, the majority—here are not North Carolinians, do not know the State, have no historical perspective of the State, and I venture to say no particular sympathetic interest. These things count a lot when an accurate piece of work must be done. I am not talking about silly chamber of commerce enthusiasm, but knowledge." Clearly, there were strong motives for Bjorkman's attempts to please local interests, given his consciousness of such local hostility toward him.[4]

Such parochialism was not only abhorrent to the Washington office; it was unrecognizable. Early in 1936, Alsberg sent down Katharine Kellock (at that stage, a field supervisor) to report on the project's progress. Aghast at Bjorkman's failure to delegate production and to accept academic authority, Kellock encouraged him to work with university faculty and tried to turn the workforce's attention away from local minutiae and toward the state guidebook, while encouraging them to assess sights in terms of *visitor* interest. Kellock could see the fieldworkers' activity only in negative terms:

I found write-ups of old homes that contained genealogies to the 4th generation on people of only local interest. (The forewoman said naively, "Everybody in Raleigh knows them—some member of the family." I asked her whether the guide was being written for local people or for tourists and how much of that stuff would interest anyone from out of town. She said, in some confusion, "I reckon it would only interest townsfolks that knew the family.")

The Raleigh file had gone extensively into the life and history of every church in town. Andrews said, "North Carolinians are great people for churches and if you do one you have to do them all." I asked him how many of the churches would interest outsiders; his answer was prompt, "Just two." . . . [All workers] are using microscopes for their own little bailiwicks.

In the assessment of one of those workers (Marguerite Yancey, again), however, the American Guide Series owed its very existence to this localism: "No doubt every Guide in the country owes its use of old letters, diaries, family records, scrapbooks, to the enterprise of some worker who *Knew Someone* in town or elsewhere." Another worker, Francis L. Harriss, explained to Harry Hopkins that localism increased workers' sense of cultural ownership and their pride in contributing to a larger picture: "The great value of these Guides lies in the fact that they will provide the information, in tabloid form, which will interest our restless people in the life progression of our country, an interest in the human chain of which they are part, stretching over the vast soil of their country in which their lives are rooted. Every part of the whole area being linked up with every other part. These Guides will provide us the knowledge of each other we need to root us in a common heritage, a common interest."[5]

Blind to the pressures of local cultural politics, Kellock also turned a deaf ear to Bjorkman's protestations about state sensitivities, blaming slow progress purely on his *propre amour* and his jealous protection of his local preeminence—what she came to call, in exasperation, his "God-complex." Washington editors conceptualized "local color" and the "vernacular" as supplements to academic expertise, not opponents of it; thus for all their enthusiasm for cultural distinctiveness, they were unprepared for the dynamics of virulent localism. In Bjorkman's words: "Mrs. Kellock is undoubtedly very able and knows a great deal about the work, but what she does not know anything about is North Carolina conditions and the North Carolina temperament."[6]

To reinstate Washington's agenda, Alsberg solicited William T. Couch, offering him Bjorkman's job. Knowing the state director's financial straits and respecting his reputation, Couch refused that position but did accept the role of associate state director, a part-time position designed to give him control over the final editing of guide copy. As Alsberg well knew, Couch was positioned very differently from Bjorkman, both ideologically and geographically. A much younger man—thirty-four, as opposed to Bjorkman's sixty-nine—Couch was well connected in the network of Chapel Hill intellectuals; clearly Alsberg believed that appointing Couch would more or less automatically enlist local faculty to the project. As a very young man, Couch had seized the reins of the University of North Carolina Press, becoming assistant director in 1925 and director in 1932. He practically single-handedly brought the organization to national prominence as a promoter of liberal, reformist, regional discourse. As Couch described the press's mission: "We want to give opportunities for intelligent, honest and direct discussion of Southern problems . . . especially by Southerners and through a Southern publishing medium. We want to help make effective the doctrine that learning begins at home. We want to offer needed stimulus and means of cooperation and thus to derive the full value of trained individuals and agencies and institutions already in the South; and to do this work on a basis of a careful knowledge of this region, of its past and present, of its economic, social and cultural needs" (qtd. in Spearman). Couch was considerably less cautious than Bjorkman and much more committed to frank self-criticism as the best recipe for southern reform. He pressed for "books that would expose middle-class southerners to conditions beyond their normal experience," as well as editing *Culture in the South*, a symposium widely noticed for its Progressive candor about the disposition of power in the South (Singal 278). And he worked in liberal southern organizations such as the Southern Policy Committee and the Southern Conference for Human Welfare. This activism leads current histories to credit him as a leader in forging a new southern cultural identity: "Couch's aggressive attitude toward regional studies filled a vacuum left by northern houses and provided the South with a publishing center, which, as an organ of the region it served, offered a means of defining and molding a 'New South' during the days of the New Deal" (Wilson and Ferris 866).

Couch's commitment to what we might call academic or specialized knowledge was inflected in fairly complex ways, however: his position was not simply the opposite of Bjorkman's allegiance to local knowledge, nor was it simply allied to Washington's New Deal pluralism. Couch did believe that academic training flushed out unknown information and challenged conventional assumptions, and he was successful in attracting guidebook contributions from members of Howard Odum's Institute for Research in the Social Sciences (as well as academics in other fields). At the same time, he was intensely critical of the limits of social science, of the tendency toward self-serving specialization and obfuscation in the academy, and deeply skeptical of claims to objectivity: "In Couch's view, detail had to be evocative, analysis explicit, and the author's own bias and belief openly set forth" (Singal 279). Heartily in agreement with Robert Lynd's *Knowledge for What?* (1939), he believed that academic knowledge was valuable only insofar as it connected with the lives of people at large and resulted in reformist action.

It was also significant that Couch was a born southerner—raised in Virginia, then North Carolina—with deep emotional commitments to the South's distinctive identity (Singal 268–75). His commitment to studying and exposing the limitations on individual lives meant that his scholarly analysis was deeply embedded in a specific place and time. The inheritor of traditional North-South tensions as well as more recent struggles over federal versus state authority, he came increasingly to distrust Washington's attempted centralization of power in the undertakings of the Writers' Project and to trust more local authorities. For example, having asked Jonathan Daniels, editor of the *Raleigh News and Observer*, to write the opening piece, he later approached him to read all the introductory essays. Although Couch appreciated the role of the Washington office in maintaining high standards, the more immersed he became in guidebook production, the more frequently he clashed with D.C. editors' directives and interventions, deeming them inappropriately rigid and disregardful of the state's particular conditions. After Alsberg had been ousted from the central office, the confrontation came to a head: flouting Washington's rule of authorial anonymity on the grounds that young writers' careers were at stake, Couch credited the authors of another project publication produced by his press, *God Bless the Devil!*, a volume of tall tales produced by Tennessee Writers' Program and illustrated by members of the Tennessee Art Project. This defiance caused a furor among what Couch called the antidemocratic dictatorship of "anonymous clerks in Washington"; in November 1939, he resigned in an eruption of charges, legal challenges, and investigation by the FBI.[7]

The processes by which this triangulation of interests issued in guidebook copy are legible in the North Carolina editorial archive. The politics of the Asheville, Chapel Hill, and Washington, D.C., offices produced editorial priorities and practices considerably at odds with each other. Driving these contestations was the assumption that representation in the guidebook legitimated a given image or discourse as the "official" account. Thus innumerable details in the guidebook—from the technical to the explicitly ideological— were subject to extended negotiations and frustrations. The pressure of official discourse seems also to have tested the limits of Couch's liberalism. In an eerie foreshadowing of his shocked reaction to the black call for an end to segregation in 1944 and his increasing conservatism in the face of 1960s civil rights movements (Singal 296), Couch ultimately denied black voice and agency entrance to the guidebook text, though in a manner much more complex and conflicted than Bjorkman's.

A fundamental difference between Bjorkman and Couch was their contrasting definitions of valuable or accurate knowledge, which led to several disagreements over the representation of socioeconomic conditions in North Carolina. The debate over the history essay was paradigmatic. Partly because they could not agree on an appropriate contributor, Couch wrote one version of the essay himself. He ended his narrative of the state's emergence and developments since the sixteenth century with a reflection on the ultimate lack of progress. In a letter to Couch, Bjorkman objected vociferously to the lack of "propriety of its final paragraph from a Guide viewpoint": "To me it is needlessly pessimistic, constituting a sort of slap at the State, and it is made dangerously conspicuous by appearing as an ultimate summary. I feel absolutely sure that the sponsoring State Department will not agree to the retention of that paragraph."[8] Bjorkman frequently acted as spokesperson for the guide's sponsors, obviating the need for the Department of Conservation and Development to enter the editorial battle. While Couch believed himself to be faithfully following the logic of academic analysis, Bjorkman felt that any representations insensitive to local pride and self-affirmation were inadmissible as guidebook material.

When the Washington office intervened heavily in editorial matters, however, Bjorkman and Couch tended to submerge their disagreements to erect a common front. They, along with Andrews and Hendricks, were fiercely united in their resistance to technical procedures imposed by Washington. They understood the ordering of information, the details of tour routing, typographical specifications, and the disposition of wordage to be constitutive of the final account and, therefore, to be the rightful domain of state editors. As Bjorkman argued to George Cronyn, "We feel that it would be advisable for the Washington office to trust our more intimate knowledge of the local situation."[9]

Particularly prolonged confrontations occurred over the representation of architecture. This topic clearly touched what the North Carolina editors considered their fundamental right: the right to define their own cultural heritage, to distinguish between the valuable and the valueless in their local environment. To Couch and Bjorkman, the state's architecture was its weak spot, revealing something about the cultural environment which they did not wish to have exposed in a national publication. The dispute also exposed a power struggle over who would define the state's appropriate place within the nation's representation.

Couch and Bjorkman disagreed about who should handle the guidebook's architectural material—Couch favored Louise Hall of Duke University, while Bjorkman strongly argued the merits of a local Asheville architect, Lindsey Gudger—but they were united in their opinion that the topic should receive limited space. Holding to traditional aesthetic measures and received notions of cultural centers, they suspected that extensive architectural material would make the state into a national laughingstock: in Bjorkman's words to Alsberg, "So many of the buildings mentioned in the Guide for historical, associational, or occupational reasons have neither style nor beauty from an architectural point of view. They are simply commonplace." Bjorkman was also adamant that vernacular description—not the technical language of Washington specialists—was the only appropriate medium for these lowly sites.[10]

In contrast, Roderick Seidenberg, a progressive architect and magazine writer, now national editor on art and architecture, considered the guidebook an unparalleled opportunity to educate both the state's inhabitants and the country at large about the cultural and social significance of North Carolina architecture. With Alsberg's support, he set about inserting copy designed to guide project workers and readers into literally seeing their built environment anew. As the confrontation became more impassioned, the North Carolina editors resorted to telegraphic resistance: "Believe Guide already top heavy with architectural descriptions and sponsors feel the same . . . North Carolina noted for scenery and sports but not for architecture." Washington editors argued that this was the precise motivation for a "pioneer job": "It is unfortunate that your ideas on what should be in the guides do not agree with those outlined by Washington from the beginning; the very fact that the architecture of North Carolina has been so much neglected is the very reason that it is important that we should give it adequate coverage." The dispute never was resolved to everyone's satisfaction: to Couch and Bjorkman's rage, publication was delayed while Washington squeezed in more and more architectural detail, even over the protestations of Louise Hall, who was ultimately responsible for most of the architectural writing.[11]

The political stakes in these editorial confrontations were raised when Washington officials also tried to effect a reconceptualization of African Americans among southern officials. Sterling Brown—national Negro affairs editor from Howard University—and other Washington officials moved to restore agency to southern blacks, as workers, guidebook subjects, readers, and travelers. Washington officials repeatedly demanded that North Carolina increase its employment of blacks. Bjorkman and Couch resisted the demand, but from different angles. Bjorkman argued the pressures of local conditions, with, typically, no question about the justice of the status quo: "So far I have employed no colored persons because the resources of the Writers' Project in this state have not permitted the setting up of separate establishments, which would be required for such employment" (Hirsch, "Culture" 17).

Couch's position was more conflicted. He was considered, and thought of himself, as occupying the far edge of southern liberalism when it came to race and class analysis. That position was a tense one: he mounted vehement challenges to racial exploitation while defending racial segregation as beneficial to blacks; in *Culture in the South*, for example, he argued the necessity of "Negro and white labor" recognizing their "community of interest" in a planned economy (457) while at the same time defending the "color line" as beneficial to black racial solidarity (469–70; King 49). The pressure by northern New Dealers to move beyond the racism of this compromise panicked Couch into resistance: he finally declared, in exasperation, that he wouldn't "discriminate for or against Negroes."[12]

The combined resistance of Bjorkman and Couch was further entrenched by their appeals to specialization. Both men insisted that guidebook work demanded expertise beyond the reach of any African American on the relief rolls but refused to use up their nonrelief exemption on black writers. Intent on thwarting centralist dictates and New Deal definitions of proper race relations, Couch and Bjorkman resisted the hiring of blacks to the point that they established one of the most discriminatory project employment records across the country (worse by far, for example, than that of the conservative, Deep South Georgia). The North Carolina project never employed more than six blacks, and that only very briefly; according to Bjorkman, black relief workers "have invariably had to be dropped after a short time because they did nothing at all."[13]

Similar resistance met Washington critiques of guidebook copy. Brown asked, repeatedly, that North Carolina expand the volume and detailed texture of copy on black lives and institutions, accusing local writers of bleaching out the population in their "unrecognizable" representations of the state. A series of editorial reports argued that instead of trading on thumbnail cultural stereotypes, city and tour descriptions should detail the domestic, professional, cultural, and religious spaces of the state's black inhabitants, while surveys of North Carolina history and contemporary conditions should accord a fuller place to African Americans than the limited role of victim. In a response to Alsberg, Bjorkman pled, again, the force of local pressures: "While I am fully in sympathy with the policy of doing justice to the Negro, and while I realize that often activities by that race are worth mentioning while similar white activities would be insignificant, I feel strongly that the Guide should not so overemphasize the Negro that it will arouse hostile criticism."[14]

Couch's response was a more complex amalgam of academic opinion and personal inclination, which led to a restrictive interpretation of black culture. Preferring to have the "Negroes" essay written by an African American but failing to find an "appropriate" candidate, Couch finally wrote the essay himself, and it was largely approved by the Washington office. When he came to position black cultural achievement in an essay on nonracially specific arts and handicrafts, however, he pitted his Chapel Hill authorities against Washington's in order to deny any originary status to black folklore or music. A bitter struggle developed, with G. B. Roberts, a black editor in Washington, finally coming very close to accusing Couch of racism. Roberts cited James Weldon Johnston on critics—like those on whom Couch relied—who insist that black spirituals derive from white religious songs: "The opinion of those critics is not sound. It is not based upon scientific or historical inquiry. Indeed, it can be traced ultimately to a prejudicial attitude of mind, to an unwillingness to concede the creation of so much pure beauty to a people they wish to feel absolutely inferior." The central office generally threw its weight against the theory that African American spirituals derive from white religious songs, recognizing that larger issues of cultural dignity and distinctiveness were implicit in the point.[15]

The upshot of this unrelenting pressure from Washington was the inclusion of more African American material. In what spirit such inclusion was made is suggested by an anonymous source, speaking of the familiar "S.A.B." initials at the head of one critical editorial report after another: "Brown came to be commonly referred to by some North Carolina Project officials as 'S.O.B. Brown'" (Hirsch, "Culture" 45). That this was an Asheville rather than a Chapel Hill response is demonstrated by Couch's continued uneasiness about the text's suppressions: "In working on the North Carolina Guide Book I have been much concerned over the problem whether we should have anything to say about the lack of decent resorts, hotels, overnight stopping places, and rest rooms for Negroes traveling through the South. . . . I am convinced that the high percentage of juvenile delinquency and crime among Southern Negroes is a direct consequence of not having satisfactory provision for use of time when not at work."[16]

Caught irresolutely in the implications of his own politics, Couch denied manifest recognition to black travelers in the guidebook but salved his social conscience in other project plans. In the same 1938 letter to Alsberg in which he voiced his uneasiness, he recommended a raft of new project undertakings which sound like a roll call of topics and information ducked by the guidebook. The list included "Negro Artists and Their Work," "Laws,

Customs, and Habits Governing Relations between Races," "Biographies of Negroes Who Have Achieved Distinction," as well as "Poor Whites in the South" and "Rural and Urban Slums."

The generation of illustrations for the guidebook was accompanied by equally delicate, though less lengthy, negotiations. Couch was convinced that there was a dearth of good photographs of the South: he wrote to Alsberg, in connection with *USA—A Democracy Looks at Itself,* "I believe the effort should be made to develop state and national photographic archives and that it will never be possible to get really good materials for the kind of job you have in mind until this is done." He commissioned his favorite local photographer, a portraitist named Mrs. Bayard Wootten, to fill the gap, insisting that she be kept on the payroll even during times of retrenchment. He gave Wootten precise directions: "She was furnished a list of places mentioned in the *Guide* and asked to get pictures of them. She was asked, also, to get pictures of the people and their occupations"; in one telegram, for example, Couch directed her to stop at a strawberry center to get pictures of picking, packing, selling, living conditions, and quarters of pickers. This was a use of project money at which Bjorkman balked, arguing to Alsberg that photographs provided by Chambers of Commerce and government agencies were adequate. Washington, meanwhile, sent down its own photographer, H. A. Highton, to cover the territory as he had done for other guidebooks. Final authority over the selection and captioning of photographs was equally contested: at different times, claims were made by Bjorkman, by Couch—both as project official and as director of the press that ultimately published the guidebook—by Alsberg, and even by the Van Rees Press, which was printing the volume.[17]

These editorial negotiations suggest how ideological positions became translated into guidebook copy. Political self-determination—a significant issue for states during the New Deal—devolved into the self-definitions implied in the selection and presentation of information in the guidebook. Once textual representation was at stake, local and academic knowledges appeared as strategies for naturalizing or exposing racial segregation, affirming or questioning whiteness as the norm in a state that reported about one-third of its population as black. Although the main architects of the guidebook were in broad political alignment as supporters of the New Deal, their disputes over foundational questions of cultural origins and cultural achievements exposed the yawning gulf between New Dealers in Washington and liberal southerners.

When the guidebook was finally published in September 1939, with a run of seventy-five hundred copies by the University of North Carolina Press, the textual imprint of these reluctant inclusions, forced exclusions, and unresolved differences was heavily masked. Like all the volumes in the American Guide Series, *North Carolina* is prefaced by a signed letter from the state governor stressing: "This Guide presents a complete view of the State, her people, the historical background, and a complete inventory of the resources of North Carolina, all compiled in one volume." Less explicitly, the omission of Couch from the contributors acknowledged in Bjorkman and Hendricks's preface—indeed the entire absence of Couch's name in the published guide—erases evidence of the contestation that informed so much of the production.[18]

Framing the guidebook with the story of that production enables what Edward Said calls "contrapuntal reading," reading for both the inclusions and exclusions, to recover the "structures of attitude and reference" regulating the published text (66). From this perspective, for example, the technical descriptions of architecture that pepper the guide read like the mapping of centralized authority and language onto local sites. More extensively, state tensions are reproduced in the guide's epistemological split. All guidebooks were divided into three parts: a section of expository essays on the state's history, geography, economics, and the like; then detailed descriptions of the state's largest cities and towns; and finally a series of tours crisscrossing the state.

In the case of North Carolina, Alsberg managed the fundamentally different orientation of Couch and Bjorkman by allotting them separate sections. The essays became Couch's preserve: the majority were written by academics, often Chapel Hill colleagues, and Couch retained considerable editorial prerogative. In Bjorkman's words: "Not only have these essays been practically taken out of my hands by Mr. Alsberg's action, but they are the part of the Guide for which the workers at my disposal are least fitted."[19] In these essays, the state is represented by statistical information, socioeconomic analysis, and a historical and geographical sweep available only to the academic or professionalized perspective, all delivered in measured tones that fold exposures of rural destitution and racial discrimination undramatically into a coherent narrative.

Knowledge takes a distinctly different form in the back of the guidebook, the fruits of the fieldworkers' "minute examination" of old documents, local informants, and their own knowledge, heavily edited by Bjorkman and his assistants, then reedited in Washington.[20] In the city descriptions and tours, history is made up of legend, tradition, supposition—not the carefully documented findings of the academic—and the local scene throngs with wildly different orders of information. Ripleyesque items—a smattering of mummified and revived corpses around the state, the adjoining married quarters of Siamese twins, the pet rooster named after the Apostle Paul—jostle alongside tales of vicious Ku Klux Klan activity, violent strikebreaking in Gastonia and Marion, taxonomies of natural and industrial production, and sites of Revolutionary, Civil War, and American Indian battles.

By one paradigm, the state is understood as a causally connected narrative; by the other, it is a ragbag of almost random incidents and tales. The alternative expository modes carried different levels of cultural currency for Alsberg and Couch. At the inception of his project position, Couch stood foursquare with Alsberg in judging the essays the only consequential knowledge offered by the guidebook. As he became more immersed in the project and found more occasions to ally himself with local perspectives, however, Couch's attitude gradually changed. In June 1936, he told Bjorkman: "I hope tours will not form the body of the work, but if we have to have directions for the nitwit who can't find his way by the excellent road maps already available (God knows how he will be helped by any more directions), then let us have more directions in the form given here [tour 1]. In fact, this tour is so interesting and well presented that my doubts about presentation of material through tours are somewhat shaken." Two years later, Couch had decisively shifted ground: "In all the discussions [with the central office] I took the position that the tours constituted the most valuable portion of the Guide Book and that although reviewers might read the essays and pay more attention to them, that in the long run the books would justify themselves by the quality of the tours."[21]

Although there was an oppositional dynamic between the front and back ends of the guidebook, they do also work together, particularly to lay North Carolina's claims to prominence on the national stage. This emphasis was achieved by Bjorkman and Couch's common front against Washington's agenda. Their preoccupation with national status functioned at all levels of the North Carolina project. A plea to Harry Hopkins for continued project funding by the fieldworker Francis Harriss, for example, ran: "The part NC has played in our national drama is very great. Seldom conspicuous, but often a stabilizer, and never absent from the general effort. . . . So much of our national basic foundations lie here in eastern and Piedmont NC."[22]

These terms reappear in the allusion in the preface to "historic associations that form an integral part of the national background" (vii) and in the framework of national standards shaping academic analysis. The opening essays' dense narratives of state characteristics and developments are regularly punctuated by comparisons on the national scale: North Carolina, we are told, is the home of the first state university in America, "second only to Massachusetts in the production of cotton textiles" (72), and site of the putative first declaration of independence in the thirteen colonies. Special emphasis is given to Sir Walter Raleigh's attempted settlements in what became Dare County, "birthplace of the Nation (1584) and of aviation (1903)" (294).

Within the myriad information given in the cities and tours sections, the one constant feature is the "George Washington Slept Here" syndrome. Countless sites are identified by their association with figures of national significance: the birthplaces of presidents, congressmen, and signers of the Declaration of Independence; the stopping places of Revolutionary, Confederate, and Union generals; and sites visited by Presidents William Howard Taft, James K. Polk, Andrew Jackson, Andrew Johnson, and Woodrow Wilson. Abraham Lincoln is dragged onto the scene by the thinnest of ruses, via the site of a no longer extant house and a misdoubted rumor: "Near the confluence of Mingus Creek and the Oconaluftee, 10.5m., stood a log house in which, local tradition says, Nancy Hanks, mother of Abraham Lincoln, lived, and in which Lincoln was born. The story, if true, would make Lincoln a North Carolinian" (457).

And George Washington, of course, is everywhere: innumerable cities, towns, houses, inns, and farms made consequential by Washington's inconsequential acts (discovering that he had mislaid his powder puff at Smithfield [380], for example, and resting under a tree near Hampstead [287]). There is even the town of Washington, which he did not visit but of which it is noted: "The George Washington Bicentennial Commission established the fact that of the 422 cities and towns in the Nation named for George Washington, this town was the first" (284). These insistent markers provide what Karal Ann Marling calls "material intimacy with important figures and great events of the past"; Washington, of course, like so many of the statesmen who throng this narrative, is a figure central to the construction and maintenance of national identity (*Washington* 18).

We can understand the cumulative effect of these emphases to be a quiet rewriting of history. Not only does the guidebook adhere to the southern euphemism of "the War between the States" (the term "Civil War" appears nowhere). Not only are the razed and the killed resuscitated by their remains or relics or sites being memorialized here. But also the guidebook documents for North Carolina a central position in any narrative of national formation.

In positioning North Carolina as the ground on which the nation took shape, the guidebook circumscribes national identity with a color line so deeply inscribed in the textual structure and so camouflaged in the language as to render it almost unchallengeable. In doing so, the guidebook contributes to what Toni Morrison identifies as the "Africanism" that "provided the staging ground and arena for the elaboration of the quintessential American identity," "a particular 'Americanness' that is separate from and unaccountable to this [black] presence" (44, 5). Morrison's analysis is directed at the canon of American literature, with its elaborate tropes and figures; her remarks ring equally true, however, for the more taxonomic and prosaic register of the guidebook.

That the negotiations between Washington and North Carolina did not lead to a balanced racial representation is evident throughout the guidebook. When information was transferred from Washington to North Carolina—that is, from one cultural matrix to another—its political meaning and textual function were radically transformed. When black editors in Washington insisted on details of black history and contemporary life, they were encouraging North Carolina writers and editors to reconceptualize African Americans as agents in the state's culture. Couch's and Bjorkman's separate handling of this material marginalized blacks in different ways.

The guidebook essays consistently aim at rhetorical balance, emphasizing the state's liberal record on racial matters while conceding continuing inequities: "In education, social welfare, and economic advance much has been done for and by Negroes in North Carolina. It is likewise true that much more remains to be done" (57). One problem with the principle of "balance" is that it produces what Paul Sporn objects to (in the Michigan guide) as "tonal neutrality," a rhetorical choice whose grounding in "racialist traditions" is exposed when the subject of the writing is immigrants, African Americans, or Native Americans (219, 227). Also, in the case of *North Carolina*, shaping this measured articulation is what can only be termed textual segregation. The opening essay, "Tar Heels All," by Jonathan Daniels, editor of the *Raleigh News and Observer*, offended G. B. Roberts in Washington: "Since Negroes have been so well treated in a separate essay it is unnecessary to include them here; but failure to identify the group would seemingly warrant a change in title."[23] As always, segregation led to erasure: once blacks had been removed to the separate "Negroes" essay, other essays were free to note the state's "progress" or the benefits for "everyone" without acknowledging the racial specificity of those terms.

The ways in which Bjorkman and his assistants more or less reluctantly incorporated African American material into the back end marginalized blacks as named absences, a people without lived culture or history. In city descriptions, we are told that blacks make up 52 percent of the population— or 37 percent or 26 percent—yet they are frequently removed to a single paragraph, characterized in group terms without further differentiation or detail. In the Charlotte description, for example, we are told: "Lying between South McDowell and South Brevard Streets is Blue Heaven, typical of the sections inhabited by the poorer Negroes" (159). A comparison with John Spivak's lengthy, excoriating exposé of Blue Heaven, in his 1936 study *America Faces the Barricades*, suggests that the appeal to typicality was the guidebook's means of escape from the details of harsh reality (28–30).

Tour descriptions repeatedly reify blacks by incorporating them into the landscape: as local color (in two senses), rather than as agents acting against a scenic backdrop. Buildings are often described as "Negro dwellings" or "Negro cabins," as if inanimate buildings possessed racial characteristics which the guidebook could fix. These sites then function to map the black presence as a margin, a sideshow to the main route: on tour 8, "Between Oxford and Creedmoor the route passes"—we might want to say *bypasses*— "the homes of white and Negro tenant farmers and traverses fields of tobacco and corn"; on tour 16, the directions read: "Left from Pineville on paved US 521 across a bridge beside a small Negro cabin, 1 m.; L. 220 yards off the highway is the SITE OF THE BIRTHPLACE OF JAMES KNOX POLK (1795–1849), 11th President of the United States" (406–7). These descriptions also suggest the stakes in the architectural dispute: buildings function here as sites onto which race and poverty are displaced. Tour copy also reinscribes the social inequities imprinted on the landscape when narratives individualize white protagonists by name while leaving black figures anonymous: "At the MCKINNON HOUSE (R), 75m., during the War between the States, Federal soldiers hanged McKinnon for refusing to reveal where he had hidden his share of the money distributed by directors of the local banks when Union troops were approaching. After the soldiers had left, a slave cut down and revived his master" (357).

The guide's role in producing racial objectification is exposed by a contextual reading of one illustration in particular. In tour 1A appears this description: "PEA ISLAND STATION (open), 15 m., is the only one in the Coast Guard service manned by Negroes. In the surf nearby is the rusty boiler of a grounded Confederate blockade runner" (300). The implied equivalency between the wreck and the black workers as tourist sites is reinforced by a page of illustrations: "Typical Wreck Near Hatteras" and "Only Negro Coast Guard Crew, Pea Island Station" (Ill. 25). The latter caption's adjective carries a suggestive ambiguity, and the content of the illustration—white officer observing black workers—demonstrates the color line in action.

The text disguises the historical specificity of this photograph. The Pea Island Life Savers, formed in 1880, were renowned both for their exclusive employment of African Americans and for the quality of their work; during the fifty years of their existence, for only three years—1935 to 1938—was there a white officer in charge. By 1939, when the North Carolina guidebook appeared, this photograph misrepresented the operation of race at the station.[24] By mapping racial segregation onto the landscape alongside historical relics and natural wonders, the guidebook produces apartheid not as a temporary nor an aberrant condition but as an established *sight* transcending historical change and quotidian contingencies.

The textual fissure of the color line extends to the treatment of Native American peoples. The local Cherokees were never a point of dissension to the degree that African Americans were, partly because they were, simulta-

25. Typical Wreck Near Hatteras

Only Negro Coast Guard Crew, Pea Island Station

neously, wards of the federal government, citizens of the United States, and a corporate body under state laws and therefore ineligible for Writers' Project jobs. There is no evidence that officials valued Cherokee "local knowledge" enough to involve them as voluntary consultants. This gap in the production process is matched, textually, by the paucity of material on contemporary tribal life. "Tar Heels All" omits American Indians from its taxonomy of state types, erasing them even from the record of the past with the statement that "North Carolina . . . has never been very long on history" (6). The essay "The Indians" is largely preoccupied with military engagements, tracing a history of diminution and vanishing, with a single sentence to carry the narrative beyond the late nineteenth century. Tour 21E covers the Cherokee Reservation: again, any sense of lived culture is limited to perfunctory details of modern administrative and social practices, the bulk of the description dwelling on past history and romantic tales. Indeed, the further into the mountainous west the guidebook moves, the more American Indian narratives attach to the landscape, but they are consistently sealed off from contemporary social and political dispositions in the categories of military history, creation narratives, and traditional stories—to the point that Alsberg protested, "We are getting pretty well loaded up with Indian legends." In perpetuating this erasure of contemporary Cherokees, as in the objectification of African Americans, the guidebook was, of course, representative of a broader set of attitudes. As Bjorkman's comment suggests, the Cherokees were palatable locally only as figures of the past: "Recently the Indians here have attracted a great deal of public interest by the revival of tribal ceremonies among the Cherokees."[25]

What is textually repressed, however, can be read to return in the illustrations. If the guidebook's written text excludes racial "others" from the central definition of the state, the positioning of nonwhite figures in the clusters of photographs insists on their originary role in North Carolina's culture. An example is the opening titled "Historical." As the series of photographs unfolds, it moves determinedly away from the anonymous typification of American Indians, the opening captions and images disposing of the race as the stuff of history: "Cherokee Types" (Ill. 26) is followed by archaeological shots of "Tuscarora Graves, Louisburg" and "Indian Mound, Mt. Gilead," then costumed scenes of "Cherokee Ball Game" and "Cherokee Bear Dance." The chronological trajectory then shifts into the individual names of military

26. Cherokee Types

heroes and statesmen attached to images from the built environment: a mansion is captioned "Cornwallis' Headquarters, Wilmington," below is "Statue of General Greene, Guilford Courthouse Military Park," and on the facing page the considerably more humble wooden homes labeled "Birthplace of Andrew Johnson, Raleigh" and "Birthplace of Gov. Zebulon B. Vance." Finally, the gathering moves triumphantly to North Carolina's progress into modernity, with the Wright brothers' technological coup: "Glider Flight by Wright Brothers, Kill Devil Hill" and "Wright Brothers' Monument, Nags Head."

Similarly, the gathering labeled "Industrial and Agricultural" opens with

27. Negro Field Hands

Cotton Pickers at Work

representations of black workers—male and female "Negro Field Hands,"
singly, then together in "Cotton Pickers at Work"—the raw end of the production cycle (Ill. 27). The individual portraits, by Mrs. Bayard Wootten,
particularly aestheticize these figures by their static pose, expression, light-
ing, and composition. Her pictorialism seeks to remove the faces from the
historical and material circumstances, casting the figures in a very different
light from the FSA's social documentary. As the illustrations represent the
increasingly industrialized stages of cotton and tobacco production—"Unloading Cotton at Gin, Smithfield," "Power Loom in Cotton Mill" (Ill. 28)
and "Tobacco Auction," "Cigarette Machine, Reidsville"—black faces disappear, only to reappear in a final "Miscellaneous" grouping, aestheticized
again by Wootten, in "Darkies Shelling Corn," a mother-and-children shot
well outside the progressive, industrial cycle. This final caption participates
in the removal of agency from these figures, "darkies" being an ostensibly af-
fectionate yet wholly infantilizing term that was moving into archaic self-
consciousness in the period (Cassidy 15).

If these groups of illustrations leave Cherokees and black workers behind, of course, they also entrench them as the beginning: there would be
no North Carolina history without Cherokees, no cotton industry without
blacks. Seeking to present North Carolina as the ground of the nation, the
guidebook includes material that can be understood to ground North Carolina's identity in the very "others" who are elsewhere removed to the margins of the state. It only deepens the irony that, in the photographs of
Cherokee types by the North Carolina Department of Conservation and
Development, the figures are wearing headdresses of the Plains Indians.
Presumably giving the tourists the stereotyped images they expect—in a
practice still extant in the state and known jocularly by the perpetrators as
"chiefing"—the Natives exceed their function as local color, seizing cultural
agency by destabilizing the history they are intended to authenticate.[26]

If racial representation exposes some of the guidebook's rhetorical designs, so too does the handling of gender. Both in the production process
and textually, the discourses of local knowledge paid significant attention to
gender; in some ways, there was more explicit attention to women as a social
category in the Asheville office than in New York City. Bjorkman was very
conscious of a certain class of women as keepers of the cultural heritage (as
was Fisher in Idaho): for best volunteer assistance, for example, he directed

28. Unloading Cotton at Gin, Smithfield

Power Loom in Cotton Mill

workers to members of the State Federation of Women's Clubs. He also knew that, again according to class and social position, women held distinctive influence in cultural politics; he made more effort to position women in supervisory roles than to place black workers. Couch also had some awareness of women's social position. Although *Culture in the South* did not devote a chapter to women, Couch's preface did recognize the gendered specificities of tenant farming: "The system is so thoroughly bad that no laws can be devised which, so long as the system lasts, can protect the women and children who are a part of it. . . . Women who have to cook, sew, wash and iron, who have to work regularly in the fields planting, hoeing, and harvesting, and who are not protected by any laws or customs regulating their hours of labour" (viii). What no one credited officially, of course, was the female infrastructure of the project, speculated on by Marguerite Yancey: "There are no figures to prove this statement, but I have the feeling that the actual compiling of the Guides was done largely by women who had to stay at home if a child fell ill, or the laundry accumulated too fast. They remained with the Project."[27]

That measure of circumscribed visibility is legible, too, in guidebook copy. Numerically, mentions of women are substantial, but predominantly they take the form of curio items. Women as a social category almost never come into focus in the essays' explanations of North Carolina's origins and development, ruled out by the focus on male sites of power, decision making, and military affairs. They do make their presence felt, in small groups and as individual figures, in the cities and tour descriptions. Still, the "Believe-It-Or-Not" tone of their representation trivializes them and the moments of national history and social description in which they appear. Believe it or not, the American Revolution was marked by "the patriotism of Edenton matrons who held the first feminine Revolutionary tea party" (182). "Mistress Barker," to the site of whose home we are directed, "was the leading spirit in the Edenton Tea Party. Tradition relates that she horsewhipped a British officer whom she discovered trying to make off with her horses" (185). Believe it or not, there were also heroic female spies and actors: "The MONUMENT TO MRS. KERENHAPPUCH TURNER, a life-size bronze figure of a woman, is one of the first erected in America to a Revolutionary heroine (1902). Mrs. Turner rode horseback from Maryland to North Carolina to nurse a wounded son" (385). In one of the few descriptions of field labor,

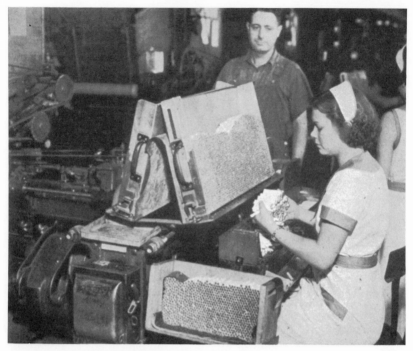

29. Cigarette Machine, Reidsville

women's presence turns sociological information into oddity: "Southwest of Fayetteville whites and Negroes of all ages work in the cotton and tobacco fields along the road. Occasionally in late summer, when immediate harvest is necessary to prevent cotton rotting on the stalks, girls and women incongruously dressed in beach pajamas or shorts work in the fields" (357). And throughout the state, women leave their mark as witches, romanticized murder victims, sensational murderers, and comical scolds: "At 15 m. is a cluster of houses and a general store, known as LOAFERS GLORY. Watching the neighborhood men gather here to swap knives and spin yarns, an industrious woman once observed tartly that this must be 'loafer's glory,' and the name stuck" (434).

Read in this context of cumulative emphases, the only two photographs that center white women take on a curious cast. Appearing back-to-back in the "Industrial and Agricultural" gathering, the two images—"Cigarette Machine, Reidsville" (Ill. 29) and "Weaving on Old-Fashioned Loom, Bur-

30. Weaving on Old-Fashioned Loom, Burgess

gess" (Ill. 30)—position women within the spectrum of state production, from domestic handicraft to factory work. In that context, they seem more curios than agents: the cigarette handler appears in a double-page spread otherwise devoted to men mobilizing the cotton and tobacco industry. More locally, within the frame of the photograph, her shuttered pose—eyes downcast in concentration—is given meaning by the gaze of her male co-worker, trained on her from center stage and variously interpretable as supervision, sympathy, or even muted desire. Over the page, we encounter another woman absorbed by her work; this time there is no defining gaze to circumscribe her agency, but she is limited in another way, by all the visible marks of an older South: an elderly figure, she sits right inside the antique loom, surrounded by the marks of passing handicrafts—the rag rug, the woven basket, the oil lamp, and the well bucket. It is because individual women are illustrated so infrequently that these images carry so much pressure of interpretation; men also appear in factory and handicraft roles, but they are equally prominent in individual portraits as sportsman, lifeboat officer, statesman, farmer, and philanthropic industrialist. As guidebook figures, photographic and written, men have a command over Old and New South, as well as the versatility to sustain their preeminence from one period to the next, that women never do.

Of all the categories of social dispossession represented, the most telling in terms of the guidebook's dynamic is the rural poor: sharecroppers, renters, and tenant farmers. Tenant farmers stood at the heart of Couch's reform projects: in the face of widespread ignorance in the 1930s, he campaigned vigorously for their cause, in the Bankhead Bill hearings, the Southern Policy Committee, and his publishing agenda; in 1935 his press published what is judged "the decade's most authoritative short work on tenancy": *The Collapse of Cotton Tenancy: Summary of Field Studies and Statistic Surveys, 1933–35* by Charles S. Johnson, Edwin R. Embree, and Will W. Alexander (Mertz 5). Another crucial study, H. C. Nixon's *Forty Acres and Steel Mules*, was written at Couch's suggestion and drafted under his guidance. Couch also spoke out in support of FDR's 1938 statement that "the South is the Nation's Economic Problem Number One," declaring: "We never can have general prosperity or a reasonable measure of wealth and health in this region unless we face the truth . . . pleasant and unpleasant, about ourselves and our land; and Southerners who attempt to obscure these truths are doing themselves and the South the greatest possible damage." His life history project (which eventuated in *These Are Our Lives* and approximately one thousand additional unpublished interviews) was driven by his commitment to make the farming poor—among other disadvantaged groups—visible and audible. Considering Couch's drive to confront Americans with images of and information about these figures, they are notably peripheral to the guidebook's landscape: not absent but represented in limited and ambiguous terms.[28]

The negotiations around production show that Couch was clearly mindful of tenant farmers as a significant part of the state's cultural landscape. He wrote to Bjorkman, for example, on tenant farmers' diet as well as on blacks and poor whites as valuable repositories of folklore. In pressing for more attention to this class, however, he found himself at odds with the local pride of most workers: when, for example, a Charlotte worker produced material on North Carolina cooking, Couch pushed fruitlessly for her to include more social classes in her representation. He was conscious that, generically and politically, the guidebook could not function as an unadulterated document of reform: "If I want to get stuff on controversial subjects into print, I am not limited to trying to get it by in the N.C. Guide, I have plenty of other more appropriate outlets. I prefer to do my boiling over elsewhere."[29]

The sense that the rural poor hovered in Couch's consciousness (and conscience) but could not come into focus in the foreground of the guidebook's landscape is perceptible, too, in the textual disposition of material. Although Jonathan Daniels's essay omits tenant farmers from the list of North Carolina types, other essays in the front section—more directly under Couch's editorial control—do make them visible in language critical enough to be considered controversial in this genre. The "Agriculture" essay devotes much of its space to a historical explanation and economic critique of farm tenancy and sharecropping, which insists that the hopelessness and desperation engendered by the system still exist: "One of the most serious economic and social problems with which North Carolina has to deal is farm tenancy" (62). The "Negroes" essay includes a small section under the heading "The Negro Farmer": "Probably the most crucial social problem in North Carolina and throughout the South is the system of farm tenancy" (54–55). When it ascribes the cause for the situation, however, the essays tread carefully: the Civil War is the only culprit named, and there is no criticism of the Agriculture Administration Act, whose "prolandlord outlook" inadvertently worsened conditions for tenant farmers and sharecroppers (Mertz 25, 99).

The intermittent analysis of rural landlessness in the front half of the volume changes, in the tours, into an unfocused presence, composed of sideways glances at and euphemisms about the condition of their existence. Tenant farmers and sharecroppers never explicitly appear in the guidebook; the omission means that this social type is never individualized, but it also means that these figures never function as local color in the way of the black boat crew and field hands. What does appear is the land to which they are tied: the tours mention "farming country" frequently, without detailing its condition; glancingly described cotton growing and picking flank several routes; and buried references, such as the following comparison, populate the landscape unobtrusively: "Southwest of STACEY, 13m. (767 alt., 45 pop.), the road follows a high ridge through a region of farms marked by tobacco barns, crude log affairs which nevertheless appear more substantial than the cabins of the tenant croppers" (372). Some allusions are so oblique that their status as euphemism is uncertain: for example, when the tour copy says "Southeast of Winston-Salem US 311 runs through an area where crops are diversified and many of the farmers supplement their incomes by employment in nearby industrial towns" (389), this may or may not be a reference to the poverty trap explained in the front half of the guidebook.

Visual representations are similarly ambiguous. In the photograph of a farmer leading two oxen drawing a load of hay—captioned "Ox Team on Mountain Road"—and in Wootten's portrait titled "Eastern farmer," there is little evidence to certify whether these are landowning or tenant farmers—though the decency of the work clothes in both cases and the access to work animals in the one suggest that they occupy the more secure end of the agricultural spectrum. The one image explicitly illustrative of tenant conditions—"Well on Tenant Farm," wooden structure and bucket in the foreground, backed by plowed field—encodes an ambiguity of a different order. As one of the few FSA photographs in this guidebook, it can function as a reminder of all the FSA images of human want not included here. Complementarily, within its gathering ("Industrial and Agricultural"), it is legible as a symbol of infertile poverty compared to the power and abundance signaled by the surrounding images of water: "Cheoah Dam, Tapoco," "Old Mill Wheel, Dillingham," "Saw Mill on Dismal Swamp Canal," and "Net Fishing at Vandemere." Equally, however, without a more analytical caption, it can be read as a curious sight or archaic hangover of the same rhetorical order as "Old Plantation Barn, Pettigrew Park," which appears beneath it and shows a woman sightseer, apparently just stepped out of her car to look at the looming building.

Hovering uneasily in this ambiguous space, neither clearly on nor off the guidebook's agenda, southern farm tenancy exposes here the limitations of New Deal rhetoric, as it did administration measures generally. The list of those dispossessed once by social polity and again by the guidebook's representation could be lengthened. It is not that the guide is uninterested in cultural difference: the Winston-Salem description devotes pages to the history, politics, education, and culture of the Moravian settlers. It is that, as the guidebook moves from essays to city and tour descriptions—that is, as it increasingly takes on the accents of commonsensical, "unmediated" observation—it is increasingly incapable of acknowledging the inequities of race and class. The more localized the knowledge, the lower the discomfort level.

If the guidebook is thick with different orders of information, it also in-scribes different orders of absence. Read from the margins and pressure points of production, these lacunae transmogrify into the most explosive sites in the guidebook.

The reception of the North Carolina guidebook, as I read it, only inscribes these emphases and suppressions more deeply into the larger discursive field produced by the American Guide Series. Reception was generally cele-bratory, with widespread notice from the press. Given the double layer of governmental authority—both federal and state—both local and national newspapers welcomed the guidebook as an official record, fixing the state's cultural identity for posterity, in the process substituting the part for the whole and naturalizing the white southern norm once more.[30]

North Carolina's official status was reinforced, too, by the ways in which the guidebook became enmeshed in a network of state cultural institutions. Project workers selected sites and furnished data for the historical markers placed across the state by the State Historical Commission, the Department of Conservation and Development, and the Highway and Public Works Commission. The project also traded writers and copy back and forth with the *State*, a weekly periodical of contemporary and historical life in North Carolina, supported by the State Historical Commission and amateur local historians. The guidebook's participation in the collective construction of the state is perhaps most evident in its distribution by the State Department of Conservation and Development, which underwrote its publication: "The department of conservation and development for the state, which is inter-ested in bringing people to North Carolina, places copies of the guide in the hands of newcomers upon their arrival in the state. Members of the depart-ment have reported that it has been found to be a valuable adjunct to their work. Many of these visitors become interested in the history of the state after attending a performance of the historic pageant on Roanoke Island, the department reports. A copy of the guide was found to be the answer to all of their questions."

Newspapers with national and statewide distribution tended to monu-mentalize the guidebook in their own way by celebrating the democracy of its achievement. Praise is expressed primarily for its comprehensiveness and popular prices, without any evident self-consciousness about the relativity of those concepts. For example, a review by "C.J.P." in the Raleigh *News and Observer* (which consistently supported project work) reads:

When the ledger of achievement is finally closed on the WPA it is going to disclose a great many things besides the leaf-raking that Republican critics discovered back yonder while the Hoover influence still hung over.

One of these achievements . . . is books—in a State where movie houses outnumber libraries 50 to 1. . . .

Change, North Carolina will, and out-of-date will go sections of the North Carolina Guide, but that is unimportant. What is important is that a foundation has been laid, and well laid.

The *New York Herald-Tribune*, in a review by Robert Watson Winston, finds the guidebook unorthodox in its focus on the common man:

North Carolina sorely needs a press agent. So ran the criticism of a state until recently laughed at and called the Rip Van Winkle of the Union. There is no longer occasion for such criticism. Tar Heelia has shed her humble motto, "To be rather than seem to be," and has fixed her gaze upon the stars: Attest the North Carolina Guide, a publication comprehensive and dramatic, throwing to the winds conventionality and artificiality and turning the Old North State inside out! Nothing indeed excluded save the stale and dull, nothing included save the racy and humanistic—a medley half Baedeker, half historical and wholly unorthodox. . . .

The theme of this guidebook is the march of Mr. Lincoln's plain man. . . . The guide is chock full of facts, it sings of deeds and not of men, though it gives credit to progressive leaders. . . . Though there are more than a hundred illustrations, not one of them is of what is called a distinguished man, *qua* distinguished.

The praise for democratic representation leads seamlessly into the valorization of the guidebook as a patriotic production. One editor, Constance Matthews of the *Nash County News*, commends its "reference value and patriotic data." At greater length, Jonathan Daniels's review in the *Saturday Review of Literature* reads: "If the book is not perfect, neither is North Carolina. But it is a good guide to a good State. As patriot that is all I ask—and a little bit more than I expected." From this perspective, by introducing a densely plotted body of information about the state onto the national stage, the guidebook has achieved iconic status.

Local newspapers read the guidebook differently. While they attributed the same official status to the guidebook, they focused more on its partiality (in both senses of the word) than its comprehensiveness. In "Concerning a

Book," the *Greensboro News* explicitly countered the claims of Governor Clyde R. Hoey's foreword, dwelling on absences in the coverage. Sixteen years later, the promotion director for the University of North Carolina Press revealed that "when the original GUIDE was published in 1939 some people incorrectly criticized the book, saying that it was controlled too much by Chapel Hill."[32] Local responses also demonstrated the intensity with which state residents read themselves into the guidebook.

Reviewers and letter writers paid close attention to the sections covering their own and neighboring districts, counting pages and fiercely resenting omissions and errors. The editor of the *Roanoke Rapids Herald* openly confessed, "It is a 577 page book which we have not had time to read," before proceeding to focus on the section covering Roanoke Rapids. The *Dare County Times*, the newspaper serving Hyde County complained: "WPA writers seem unfamiliar with Hyde," despite "all its rich history and the attractive area that is helping to make Hyde County nationally known." In a piece titled "Is It History?", the *Chowan Herald* damned the guidebook— "Inaccuracies galore fill it from stem to stern"—because it slighted Edenton's history in favor of Bath. The *Elizabeth City Daily Advance*, on the other hand, was delighted with the guidebook because, in the words of its headline: "North Carolina Guide Is Delightful Adventure; Elizabeth City Has Prominent Place in Book and in Its Making." Bjorkman found himself entangled in endless letter writing to local newspapers: apologizing for errors, for example, in letters to the *Daily Advance* which conveyed "my profound apologies to your city" (10 November 1939), refuting a correspondent's criticism in the *Greensboro Daily News* as "another unwarranted attack on the North Carolina Guide" (5 November 1939), and soliciting opinions from the local populace (29 October 1939). Learning from this lesson, in 1941 Bjorkman also invited nominations for inclusion and suggestions for one publication of North Carolina biographies and another calendar of North Carolina events. Privately, both Couch and Paul Kelly (of the sponsoring Department of Conservation and Development) confessed that they were taken aback at the bitterness of criticisms by the local press and apprehensive that the response would kill sales.[33]

One of Sterling Brown's main objections was that guidebook copy always oriented itself, rhetorically, toward a white readership: the agency of blacks, as travelers or readers, erased yet again. Tellingly, the soberest and most coded review appeared in the black periodical *Opportunity*. Echoing the even tones of the guidebook, Henry R. Jenkins weighs up the precise limitations of North Carolina's reputation for favorable race relations and the guidebook's complicity in promoting that image by avoiding hard questions. The final paragraph reads like pure irony: "So the contrasts persist, shadowing every sphere of life that vitally concerns the Negro. And yet, somehow, in spite of them (perhaps, because the neighboring states are so far behind) North Carolina will occupy a commanding position in the enlightened social order emerging in the South for its many contributions to American life, not the least of which have been cigarettes and furniture, textiles and Tar Heels, a Sunday brand of racial good-will, Bull Durham, and 'bunk.'" That final term is glossed in the guidebook "as meaning anything said, written, or done for mere show" (138). Its origin is traced to a political speech by Felix Walker, congressional representative for Buncombe County: "The address was a masterpiece of fence-sitting, and when a colleague asked the purpose of it, Walker replied: 'I was just talking for Buncombe'" (139). With knowledge of the production history, Jenkins's sly remark can be understood to dismiss not only the guidebook as sham and show but also Bjorkman, who always spoke for Buncombe, and Couch, who sat on fences.

Jenkins's analysis of "Sunday good-will" was also borne out the same month, when the most sustained note of dissension from the local press occurred in response to African American material. In the brief description of the small town of Rockingham, the guidebook matched population to copy in unusually close proportions. One paragraph sketched the town's history and industry, then the second paragraph read: "In Rockingham, Saturday is still 'Negro day.' The Negro population of the section is almost as large as the white. Since they live mostly on the cotton plantations, where the land is level, the rows long, and the summer sun scorching, Rockingham grants them one day to call their own. The carnival spirit prevails as whole families stroll about in their best clothes. In picking time cotton hands discuss the price of cotton and the wages planters are paying for labor in order to bargain with their overseers" (351). As soon as the guidebook appeared, the *Rockingham Post Dispatch* rushed out a response titled "Shameful": "On page 351 is a grossly unfair and false description of Rockingham. If this sort of reading matter depicts other towns as inaccurately as it does Rockingham, then the book should be consigned to the furnace. It certainly should not be circulated in this or any other State." The review proceeds to quote only the second paragraph of the Rockingham description, commenting:

Can you imagine any group or individual writing or sponsoring any such tripe as that? And to think the Government has PAID some smart-alec WPA writer for such a libel!

It is disgraceful.

When such interesting matter could have been written about this town—its history, its railroad facilities, the fact that it is on U.S. Highway No. 1, fine system of schools with nine months and twelve grades—in fact, a wealth of worth-while matter. And in the matter of history, the town has an enviable distinction: the fourth cotton mill erected in North Carolina was at Rockingham in 1834. . . .

Instead, it is classed as a Saturday Negro town, with rich land-lords oppressing the toilers and the people working like peons.

Letters were fired off to New Deal officials in Washington, while the *Greensboro Daily News* and the *Richmond County Journal* kept up the public pressure: "What we are ashamed of is the fact that WPA writers who authored the book in question are so dumb, so ignorant, so simple that the only thing they see when they come to Rockingham is the parade of negroes strolling up and down the street on Saturday."[34]

This attack in turn provoked a response by the *State*, the magazine most symbiotically enmeshed in the guidebook's discursive framework. On 21 October 1939, its editorial mounted a defense: "*The State* magazine advised: 'Take It Easy Ike!' and noted that the guide had not dismissed Rockingham as a 'nigger town.' The first paragraph of the guide's description, commented *The State*, noted interesting facts about the city's history and resources, and as for the paragraph that so offended London, 'It applies to most every other town in the state'" (Hirsch, "Culture" 47).

What the guidebook saw, or failed to see, was clearly an issue of intense political interest to a wide constituency. Those closest to the sites of representation read the guidebook as a map of their social identities. The investments, emphases, and lacunae of the guidebook text became writ large across the state's—and to some extent the nation's—public discourses.

It is instructive to return again to *These Are Our Lives*, a work that contained much more implicit and explicit criticism of the state's living conditions than did *North Carolina*. *These Are Our Lives* received extensive and even more laudatory national attention than the guidebook, but it was also greeted enthusiastically by local reviewers. The difference was that the life history volume was received as a new genre, one unencumbered with the conventional expectations of an established genre. Also, its authority was that of personal witness—a series of clearly located voices—rather than the ostensibly transparent, definitive, and unlocated voice of the guidebook. In the life histories, local knowledge is explicitly complicated, personal, and politically interested. And finally, *These Are Our Lives* was read as a regional work rather than one attempting to map the state onto a national grid.[35]

All of these attributes gave this volume a freedom of composition, circulation, and reception denied the guidebook. Discussed variously as literature, documentary, newsreel, folklore, "phonographic literature," and sociology, the book escaped stable categorization, whereas the guidebooks were all about categorization and taxonomy. One exhibit brought together FSA photographs with *These Are Our Lives* text, thus making manifest the implications for farm tenancy that were suppressed in *North Carolina*'s representations. Some reviewers came close to valuing the life history book in contradistinction to the guidebook genre: Ralph Thompson in the *New York Times* judged that *These Are Our Lives* was about "ordinary people" in a way that the American Guide Series ultimately was not; the *Providence Sunday Journal* said, "It is another kind of guide book; and better than any road descriptions it points ways of knowing what America is like"; in *So You're Going South!*, Clara E. Laughlin *almost* says that *These Are Our Lives* offers what the guidebook omits: "There won't be much else to think about for the next thirty miles or so, unless you have read that remarkable book called *These Are Our Lives*." Alsberg considered the volume and its reviews important ammunition in the fight to persuade Congress not to dissolve the Federal Writers' Project, telling Couch to send the book to southern senators. And Couch himself obviously considered *These Are Our Lives* his major accomplishment on the project.[36]

Yet in its inclusions and exclusions, the guide to North Carolina is an equally complex and valuable cultural document. Read contextually, it plays out the politics of knowledge in a particular southern location at a specific historical moment. Parties interested in the guidebook's making attempted to map onto North Carolina's landscape—and thereby naturalize—competing agendas. The Washington office conceived of the guidebook as an educational work: by representing social pluralism in factual, ostensibly unmediated accents, it would bring about social change. Although Couch was committed to reform, he came to feel that the view from Washington obscured the meaningful nuances of southern society. He also came to suspect that project rhetoric about regional self-discovery was a ruse by which New Dealers could remake the state in their own image. Determined to protect the state's right to self-definition, he was driven into an alliance with Bjorkman and his identifiably local constituency. In turn, the claims of local knowledge mounted by this alliance—the claim, for example, that it is a democratic mode producing authentic representation—emerge in the production history as a strategy for excluding undesirable voices, for limiting the scene in the interests of "cultural insiders" vying for local power. "Local pride" emerges as a code word for the deep anxieties of a southern class determined to preserve its privileges.

Thus the guidebook demonstrates that, at the discursive level (as at the material), southern conditions tested and found wanting the New Deal's patchwork of pragmatic measures. What were intended as progressive interventions foundered against the localized dynamics of race, gender, and class, exacerbating reactionary responses. The convergence of federal authority and the expectation of exhaustive taxonomy put pressure on sociopolitical fault lines, which then indelibly marked the representation of cultural identity. Far from liberating North Carolina from the color line, federal pressure drove it more deeply into the structure of the guidebook, wove it more invisibly into the national perception of natural conditions in the state.

And yet the guidebook remains largely uncontested as a source of state self-definition and self-representation. It was condensed and revised for republication in 1955 but was restored to its original form in 1988, in a reprint that marketed the work as a "State Treasure" (Powell, "Introduction" [v]). As recently as 1992, William Powell, North Carolina's preeminent state historian, judged the guidebook unsupplanted as an authoritative source of historical and cultural knowledge. Recognizing that state interests informed the guidebook's making and that the work "fed local pride," Powell nevertheless continued to subscribe to the guide's transparency: "I doubt that there was much regimentation . . . it was just the obvious way to do things."[37]

Missouri

Recovering Voices of Dissent

In the late 1960s, Jerre Mangione interviewed two men who had contributed to the Missouri guidebook: Jack Balch, who had been state editor in St. Louis, Missouri, and Harold Rosenberg, the national art editor who had been sent in from Washington, D.C., in 1939 as a troubleshooter to pull together the languishing guidebook. Rosenberg clearly remembered the Missouri Writers' Project as an adventure. For Balch, thirty years later, it was still a betrayal. The difference in the two reactions—palpable and vibrant in the taped interviews—is a mark of the difference between the guidebook's meaning to the local and the cosmopolitan. For the former, the guidebook was an expression of idealism, an opportunity to overstep corrupt state politics and bring together the best of national (indeed, international) and local radicalisms. For the latter, the guidebook was essentially a mechanism for managing regionalism from, and according to the designs of, the federal center.

The story of production in Missouri is more complicated than these two poles. The guidebook was seized and imprinted by a spectrum of competing interests—the state party political machine, various local voices on the left and right, progressive editors and officials from Washington, D.C. (who did not always agree on policy)—so many interests that the project disintegrated under the strain. In the end, the imperative toward central management—what Harold Rosenberg later called the "fantasy of One America"—produced a guidebook visibly distanced from the locality it pretends to represent and not even authored by the project members who had invested so much energy and such a range of personal and political hopes in the volume (99).

In the early days, fieldworkers across Missouri produced material typical of the cliché and boosterism to which Washington objected, but part of the state's editorial staff—whose job was to transform this raw material into essays, city descriptions, and tours—was unusual in having the central office's imprimatur. As national director, Henry Alsberg was able to intervene directly in the Missouri hiring, putting on the payroll both Jack Conroy, a Pulitzer Prize–winning novelist renowned for his proletarian fiction and left-wing politics, and Jack Balch, a second-generation, working-class Russian immigrant who was beginning to publish socially conscious fiction in the "little" magazines. Alsberg had wanted Conroy for Missouri state director, but the powerful, conservative Democrat Pendergast machine insisted on a local socialite, Geraldine Parker, for that position. First sight suggests that the national director aimed to turn the Missouri guide over to radical forces; the unfolding evidence of the guidebook's composition suggests, to the contrary, that his purpose was to harness powerful voices of the era to the master narrative of the New Deal.[1]

The Missouri state office is best known now—as then—for its employees' political activity, the most visibly tumultuous in the Writers' Project outside New York City. The fault lines ran in different directions in Missouri, however. There is no evidence of the Stalinist-Trotskyite battles that rent New York's radicals, no raging debates over ideological programs. Being on the cultural left in St. Louis, Missouri, during the Depression, meant being in fundamental alliance with the unemployed and the working poor and trying to make the perspectives, voices, and experiences of working people visible and audible through cultural forms. The connection with New York and Washington on the Writers' Project was crucial: the writers in Missouri saw it as a way to link local with national and international developments—in both radical politics and artistic movements—overstepping corrupt state party politics and parochial cultural standards. With the aid of the American Writers' Union and the New York chapter of the Workers' Alliance, they started up local wings of both those unions.

Against these hopes and ambitions, Parker seemed everything parochial and self-interested that the young idealists on the left abhorred. As a beneficiary of state political patronage, and with ambitions toward future political appointments, she dedicated her loyalties entirely to the Democrat Pendergast machine. Parker not only encouraged puffery in guidebook copy and censored criticism of the state; project employees also believed that she submitted their writing to the state WPA administration for approval, that she put considerably more energy into public displays of the project than into its production of material, and that she was corrupt in her financial dealings. She also refused to hire black workers: on several occasions, she turned away black applicants with advanced academic qualification in favor of whites acceptable to the Pendergast machine (Mangione, *Dream* 194).

This volatile mix erupted in October 1936, when Parker dismissed Wayne Barker, head of photography in the St. Louis office. Accounts differ—then and now—as to the motives (ostensible and real) for the dismissal. Supporters of Barker claimed that he had been fired for his role in union organization. Representatives of the American Writers' Union identified an additional cause in some articles he had published (in *New Masses*), which exposed anti-Semitic activity threatening official circles in Washington, D.C. Barker added to those reasons his public accusation that Parker had mishandled funds. All that Parker would say on the record was that he had been dismissed for inefficiency. But Washington officials (including Alsberg and Reed Harris, assistant director, who was sent to Missouri to investigate the situation late in 1936) were also told, and accepted, a story that Barker had misappropriated project photographic equipment for pornographic purposes (Mangione, *Dream*, 193–200; Penkower 162–63).

What is sure is that seventeen members of the project, led by Balch, Conroy, and Edwa Moser, went on strike in October 1936 in protest against Barker's dismissal, Parker's corruption, and the conditions of their employment. As the first Federal Arts Projects strike (according to Jack Conroy), it hit both the local and the national headlines: charges of communism flew, but support came forward not just from the Writers' Union and Workers' Alliance but also from the considerably more conservative Newspaper Guild and the Authors' League, not to mention the Women's Labor League. In the flurry of documented telephone calls from this period—among the Missouri office, the regional office in Chicago, and the Washington, D.C., office—Alsberg is audibly panicking, attempting to keep the lid on both the strikers' actions and the state officials' reactions. The pressure erupted when the strikers picketed the St. Louis office, they were arrested by the police, two of them charged, and many of them dismissed by Missouri's WPA administrator.[2]

The strike opened fissures among the project workers as well as between Missouri and Washington, D.C. In a familiar irony, wryly noted by Balch himself, the Missouri chapter of the Writers' Union was entirely composed of nonrelief workers. The "reliefers," in whose name the proletarian authors wrote, wanted no part of the strike, which was driven (as they saw it) by outsiders from the East and threatened their survival: about fifty of them signed a statement in support of Parker, which she brandished before the local press (although, according to some newspaper accounts, the statement also supported workers' rights to unionize and strike). This action was easily exploited by the local WPA administration—and the Democratic Party machine—who were representing union activity as "outside agitators" driven by New York.

In his frustration, Alsberg, who had been trying to edge Parker out for some time and who was fundamentally in sympathy with the left-wingers' aims, now revealed a deep-rooted paternalism toward the strikers. In a telephone conversation with Florence Kerr, he declared: "They had been disorderly and I told them they were putting their foot into it, that they should have borne the thing patiently until we got around to it." For Balch, this was the moment of betrayal:

In a way, we felt then—and I feel now—that it was an act of patriotism for us to do what we did. When we went out on strike, it was almost like we were a kind of an outpost waiting for relief columns to reach us. What we were doing was doing our small part in the concept . . . that America was falling apart and that in the middle of falling apart we had the job of pulling it together. And in the act of pulling it together there was this business of the same old stand; we couldn't allow that to happen because that was what had sunk us, and then Washington . . . just fell out of it. So there we were left, we were expendables . . . not only we but the dream.[3]

Eventually, through various interventions by Washington officials, some strikers (among them, Balch and Conroy) were offered reinstatement, which they refused when it became clear that others (including Barker) were not included in the offer. Geraldine Parker gracefully resigned giving the public excuse that compilation of guidebook material was almost complete and labor disturbances had been resolved. Esther Marshall Greer, who had been serving as district supervisor in the Sikenton office of the Missouri Writers' Project, was brought in as state director, but she proved every bit as inefficient and boostering as her predecessor. At a loss, Washington temporarily closed down the Missouri project in May 1938, its employment rolls having shrunk from about two hundred to forty-six.

Finally, in 1939, Charles van Ravenswaay was instated as the project's state director. His arrival introduced another ideological strain. Van Ravenswaay was a young Missourian independently involved in what he called "cultural conservation": a collector of local Americana, he and the Piaget brother photographers had undertaken a survey of early Missouri buildings, a visual and verbal record of vernacular architecture that ultimately became part of the Library of Congress Historical American Buildings Survey. Van Ravenswaay spoke the language of preservation, custodianship, and cultural heritage; he understood material culture as a manifestation of stability that was particularly precious in a time of economic dislocation. He came to characterize the American Guide Series as a bulwark against social and cultural transformations—that is, against some of the very processes of modernization that inspired Balch, Conroy, and others:

Traditional ways of thinking and doing were being swept away by the onrush of change . . . Americans were now on the move, eager not only to explore their own states but also to go far beyond to see the nation's scenic wonders and historic places, along with the natural and man-made diversions that they had read about. Travel broadened their vision and gave them a new appreciation of the size and meaning of their country, along with a deeper realization of the rapid, seemingly incomprehensible changes taking place. The time had come for books that reviewed, charted, and explained. . . . I can still feel the excitement of taking part in a great national act that rediscovered and reaffirmed faith in America during a time of fearful uncertainty.[4]

Van Ravenswaay seems to have understood the Writers' Project not as the empowerment of the voices of the dispossessed, nor as a great opportunity for political patronage, but as part of the institutionalization of cultural custodianship, a process to which he dedicated his career. A contributor to the Missouri Historical Society before his tenure with the Writers' Project, he later became president of that body, was appointed to the directorship of various museums, and ultimately received the Conservation Service Award of the U.S. Department of the Interior, "the highest honor that can be bestowed upon a private citizen or group by the Secretary," for his outstanding contributions "to the preservation of this Nation's cultural heritage."[5] With these institutional affiliations, van Ravenswaay was centrally positioned within debates about the authenticity, aesthetics, and national uses of historical preservation which raged from the 1920s (Kammen 29, 325, 561).

Anxious to ensure an acceptable completion of the volume, the central office dispatched to Missouri Harold Rosenberg, who had served first as magazine editor in New York City, then as national art editor in Washington, D.C., as part of "a flying squadron of troubleshooters" sent around the country to bring closure to recalcitrant publications (Mangione, *Dream* 337). Rosenberg was very much the Jewish New York intellectual of those years. "A sort of freelance Marxist, way up in the clouds, a Hegelian Marxist," according to Vincent McHugh, he had been embroiled in the factionalism of the New York Writers' Project, attacked by Communist Party members in the Writers' Union as a Trotskyite because of his anti-Stalinism and his refusal to articulate the connections between art and society as deterministically as wholesale social realism demanded. Missouri was utterly foreign to Rosenberg; he could have said of it what he said—in his interview with Mangione thirty years later—of his troubleshooting team's relationship to Washington State (his next guidebook): "We fell in there like a couple of commissars from Moscow who didn't know how to speak Hindustani or whatever the hell it was." Throughout his work on the guidebook he remained the outsider who lacked "local knowledge" but lent his editorial expertise, literary flair, and Washington office perspective.

With Rosenberg as some mixture of overseer and assistant and a staff of five, "mostly stenographers and clerks," van Ravenswaay managed, finally, to publish *Missouri: A Guide to the "Show Me" State* in June 1941.[6]

The battle over controlling the means of expression in Missouri was not just a scramble over pork barrel. As a midwestern state, Missouri was seen in the 1930s to belong to what Howard Odum called the "real America," site of the country's most distinctive (least European) culture. This was very much a fledgling sense of identity, however; Frederick Gutheim articulated a common perception when he described "Wisconsin, Missouri, or Kentucky, the newer states, the indeterminate states . . . whose history is fresh, whose people face the future, and where you are more likely to find 'the typical American'" (3). To control the representation of this state was, as some understood it, to strike at the heart of America's burgeoning self-discovery.

In effect, two versions of Missouri were created in the project. An "ur-guidebook" survives in the manuscripts composed by the local editors, all of which were rejected by Washington. D.C. Thirty years later, Jack Balch still sounds bewildered by reactions to copy which, as he said, was not digging up anything subversive: "We were trying, in our own small way, to fight for the integrity of the social vision, which was what this project was all about."[7] In their different ways, however, the rejected manuscripts can be read as offending the narrative of progress (cultural, economic, political) so strongly encouraged by the central office (and so palpably imprinted by Kellock on the Highway Route Series). Then there was the published guidebook, which appeared in 1941, having been composed by Washington's sanctioned representatives. While the manuscript essays speak in a range of discordant registers, representing competing aesthetic and political impulses of the period, the published guidebook scripts its narrative much more harmoniously.

In the production of the unpublished volume, the opposition between local and central points of view occasionally crystallized around the selection of content. For example, Donald P. Beard, a worker in Independence, Missouri, sent Reed Harris two photographs of dilapidated shacks inhabited by black families on relief. His letter underlines the point: "They are not very pretty. . . . The worst of the two inclosed dwellings, at North Dudgeon and Van Horn Road stands within a stone's throw of the pretentious Colonial court house in Independence. The photo I enclose was taken in 10 above zero weather in January, 1937. The tenants threw slops out of the door just to the right of the telephone pole, while scraps of fiberboard from grocery cartons replace broken window panes. The average hog pen is luxurious by comparison, yet human being [sic] dwell there."[8] This was certainly the voice of the local witness, one of the "men and women who knew the particular locale in all its richness," about whom Roosevelt had proudly boasted as the authors of the American Guide Series, but this voice was firmly suppressed. Neither of the photographs was included—the only guidebook photograph of Independence portrayed the colorful "Old Settlers" parade—nor did the verbal description of the city acknowledge the presence of poverty; as far as the guidebook was concerned, these shacks were not part of Missouri's landscape.

More often, however, the politics of style was at issue. Jack Conroy, for example, wrote essays and city descriptions in the vocabulary of competing class interests. In his essay "Literature," he cited Whitman as his model (a formulation common to 1930s' writers of social realism), championing the taste of the "masses" and the "people" in his aesthetic and political judgments on a variety of Missouri writers. Conroy's class allegiances were also played out geographically: in the same essay, the artistically nurturing environment of the Midwest is privileged over the pronouncements of the "brahmins" whose vision of art, society, and gender roles was constricted by their obeisance to "Eastern refinement." Conroy characterized the confrontation between western and eastern writing of the nineteenth century as follows:

> The characters in stories mirroring the frontier milieu and written by those on the scene were considered far from decorous and civilized to eastern readers and critics. The genteel females pictured in novels turned out by contemporary residents of the seaboard were delicate hothouse blossoms indeed, invariably swooning at crises, while the husky self-reliant dames of the Missouri settlements, standing squarely on two feet, fighting bears with knives, shouting encouragement to lovers locked in life-and-death combat with rival swains, earned the disapproval and incredulity of those whose opinions on literary matters were presumed to carry weight.
>
> Not only did the wild and woolly westerners behave in a most unorthodox manner, but their speech was barbaric. Dialect was still frowned upon by the effete eastern arbiters of literature, so the embattled westerners, goaded to more violent revolt against the stylistic straitjackets imposed by those cloistered in the library and classroom, deliberately scorned grammar and encouraged misspelling. Such eccentric spellers as Artemus Ward and Petroleum V. Nasby reflect the ultimate extent of this rebellion.

Similarly, at Conroy's hands, Mark Twain becomes a rich native talent discovered by the masses and spoiled by contact with the artificialities of the eastern leisure classes. Conroy's essays "Art" and "Music" value community and folk creativity over the technical proficiency of concern to "academicians." His style, consistent with these ideas, is conversational, spirited, and impressionistic, an attempt to express the region's vernacular accents.[9]

All of this sounds acceptable enough in the context of 1930s' liberalism, yet Conroy's work was consistently rejected. Washington editors objected to his "proletarianisms" and to his conversational, freewheeling presentation. His description of Kansas City was commended by several Washington editors as lively and substantial, yet they required that it be resequenced according to the central office plan: "Its present arrangement gives a disconnected and imperfect picture"; "The material is all there for a picturization of the city as a whole. We should like it woven together in a smooth narrative . . . told through its history and the story of its development." Most ironically, Conroy's work was criticized for its attitude to local culture: one editor asked for "a more reserved statement of regional pride" while another ruled:

Folk songs, hillbilly "music," Negro ballads, and the like should be treated under Folklore. What is wanted here [in the "Music" essay] is an article on music as an art, showing its progress as such in your State. . . . Both St. Louis and Kansas City have excellent symphony orchestras. Why not tell us something about them, rather than Frankie and Johnnie? . . . [Include] native composers and artists, if nationally known.[10]

Two principles seem to underlie these objections. The last comment demonstrates Washington's desire to demarcate regionalism, the center defining the margins by grading a locality's accomplishments on the basis of their impact on the cosmopolitan sites of political and cultural power. More generally, the objection seems to be that Conroy's choice of terms such as "class," "masses," and "the people"—which belonged to an identifiable discourse of the 1930s—is too divisive, too clearly a matter of political allegiance. One of Washington's key terms was "panorama": Conroy was advised, in describing Columbia, Missouri, for example, that "the panoramic method from a suppositious vantage point (or an actual one, if available) is best." The boast of all the guidebooks (including *New York Panorama*) was their sweep and inclusiveness, and Reed Harris promised that "point of view" would be edited out of final copy. As Alan Trachtenberg has said of the FSA file: "Its encyclopedic intention alone inscribes a signifying order upon the variegated materials it holds . . . making the file seem permanent and authoritative, a sure guide to reality" (55–56). This was precisely the authority at which the architects of the American Guide Series aimed. Their publications were to rise above all viewpoints, to look like reality. Conroy's vision was too obviously informed by opinion and conviction, too insistently a representation manifesting its mediation.[11]

Jack Balch also failed to lay an invisible template over the Missouri scene. His vision seems akin to that of fellow Missourian Thomas Hart Benton in the visual arts in his celebration of quotidian activity (including the culture of manual work) and his efforts at mimesis in articulating the sometimes brutal dynamism of everyday life. In his Bentonesque technique, Balch worked totally at odds with the declared aim of the Writers' Project to control and demarcate America, an aim actualized in the "American Guide Manual" and its many supplements to which all workers were directed to conform in their writing up of copy. Balch asserted in his guidebook essay on St. Louis: "It is hard to chart a course too carefully, for as in all big cities, the most beautiful or shocking things are seen at the oddest and most unexpected times, and in the strangest places"; this is "a brief review of the city, one designed to give some idea and feeling into what the poet . . . calls the 'movements that make her tick,' rather than a plain survey of facts." In Balch's handling, St. Louis ("outside of the established and self-conscious islands of the aristocrats and business men") becomes a site of sheer human energy which defeats plan or system: "The city spreads out . . . with the splashing abandon and planlessness of waves. . . . This hodge-podge . . . a city swirling and blaring to the joyous and deep laughter of men moving in it without perspective or memory." Balch's style is equally swirling and blaring as he rushes from historical detail to contemporary anecdote to local joke and back again, the whole mass of moments swept along in a rush of participial clauses and idiomatic interjections.[12]

Implicitly, Balch challenged Washington's procedures by equating this kaleidoscopic representation with the true impulses of the region's culture. His description of Springfield opens with an extended trope personifying the city as a face full of lines, then dwells at length on the "Trading Lot," a patch that brought together farmers, townspeople, and soap-box orators in a Bentonesque scene swirling with gossip, social intercourse, and trade. Balch then asserts, "It is the symbol contained in this 'trading Lot' which reveals the true history of Springfield. Dates, facts and figures can but add to one's knowledge of the city's growth, not its nature."[13]

Balch's pronounced class allegiances led him not only to defy Washington's dictates about impartiality but to expose some of the constructedness of the historical material which the project sought to naturalize. Sensitive to the industrial conditions shaping working people's lives, Balch's essays locate conflict particularly at the intersection of class and ethnicity. His submission on St. Louis attacks the leisured French classes of an earlier era, tracing continued discrepancies and tensions among the contemporary descendants of French, German, Irish, American, and African American settlers:

> The all-pervasive but anemic French culture in St. Louis is to be found mostly in private Catholic schools and in exclusive homes on Vandeventer Place and in outlying incorporated villages, complete with millionaire sheriffs and mayors and home taxation. . . . Its single most public appearance is during the Ball of the Veiled Prophet, St. Louis' equivalent of New Orleans' mardi Gras.
>
> This event, paradoxically, is held at the Coliseum, a building devoted usually to the groaning and slugging of boxers and "rasslers"; the guests, admitted by invitation, and then only when the men guests "wear correct white bow-ties and vests" roll up in limousines and sometimes a cabriolet, through grown-dark business and slum streets, to step out in top-hats or trailing gowns, ushered past the silent and admiring crowds of poor whites and Negroes of the district by policemen. . . . Next day the populace-at-large reads with great concentration and interest what the various debutants and matrons wore, who escorted whom, and usually there are pictures in the rotogravure sections of all the newspapers featuring the new "Queen of Love and Beauty" and the twelve smiling young women who were her "Maids-of-honor." These pictures, side by side sometimes with pictures showing a man who has just committed a holdup or a murder or showing a woman and five children found hungry in a shack in the slums, are interesting contrasts in the variety of life in a big city.

Balch's reading of class is clumsy and simplistic in some of its generalization, but he does identify persuasively the function of historical pageantry as social control. Similarly, he rehearses the well-known class and ethnic markings of organizations such as the Daughters of the American Revolution, the Daughters of the Confederacy, the American Legion, the Chamber of Commerce, the Rotary, and the Knights of Columbus, making explicit some of the social and economic interests driving the construction of tradition.

The gulf between Balch's submissions and Washington's designs is evident in the central office's editorial comments. A typical response reads, "The enclosed St. Louis article is nearly hopeless." Repeatedly, editors sidestep questions of interpretation or political sympathy, articulating their criticism as a matter of stylistic policy (though, in Balch's case particularly, style and interpretation are inseparable): "We are returning the Springfield article for a complete rewrite. The English is so odd that we do not feel we should go into detailed editing until it has been properly rewritten"; "We strongly suggest that it be given to some other person to write according to the plan established for city treatment." Apparently throwing Balch to the wolves, Reed Harris declared to the WPA administrator in Missouri (a prominent Pendergast man): "Recent copy received here and bearing Mr. Balch's name (city copy for Hannibal and St. Louis) has been very poor. I am forced to conclude that Mr. Balch's writing ability is either being hidden by him or that he cannot write guide book copy. On the basis of editorial study alone, Mr. Balch should be relieved of his duties." Chronology, order, and the excision of "irrelevant" matter were demanded. Dismissing the St. Louis essay in its entirety, one editor took on the collective voice of officialdom to underline the need for systematization: "Regarding all this the Central Office is bound to suggest that reorganization of text and revision of rhetoric is necessary to put the copy in the running with that from other cities of these States. The Missouri Guide shouldn't be a guide to chaos." From Balch's perspective, of course, some textual approximation of chaos authentically captured the vitality and material conditions of his locality.[14]

If Conroy submitted "proletarianisms" and Balch "chaos," another rhetorical mode—also rejected by Washington—was the false cosmopolitanism of Geraldine Parker. Parker and her political backers suffered from what Calvin Trillin calls "rubophobia": fear of being taken for a rustic or a rube (Kendall 14). Symptomatically, they objected violently to Benton's representation of Missouri, seeing his works as clumsy, ugly atrocities: the state WPA administrator declared, "I wouldn't hang him on my shithouse wall" (Mangione, *Dream* 195). It was not just that Parker was wholly opposed to the radical politics of some of her workers; her statements as administrator of the state project plus the essays "Racial Elements and Folklore" (to which she and her successor as state director contributed) and "Folkways" (which she wrote alone) fundamentally refuse the terms articulated by Conroy and Balch.

Parker's Missouri was mainly a Hollywood vision of urban sophistication offset, in one carefully segregated area, by hillbilly quaintness. She argued that a guide to her state should allot more space to the formal arts and fine architecture than to agriculture and that—apart from in the Ozark highlands—Missourians' "way of living is much the same as the country at large": rhetorical strategies that aligned the state with urban centers in the

East, displacing its substantial rural population to the margins of the narrative. The "backwoods hillfolk" are singularly "othered": "The cities and larger towns of Missouri do not differ essentially from cities and towns elsewhere, but the settlements in certain isolated Ozark 'hollers' are like nothing else in America."[15]

This social schematization in turn delivers a narrative of cultural production diametrically opposed to Conroy's. Where Conroy—in "Literature," "Music," and other essays—identifies folk art as Missouri's distinctive, and superior, aesthetic contribution, Parker and her coauthors situate folk culture where they do the Ozarks, at the quaintly irrelevant margins. In a telling sequence of epithets, Parker et al. assert of folk beliefs, "Even the most unprogressive of the Ozark people are becoming more enlightened in these matters, and folklore here as elsewhere is disappearing very rapidly." Parker's essay "Folkways" proposes a narrow definition of folk culture which rules out contemporary forms and practices that transcend regional demarcations. Indeed, Parker clearly rejected the identification of the forms of everyday life *as* culture. One result is that, where Conroy saw vivacious folk culture everywhere in Missouri, almost to the exclusion of more formal artistic activity, Parker recognized only an atrophied remnant of folk culture in the primitive Ozarks.

In a parallel ethnocentric move, Parker also effaced racial difference, claiming that the state's surviving folklore was a European heritage free of black influence. Despite its title, "Racial Elements and Folklore" depicts a state almost devoid of blacks, going out of its way to dispute a claim that Ozark superstitions might be "relics of some primitive African culture"; "it is now well established that they came originally from the British Isles, and were preserved by the Negroes long after their more sophisticated masters had forgotten them." "Folkways" erases African Americans from the state's population by ignoring their existence, an imbalance Parker reproduced on the project by strenuously resisting the employment of black writers. The contrast with Conroy's and Balch's submissions is, again, dramatic. In the essay "Drama," Conroy addresses the efforts by African Americans in Missouri to develop distinctive theatrical forms, a topic that was excised in the published guidebook. In "St. Louis," Balch declared that "no story of St. Louis could be complete without the picture of the Negro," and he made palpable efforts to resist both sentimentalizing and homogenizing his subject: "It is not hard to visualize that Negro life of yesterday, so unchanged in this city where his material opportunities are, as compared to the white man's, so limited. . . . Look . . . [at] the wide range of peoples the term Negro compasses." His exhortations make visible much that Parker's essays conceal.

Parker's progressivist, circumscribed narrative was clearly intended to foster the state's "official image" of itself: as Lawrence Morris reported to Alsberg, "She has a fear of saying anything in the Guide that could possibly offend any one. Behind this lies the fact that . . . Mrs. Parker hopes to make her success in this job the stepping stone to a future political career in Missouri." In the same vein, Parker supported the Springfield Chamber of Commerce's censorship of a local, partly critical guide pamphlet written by Jean Winkler, another young leftist writer on the project. Washington did not want this boosterism any more than it wanted Balch's chaotic vitality: Parker's copy was criticized (by John Lomax) for ignoring black contributions to Missouri's culture and for relegating the topic of folklore to the Ozarks alone, and her role as censor was censured by Alsberg himself.[16]

As a complete volume, the "ur-guidebook" of unpublished typescripts reads like a pastiche of many 1930s' discourses with which the Writers' Project was competing. The work also seems to speak for its place with a potent accuracy, in that its polyvocality both describes and manifests the region's competing interests. The central office responded by rejecting the entire manuscript, closing down the Missouri project, then, in 1939, sending in its own representatives to bring the volume to publication.

Washington boasted that the two men selected for the job were "experts" whose institutional credentials qualified them to undertake a thorough revision of the guide (Mangione, *Dream* 338-40). The *St. Louis Post-Dispatch* echoed this claim in its explanation, under the heading "Only Director and Supervisor Left—200 Once on Payroll," that the Missouri Project was being closed down temporarily until the central office found an "'expert' editor" to finish the guidebook work. That designation promised a kind of political free zone, overriding the tension between the local and the national. Certainly, then and later, van Ravenswaay was prepared to echo the harmonious New Deal formulation that the guidebook was "written by the people of Missouri" and to assert that "I was . . . given a free hand."[17]

The working practices leading to the final version of the guidebook—inasmuch as they can be reconstructed—seem to have involved a little more negotiation than these claims imply. Clearly, van Ravenswaay felt himself to be starting from scratch. Working with an extremely small staff, he relogged tours, checked information, and wrote final copy. Rosenberg joined him for three intensive weeks, working six or seven days a week, going over copy for the entire book. Van Ravenswaay and Rosenberg seem to have agreed on a basic content-form split characterizing their separate contributions to the process: retrospectively Rosenberg judged, "It's one of the best books in the whole series, and the credit all goes to him for the content"; van Ravenswaay said, "Our ties with the Washington office remained close . . . Harold Rosenberg . . . came to help shape the final manuscript, to cut and tighten, and to otherwise ensure that it conformed to the format that had been established for the American Guide Series." Contemporary project correspondence suggests that there may have been a little more friction in the relationship—and more of a hierarchy—than the two men remembered. Billie Jensen, van Ravenswaay's assistant, more than once showed her irritation with Rosenberg's high-handed revisions, complaining that "Rosie will undoubtedly do as he darn pleases, as always" and "Rosie sure changed things," alterations van Ravenswaay sometimes judged "phony" and which produced "a crisis a day." Textual evidence suggests that the guidebook was heavily informed by van Ravenswaay's project of cultural conservation, with some key interventions by Rosenberg, and precise application of Washington's organizational principles, especially in the handling of illustrations.[18]

The result, *Missouri: A Guide to the "Show Me" State*, is an intricately worked manifestation of harmony. The first rhetorical move comes in the preface, which excises the visions of all the original contributors: neither Conroy, Balch, Parker, nor any of the demonstrators receives an acknowledgment. (By the 1980s, in "The Making of the Missouri Guidebook," van Ravenswaay dismissed his predecessors on the project as "scheming politicians" and "disruptive hotheads.") The prefatory matter by Lloyd C. Stark and van Ravenswaay insists on the neutrality of the work by emphasizing the form's transparency: "Information [is] presented objectively and dispassionately"; "Every effort has been made, not to editorialize, but to present the salient facts." Only when read against the "ur-guidebook" does the pub-

lished version seem marked by emphases and omissions spoken by a particular voice (or set of voices) speaking from a particular place.

One avowed ethic of the guidebook is inclusiveness, an aim in stark contrast to Parker's suppression of uncomfortable details. To a degree, the essays acknowledge social upheaval in the state: "Industry, Commerce and
Labor," for example, focuses largely on unionization and strikes. Attention is
also paid to the racial mix: "Folklore and Folkways" judges both that "the
memories of half a dozen national strains are preserved in [Missouri's] lore
and its customs" (131) and that "Negro parlance has added much more to
Missouri speech than have the French and German tongues of the socially
isolated communities" (132). Quintessential of the guidebook's proclaimed
breadth is the opening essay, "People and Character," with its endless taxonomy (of historical characters, ethnic groups, topographical details, foods,
wildlife, place names, events), which positions Missouri—with symbolic
repetitiveness—as the sum and center of these various manifestations of
abundance.

Unlike Conroy's and Balch's accounts, these essays celebrate diversity
with a formal harmony that inscribes social harmony. Unifying the discourse
of the published guidebook are the organizational principles of the central
office, married to van Ravenswaay's preservationist ideology. The chronological line that orders all the pieces stabilizes regional culture, first by shifting the central narrative, with its episodes of social and economic
turbulence, to the past. Although the contemporary scene is described, in
terms of topography, industrial developments, and political systems, narra-
tivization—what Mieke Bal calls "the most powerful form of address"
(561)—is largely reserved for events, practices, and individuals from times
past. The ground is thus prepared for the representation of a stable present
and an optimistic future. The opening essay invokes this rhetorical strategy
when it ends, "If Missouri may judge its future by its past, progress is as certain as the cream-white petals of the dogwood trees on its hillsides every
April" (10). When "History and Government" tells of the corruption of the
Pendergast political machine, or when "Agriculture" speaks to the "tenant
problem" and recent demonstrations by sharecroppers, these stories are succeeded by accounts of New Deal legislative and social reforms. Thus the
palpable crisis of 1939, when over a thousand evicted sharecroppers—90 to

95 percent of them black—demonstrated along over one hundred miles of highway in the Missouri Bootheel, is defused in the guidebook's account, which ends with its list of officials and their plans: a conference called and a plan developed by the governor, an allotment of WPA work, rehabilitation by the FSA (for a fuller account of the protests, see Natanson 113–41). This closure suggests a house now in order, a message writ large in the repeated reminders that the guidebook's narrative voice is speaking from the vantage point of 1941, when the economy was on the rise.

Order is achieved, too, by the guidebook's taxonomic practices. Van Ravenswaay worked by the "ideology of distinction" which Bal cites as a central rhetorical strategy of museum (re)presentation (562n). All material becomes classifiable into specialized groupings, providing an effect of diversity without friction, cultural richness without rivalry. Van Ravenswaay's city descriptions, for example, mark each town with a distinct character, an impression that is reaffirmed in the selection of "Points of Interest": Jefferson is the political city, Hannibal is dominated by Twain memorabilia, Columbia is the college town, Jefferson the mining town, and so on. For all the gestures to social context, lists and juxtapositions construct their own orders of reality, avoiding explicit commentary, judgment, and definition, as if material culture floated free of political implications. The architecture essay, for example, records a vast range of buildings, from the stately home to the lowly cabin, the industrial plant to the rural barn, without reading for economic and social tensions (or even distinctions) in the way that Balch's submissions do. Geographical tensions are also effaced in a taxonomic system that fits the local and the national seamlessly together: "The history of America speaks through the things and events that have made Missouri" (8); Missouri has a secure place in the "national family" (10).

The claims to panoramic truth-telling notwithstanding, a particular version of the past subtends the Missouri of the guidebook. Particularly in the tours to be driven around the state, stories of individual lives predominate; in an emphasis familiar from Katharine Kellock's tour guides, history is made by individuals of character. These individuals are selected by their public manifestations, largely located in nineteenth-century Missouri: the person who built this house, platted this town, began this railroad, orchestrated the Civil War battle commemorated by this monument. Inevitably the stories are predominantly of Anglo-Saxon men. Only the exceptional white woman, African American, or Native American who drew notice in the public domain of mainstream culture is narrativized here: Calamity Jane, Carrie Nation, Dred Scott. To an extent, this emphasis typifies dominant attitudes in the 1930s to gender and race, as well as the blindness of the preservationist who conserves rather than interrogates public culture. But it is notable that Conroy and Balch attempted to traverse some of these limitations, to suggest that important voices (in the arts, in politics, in society at large) can be blocked from public expression and require special efforts of reconstruction—not just preservation—if their contribution to a complex, problematic history is to be recognized.

These strategies—systematizing, historicizing, and naturalizing Missouri's social landscape—are reinforced by the guidebook's illustrations, gathered into what can only be called ideological tidiness. Each gathering conforms precisely to its announced classification and is ordered into formally balanced compositions. So, for example, in the gathering labeled "Historic Buildings," three interiors are followed by three porticos. In "The Missouri and the Mississippi," a nineteenth-century print of "The Levee at St. Louis" faces a photograph of "St. Louis Levee" in the twentieth century; the exterior of the steamboat "The Grand Republic"—"Built in Pittsburg, 1867, and was the largest steamboat in the world"—appears above an illustration of its lavish interior. The only manifest flourish comes in "Industry," with its two-page spread—very rare in the guide series—of the "Sheffield Steel Plant, Kansas City" (Ill. 31) with its massive hooks, iron frets, and stacked equipment lined up in industrial orderliness. This last display could be read as lingering homage to the power of the Pendergast machine, whose base of operations was Kansas City. In the immediate context offered by the guidebook, however, the scene reads more persuasively as a celebration of the rewards of industrial production. The two-page photograph appears as the pivotal opening between, on the one side, images of machines biting into the earth for coal, lead, and zinc mining and, on the other, tidy evidence of industrial production: vats of wine, barrels of champagne, crates of bottled beer, a row of brew kettles, ranks of boots under inspection in a shoe factory, shelves of ceramic tiles being pushed into a kiln. These are the orderly lines of modern productivity cherished by Progressivism.

The case of Thomas Hart Benton is symptomatic of these formal effects. In the published essay "Art and the Crafts," Benton figures as an important

31. Sheffield Steel Plant, Kansas City

Missouri artist, though his entry is considerably reduced from Conroy's version. Among other points, Conroy detailed the storm of controversy provoked by the unveiling of Benton's mural for the Missouri state capitol in 1937. Intended by its official sponsors as a major witness to the state's progress, the mural was understood to deride local pride by focusing on some of the least flattering, least progressive aspects of Missouri's history in a style that broke with all propriety by magnifying ugly physicality (Benton 6, 70–74, 150). In Conroy's essay, this battle exposes significant, unresolved oppositions that continue to fracture local culture, as well as the repressiveness of state institutions. In the published essay, a voice that is surely Rosenberg's closes off the incident from a cosmopolitan perspective, characterizing it as slightly absurd and ultimately beneficial: "When the mural was completed, Benton was charged with 'deliberate insult and painting a lie.' The controversy that followed provoked much discussion and absurdity, and proved highly stimulating to Missouri's art" (176). Subsequent references to Benton, in the city descriptions and tours, direct the reader back to this statement, with the effect that it becomes definitive. A panel from Benton's mural is also reproduced within a cluster of illustrations chosen and ordered by the Washington office.[19] The mural is framed by a gathering of historical figures (George C. Bingham, Daniel Boone, Jesse James, Dred Scott, the

Louisiana Exposition) labeled "Old Missouri," which consigns Benton's vision to the past, a fleeting moment now as dated and picturesque as its adjacent images (Ill. 32). The context also encourages the reader to "look past" the controversial style of the painting, focusing attention on the historical content. Katharine Darst, reviewing the guide in the *St. Louis Globe-Democrat*, pays witness to the composition's effect: "Gazing at the reproductions of Bingham and Benton, one above the other, we realize that these two are as closely related from the standpoint of Missouriana, as the Kansas City–St. Louis grouping." By 1941, the Missouri guidebook—a discursive space as official as the capitol—could efface the challenge and subversive potential of Benton.

Prominent images from the Farm Security Administration were also subjected to a rhetorical charge by their position in the guidebook. Russell Lee's photograph "Flooded Farmland after a Mississippi Rampage" is a case in point (Ill. 33). Richard Pells has posited that, during the Depression, "Men became preoccupied with floods, dust storms, and soil erosion not only because these constituted real problems but also because they were perfect metaphors for a breakdown that appeared more physical than social or economic" (72). Thus the documentary photographs of the 1930s could be read as metaphors for social catastrophe and Lee's photograph of a house and farm buildings submerged in floodwaters specifically representative of the loss of security, the flood of problems suffered by the Midwest. Here, though, the photograph is recontextualized: it appears below a photograph labeled "Flood Control, a Lumber Mattress Is Constructed as Revetment" and among images of bridges, boats, and dams that tame the great rivers and are organized into an old-new, exterior-interior rhythm of balance. In this company, the landscape connotes problems overcome by human ingenuity, not the opposite. Again according to Katharine Darst's review, in a simile that suggests the guidebook's undertone of calm control and rational direction: "The industry, history, agriculture, manners and customs of Missourians flow through this volume as the channel of the Missouri and Mississippi."

Similarly, the three FSA photographs in the gathering "The Farmlands" seem selected and framed for harmonious effect. Russell Lee's photograph of black laborers, "Chopping Cotton on a Southeast Missouri Farm," John Vachon's "Sharecropper Cabins," and Arthur Rothstein's "Farmer" pausing

32. *Stump Speaker,* A Painting by Bingham

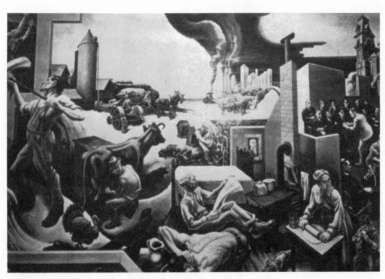

Panel from Missouri Mural, State Capitol, Jefferson City, by Thomas Hart Benton

33. Flood Control, A Lumber Mattress Is Constructed as Revetment

Flooded Farmland after a Mississippi Rampage

momentarily from his toil are surrounded by scenes of pastoral peacefulness and agricultural productivity: "Herefords" and "Wheat Field" on one side, tobacco barn and cotton field on the other. In that company and with similarly picturesque skies and vistas, formal lines of composition and still poses, there is distinct encouragement to read these images of black and white sharecroppers and their ramshackle living quarters for their sense of order. Rothstein's "Farmer," for example, has none of the confrontational exposure of his 1939 coverage of the Missouri evicted sharecroppers' protest. (See Natanson, 113–41, for a detailed analysis of Rothstein's photography in the Missouri Bootheel.) The guidebook works to position all images as equal signs of the state's variety, and potentially explosive photographs have the edge of their social criticism blunted, at the very least.

In these ways, the guidebook harnessed powerful voices and representations of the age, fitting them to the guidebook's myth of harmonious plurality. Diverse races are brought together; problems of politics, corruption, and poverty are folded into a larger picture of social health; rural and industrial worlds coexist happily. The published guidebook locates itself at the intersection of apparent opposites, bringing them together not in the clashing excitement of Balch or in the class friction of Conroy, but in a formal harmony and predictability that imply sociopolitical harmony and confidence in the future. Voices no longer quarrel with each other, on or off the page.

To Jack Balch, long off the project, the revision was clearly a "whitewash" (Penkower 164). In *Lamps at High Noon* (1941), Balch's novel about his project experiences, the author satirizes the manipulations of the "expert" view, the outsider's dislocation from the felt realities of everyday life. The protagonist's parents, working-class immigrants, marvel over Washington's instructions that assign consultants and experts to interpret and articulate the visions of the common folk. Taking the example of his wife's chest problems, the father declares: "The man (how do you say it? The consultant?) who speaks for everybody is a wise man. . . . But the man who speaks for himself, even if he is—forgive me—as mixed up as your mother, speaks from a closer place; his truth, in short, is . . . a truer, a finer, truth, even if it is not accurate. Your mother . . . is wrong. But she is right. And if she says she breathes with difficulty, then this is how she breathes, even if the consultants write learned books on the business of the lungs" (102). If there was some tension between nonrelief artists and relief workers on the project, how much greater was the gap between the "experts" and the common folk of whom they wrote? For Balch, by 1941 it was clear that the entire project was "a fake" and van Ravenswaay's necessarily "a salvage job."

When the guidebook was published, its blurb asserted—in a formulation once again attempting to efface the work's constructedness—"Missouri shows itself at last." The documented reception, local and national, indicates overwhelming acceptance of this claim. Although the Missouri project had been generally vilified as politically suspect and wasteful of public funds, the guidebook was uniformly praised, partly because it was as strongly identified with Charles van Ravenswaay as Idaho was with Vardis Fisher. For example, Estelle Asckenasy spoke on Station KMOX, on 20 July 1941, about "the very charming young man whose efforts made the MISSOURI GUIDE the successful book that it is"; the review in the *Missouri Historical Review* identified "Charles van Ravenswaay who is responsible for the editorial excellence of the book"; and the *St. Louis Globe-Democrat* judged that "the anonymity of WPA cannot eclipse the sensitive intelligence of Charles Van Ravenswaay." More privately and retrospectively, Billie Jensen wrote to Mangione: "We put out a really good book, but that was entirely thanks to CvR."[20] Harold Rosenberg is nowhere mentioned.

At the same time, the press lauded the guide as a model of inclusiveness. In a dynamic reminiscent of Idaho, van Ravenswaay's ideological profile allowed most reviewers to identify both a single dominant author and comprehensive coverage. The *St. Louis Post-Dispatch* of 10 June 1941 declared that the guidebook contained "literally everything"; local newspapers such as the *St. Louis Globe-Democrat* and the *Kansas City Star*, though usually hostile to centralized power, were delighted to report that the guidebook was an "eye opener" for locals, who had not appreciated the richness of their own state; H. J. Haskell in the *New York Herald-Tribune* welcomed the guide for putting on the map a state that had previously been "only a vague name" to easterners. These judgments were echoed by the phenomenal sales figures which turned the guidebook into a local bestseller outpacing *Gone with the Wind*, according to the *St. Louis Post-Dispatch*: in the first five months the guidebook sold forty-eight hundred copies and went into a second printing. The lone dissenting voice is, again, Balch's: "I never read the book that finally came out. I picked it up once and I started to go through it. I read one or two chapters or tried to read one or two chapters and it was what in my

newspaper days we would call a handout. The whole thing was a handout. . . .
It had no flavour, no taste, no charm, no sense of exploring."

The vast majority of readers—local and foreign—were persuaded to look
at Missouri through eyes sanctioned and directed by the Washington, D.C.,
office. Again it seems suggestive to follow Mieke Bal's reading of another national institution, the American Museum of National History: "The repressed story is the story of the representational practice exercised . . . the
story of the changing but still vital complicity between domination and
knowledge, possession and display, stereotyping and realism, and between
exhibition and the repression of history" (588). The specific terms of the
American Guide Series are different from the museum's, but the model of
colonization is useful for thinking about the power relations involved in the
production of cultural knowledge and cultural identity under the New Deal.
Centralized administration supplanted the folk efforts of the local populace,
the creative endeavors of the state's artists, and the puffery of its boostering
spokespeople, transforming the local discourse from a lively quarreling into
a managed harmony. Read from the story of its production, *Missouri* seems
most precisely a guide to how national myths of social cohesion and self-
confidence were imprinted on the disputes, rivalries, and ideals of one midwestern state. Missouri's culture had come of age not by showing itself but
by being fitted to the progressivism, pluralism, and professionalism of the
New Deal.

Conclusion

The Afterlife of the Guidebooks

This Guide Series will stand as a heartening monument to the stability of America long after the bitter years of the 1930's have been forgotten.

—Harlan Hatcher, 1941

For a utilitarian genre tied to a particular time and place, the American Guide Series has had a remarkably long shelf life. All the volumes have been reprinted, some more than once; several have been revised as updated editions; excerpts have been recombined into anthologies and compilations; there remains a steady audience of collectors, local historians, and even a kind of fanzine (*American Urban Guidenotes: The Newsletter of Guidebooks*, edited by John Fondersmith, contains frequent references to the WPA guidebooks and ran a special issue on the American Guide Series in October 1983). Much of that life has been achieved by omitting the production contexts foregrounded by this book: the institutional record, the negotiations over the representation of cultural diversity, the tensions between local knowledge and centralized notions of expertise.

Since 1941 (when the American Guide Series was completed), it seems that the WPA guidebooks have been predominantly read as Harlan Hatcher predicted: as cultural touchstones of a vanished past. Reprints, revisions, and anthologies celebrate them as transparent representations of a society not yet "conglomerated and microchipped," a country that was pleasingly "incoherent, piecemeal, a hundred aesthetics each doing his own thing with never a thought for Overall Style"—a land of random diversity killed by "Franchise America" (Weisberger xv; Stott in Hobson 274). In other words, they are read not as part of but apart from historical change.

This book has read the guidebooks otherwise, arguing that the American Guide Series is not only harbinger but facilitator of contemporary culture, including the increased homogeneity lamented by the guidebooks' champions in recent years. Kenneth Bindas makes the case that the Federal Music Project, among other New Deal agencies, laid the foundation for post–World War II social consensus (116). The production record of the Writers' Project suggests that cultural diversity was neither a guaranteed nor a self-evident quantity for editors and writers at federal, state, or local levels. There was ongoing struggle among these very differently situated contributors over what cultural differences should be promoted and made visible in a national, publicly funded publication. Local and centralized interests hammered out compromises over representation, thereby producing cultural identities for the future and taking America one step toward the "ceremonial agendas" of mass tourism that dominate post–World War II society (MacCannell 43). Michael Denning argues that the 1930s generally and the federal arts projects specifically were a decisive moment in the modern bureaucratization of cultural production (48-50). I would argue that it is the guidebooks' bureaucratic framing that makes them legible and attractive well into the 1980s; the modernity of their presentation of the past makes them available for nostalgia.

An early sign of the guides' political usefulness to the regulation of national remembering emerged during World War II. American Guide Week was declared by Franklin D. Roosevelt to coincide with the publication of *Oklahoma*, the final volume in the series, 10–16 November 1941. In the midst of heightened nationalism only weeks before U.S. entry into military combat, the week's slogan, "Take Pride in Your Country," and other public rhetoric—echoed by state and municipal officials across the country, in newspaper releases, radio programs, exhibits, and public speeches—used the guidebooks' representations to consolidate the national "we." The rhetoric reinscribed lines of cultural citizenship, inclusion and exclusion, and, of course, erased any memory of dissent in their production, circulation, or reception. Typically, one radio announcement welcomed "the vast heritage that is ours"; another affirmed: "These American Guide books, State by State, tell the story of our America." This patriotic, unifying presentation of the guidebooks helped national loyalties to override other identity claims: again in the transcription for the Kate Smith program, the guidebooks are said to contain "everything that has gone to make each of us what he is"; "in the 12,000,000 words which make up these books each of us can, perhaps, understand a bit more clearly why he is the American that he is."[1]

The nationalist rhetoric of American Guide Week also nicely balanced the guides' affirmations of cultural diversity and national unity. Indeed, the guidebooks' patriotism ("the finest contribution to American patriotism that has been made in our generation"; "an educational force and even a patriotic force, an honorable addition to our awareness of ourselves and of our country") came to be equated precisely with their balancing of local, regional, and national interests (Mumford, "Project" 306–07; DeVoto, "Project" 222). Roosevelt, for example, declared that the American Guide Series delivered "for the first time in our history a series of volumes that ably illustrate our national way of life, yet at the same time portray the variants in local patterns of living and regional development. . . . I am sure that this shelf of books . . . will serve to deepen our understanding of ourselves as a people, and hence promote national unity" (qtd. in "WPA Guide Series," *Daily Worker,* and elsewhere).

In the postwar world, the balance between unity and diversity began to seem less and less sustainable—even as a public trope—and the American Guide Series was refitted to changing political contexts. When the guidebooks were revised in the 1940s and 1950s, the world and the voice that had made them possible were written out: their New Deal politics were overwritten by consensual Cold War ideologies, however liberal in orientation, and their authorial voices became less engaged, more distanced from the material, less stylistically, regionally, and politically diverse. After a hiatus in publishers' interest, the guidebooks resurfaced in the 1980s, now in their original editions, reframed by contemporary introductions or as more interventionist compilations. In a climate in which positive notions of cultural unity have devolved, in many quarters, into apprehensions of cultural homogenization, the framing voices stress the guidebooks' service to cultural diversity while sealing that diversity off into an idealized past. What is common across these very different periods and instances of the guides' recirculation is the impulse to play down the guide-makers' struggles and compromises with bureaucratization, modernization, and the public purse—in other words, to take politics out of the guidebooks.

The first postwar trace of the American Guide Series was *The American Guide*, published by Hastings House in 1949, and edited by Henry Alsberg, with an editorial team drawing heavily on former project members. This one-volume guide (also produced as four continuously paginated books) was Alsberg's chance to fulfill his original conception of a national guide: demarcating the country by regions instead of the state lines dictated by political exigencies, while sustaining the tripartite organization of information into essays, tours, and city descriptions. The guide used material from the American Guide Series, but there was also a great deal of updating, new research across the country, and rewriting; Alsberg said that he wrote "about 20 thousand letters" to knowledgeable people in the states, many of whom were eager to help out of loyalty to the earlier WPA series.[2]

What is known of the production record suggests how different the enterprise was from the Writers' Project. Walter McElroy joined Hastings House Publishers after his service on the California Writers' Project, then his very brief stint as national director of the Writers' Program in its dying days. McElroy eventually persuaded his employers that a one-volume guide to the United States, spearheaded by Alsberg, was a viable option. But without government sponsorship, the book had to be priced at $10—an expensive purchase—and available evidence suggests that neither sales nor public impact was massive.[3]

As a private, commercial undertaking, the book also lacks the collective markings of the American Guide Series—essays, for example, were all individually authored, sometimes by former project members. The dominant style and tone here are driven by pragmatic calculations: to cram "A Source Book and Complete Travel Guide for the United States" into just over a thousand pages, the work dispenses with illustrations, resorts to tiny, densely packed typeface, abbreviates almost two hundred frequently repeated terms, eschews definite articles in the tours and city descriptions, and uses the ampersand throughout. The genre seems closer to a reference work than the kind of guidebook with literary aspirations promoted by Alsberg in the 1930s.

This highly condensed, sometimes cryptic style also contributes to a sense of cultural diversity on the wane. Although heterogeneity—ethnic, racial, occupational—is regularly recorded, it is not voiced, not admitted to the fabric of the guidebook: the style flattens out differences among the authorial voices and tends to expunge details of human presence from the passing scene. Grammatical constructions also imply difference under threat: even in New York City—"more than merely polyglot . . . the world's cultural center" (273)—ethnic and racial districts are said "still" to retain their distinctive characters; various buildings have "escaped destruction"; Patchin Place, "haunt of famous writers & poets, still hides away, off 6th Avenue, as if it hopes to escape destruction by remaining inconspicuous" (272).

The reduction in the range of voices is also about changed political perspective and historical context. Because this guide was not forged out of the give-and-take between federal and local interests, it carries neither the localist accents nor the tones of cultural insiderism that so distinctly mark some of the WPA guidebooks. For example, although some of the information on Idaho echoes Fisher's material, the masculinism of its presentation is greatly toned down. Wilderness conditions still challenge the (male) visitor, but the voice of the guidebook no longer aligns itself rhetorically with the rugged insider. This voice directs the visitor toward information and sources but has no particular mastery over the terrain: a typical description is Bruneau Canyon, which "ranges in depth from 1,200' to 2,000', & at almost any pt. a man can throw a baseball across it, but in all its 100^m there is only one place, it is said, where a man can cross it. A guide is needed, an old timer of the valley" (1142).

When the guidebook turns its attention to the South, the location of the outsider's voice becomes clearer: this is a liberal, northeastern perspective operating at a critical distance from southern loyalties. Acknowledgments of the South's progress are regularly tempered by recollections of its recent barbarism and ongoing racism: "Although the thumbs of lynched Negroes are no longer exhibited in butcher shops, as they were not too many years ago, the southern bloc in Congress has consistently (on the basis of state

191

rights) prevented the passage of an anti-lynching bill" (716); "Immensely proud of its aristocratic tradition & comparatively wealthy, Virginia is also immensely conservative. It has not had a lynching (1949) in 20 years, but it has still not abolished the chain gang" (717). This voice also exposes systematic segregation to a degree not typical of the WPA guides—in the process exposing, retrospectively, some of the mystifications, erasures, and targeted audience of those earlier volumes. Lumberton, a small North Carolina town that received almost a full page of coverage in the 1939 guide—for its industry, history, architecture, and the racial composition of its settlement (Croatan Indians, Scottish Highlanders, English, and French are mentioned)—is represented in 1949 by one and a bit sentences: "trade & lumber center of Coastal Plain reg. Town's theater has 3 entrances: one for Inds., Negroes & whites" (777).

If a range of regional and local loyalties presses less heavily on *The American Guide* than on the American Guide Series, the 1949 volume also has a distinctly different rhetorical relationship to federal power. Basically, the guidebook writes out the Roosevelt administration, which made the original series possible and gave several of this work's editors congenial employment. The New Deal draws little attention, either in the essays' narratives of American development—in contrast to the WPA guides, the New Deal never figures as the logical culmination of historical progress—or in the cities and tours. Most of the numerous federal initiatives in the natural, built, and cultural environments of the 1930s seem to have vanished. When the description of Missouri dwells on the economic depression of the 1930s, for example, post-1933 recovery is "aided by Federal & State legislation" (611); the New Deal's extensive agricultural programs go unnamed. In the New York City description, there is only the most occasional reference to a WPA-built structure. And the WPA Arts Projects—consistently celebrated in the American Guide Series for their productivity and sustenance of American talent—have left not a mark on the cultural scene. Weldon Kees, an alumnus of the Nebraska project, sweeps the 1930s wholesale from American aesthetic development in his "Literature" essay: "The crash of 1929 ushered in a period more notable for its meetings, manifestoes & controversies than for its creativity" (79).

The shift from the American Guide Series to *The American Guide* points up the constructedness of both representations as well as the genre's susceptibility to changing political climates. In this comparative context, the WPA series seems distinctly marked by its New Deal paymaster (including the stresses and strains of that administration's accommodations). The 1949 volume could be labeled Trumanesque only, perhaps, in attenuated ways: in the consensual implications of the uniform authorial voice, in a centrist perspective enabled by private-sector production, and in the dwindling imprint of diversity, with the negative meanings of difference becoming concomitantly starker.

Revisions of individual volumes in this period also demonstrate significant shifts in voice and perspective, though the political implications differ from Alsberg's production. In 1950, for example, an abbreviated, lightly revised version of *Idaho: A Guide in Word and Picture* was published by Oxford University Press. Taking the New Deal out of the Idaho guidebook was not a big job because Fisher had given short shrift to federal initiatives in the 1937 version. But the 1950 edition does reframe the account with a Progressivist emphasis that makes the voice of the tours sound more quaint, more contained to the past than in 1937, when it was the dominant voice, consistent with that guidebook's celebration of wilderness and the primitive.

The new foreword, by J. D. Price, secretary of state, declares that "no State is on the threshold of such a vast development" as Idaho ([ix]), and the revisions to the essays that follow are all about evidence of the state's progress: in its legal dealings with Native American peoples, its technological improvements, its management of natural resources. The future, envisaged so distantly and resisted so energetically by Fisher, has arrived. Where the 1937 guidebook spoke of hydroelectric developments—"Idaho's power, like much of its mineral wealth, belongs for the most part to the remote future" (168, 1937 ed.)—the revised copy reads: "Idaho's power and mineral wealth are entering upon developments not dreamed of a few years ago. The immediate future, as well as the present, demands that they be completed as soon as possible" (110, 1950 ed.). Again, this is not a future facilitated by the New Deal: examples of progress are tied either to state initiatives or to changes wrought by World War II.

In this version, the state's natural forces are harnessed to the process of modernization; they guarantee Idaho's future development much less ambiguously than in Fisher's copy. This impression is reinforced by the selection of illustrations. Only about one-third of the original display is included, and the most obviously gendered photographs disappear. In the new edition, wilderness scenes and natural resources predominate, bracketed by the "Fort Hall Indian" at one end and Sun Valley recreational facilities at other, a positioning that lightly suggests, again, the story of progress.

A more wholesale, more textured, and more locally invested revision than Idaho's was applied to *North Carolina* by the University of North Carolina Press in the early 1950s. Spearheading the effort was Lambert Davis, director of the press, who managed to persuade the North Carolina Conservation and Development Department to sponsor the revision, both because the first edition sold so successfully and because they accepted Davis's argument that "any sound program of conservation and development requires as its first step an understanding of the past, and as its second step a survey of the present." This money enabled the hiring of an editor—Blackwell P. Robinson, a historian from High Point College—who was advised by a board of academics, newspaper editors, local historians, and other local authorities. It was of some concern to the production team that the revised guidebook not be seen as in thrall to Chapel Hill academics—one local criticism of the 1939 guide; in the words of the University of North Carolina Press promotion director, "We are leaning over backwards to avoid this criticism with this book." Robinson pursued this outreach to other forms of local knowledge in his editorial work, overseeing the five new essays (three by academics from the University of North Carolina, Duke, and North Carolina State College; one by the associate editor of the *Greensboro Daily News*; and one by the president of *Time,* Inc.) and revising tours with the aid of "County Representatives," all 127 of whom are listed and thanked in the preface.[4]

The combination of state money and local consultancies positioned the production of the 1955 guidebook quite closely to its 1939 predecessor in terms of competing interests. One crucial difference, of course, was the lack of federal input—a lack that, again, reverberated historically. The new guidebook's appearance was accompanied by a flourish of publicity, which—in the style of the 1930s—played up the work's patriotic associations but expunged all mention of the Federal Writers' Project or the Works Progress Administration as the source of the original edition.

Consistent with this publicity, New Deal initiatives in material, social, and cultural conditions receive scarcely any notice in the guidebook's es-

says: on the one occasion when the New Deal is named, it is lumped together with President Harry Truman's "Fair Deal" as a single period
(1933–53) of North Carolinian participation in national administration (105).
When William T. Couch is mentioned, in the "Folkways and Folklore" essay,
it is not as one of the main architects of the 1939 guide but for his "creative
editing" of *Culture in the South* and *What the Negro Wants* (17); Edwin
Bjorkman, similarly, is listed as an Asheville notable not because he was
state director of the North Carolina Writers' Project but because of his work
as "author, critic, and translator" (136). If their work for the Writers' Project
has been quietly forgotten, so has all the Arts Project teaching, performance,
and production noted in the 1939 guide. Some 1930s' reclamation work
demands to be noted in the tours section, but even then only anonymous
"Federal agencies," working to curtail beach erosion, for example, are acknowledged.

The withdrawal of federal pressure may also partly account for the reduced attention to racial difference in the front half of the 1955 edition. The
reduction in the number of essays, with more sweeping mandates—"Folkways and Folklore," by William T. Polk; "Natural Setting," by B. W. Wells;
"History," by Hugh T. Lefler; "Architecture," by Louise Hall; and "The Big
Change," by Roy E. Larsen—does, in a sense, erode the "textual segregation" evident in the 1939 guidebook essays. Folding Native and African
American subjects into more general essays, however, only further reduces
their visibility: they are tucked into the early periods of the "History" essay,
for example, and appear very fleetingly in "Folkways and Folklore"; blacks
have also been excised from the Rockingham entry, which had caused so
much local furor.

This phenomenon is evident in the photographic selection, too, which
combines some original and some new illustrations. Some of the most troubling representations of race have been excised—gone are "Cherokee
Types," "Only Negro Coast Guard Crew, Pea Island," and "Darkies Shelling
Corn," among others—but the net effect on African American presence is to
reduce it. The dilution of the Cherokee presence in North Carolina is more
complex. New portraits of group activity are added—a village gathering, the
Eagle Dance, and the Medicine Dance appear alongside "Cherokee Ball
Game"—and the cluster is moved away from a "rise of civilization" pattern.
Instead, Native American peoples are positioned within a series of perfor-

mances: the Wright brothers' flight before witnesses on the one side and the *Lost Colony* dramatic production on the other. Representing the Cherokees as exclusively performative is troubling too, of course: witness the *Lost Colony* scene, which brings all the implications of dominance, subjection, and containment to the surface in the image of two Native American men genuflecting before Elizabeth I.

What happens in the back half of the 1955 guide is chilling in a different way. The tours marshaled by Blackwell Robinson are considerably less quirky than those compiled by Edwin Bjorkman. Robinson notes evidence of "official progress"—new courthouses, schools, highways, recreational facilities—more often than freaks of nature or accidents of history. He also adds a rationalizing voice that counters legend or superstition with a more logical explanation. Thus the following explanation is retained from the 1939 guide ("romantic" is Robinson's addition): "A romantic explanation for the name 'Nags Head' is that in the early days of the settlement 'land pirates' deliberately sought to wreck ships. On a stormy night a lantern was tied to the neck of an old nag, which was then ridden along the beach. Mistaking the light for a beacon, ships were lured to the treacherous reefs, there to be boarded and looted by the wily shoremen." The 1955 disclaimer follows immediately: "Those who hold to this story should try tying a lighted lantern around the neck of a banker pony. A more reasonable explanation is that it was named for one of the highest points on the Scilly Islands, off the coast of Devon—the last sight of old England" (310).

This rational voice also quietly and unrelentingly documents racial segregation: "Throughout the town [Durham] are parks and playgrounds for both races" (169); in Winston-Salem, "A new City-County Library was completed in 1953, as was a new Negro YM-YWCA" (276); there is also "the WINSTON-SALEM TEACHERS COLLEGE *(Negro, coed)*" (xxx); in Rocky Mount, "MANGUM'S WAREHOUSE . . . is the scene of the annual all-night June German . . . attended by thousands of guests from several states. . . . On Saturday night after the ball Negroes use the same warehouse and decorations for their June German" (335); two miles west of Goldsboro stands "THE STATE HOSPITAL FOR NEGRO INSANE . . . established in 1884, the first mental hospital for Negroes in the world" (343); forty-five miles from Winton, "a dirt road (R) leads to CHOWAN BEACH *(for Negroes)*" (419). This roll call of apartheid is delivered not from the identifiably critical perspective of *The American Guide* but by a voice whose accents are determinedly factual, informative, and reasonable and whose politics, therefore, are inscrutable. When this voice updates 1939 copy to tell us that Hope house, "one of the most impressive ones built in colonial North Carolina, is now occupied by Negro tenants" (293), there seems no way to guess whether the intent of this information is ironic or culturally affirmative, only that the very undecidability of the rhetorical position is deeply disturbing.

Whatever meanings we attach to the internal dynamics of the 1955 guide, its relationship to the 1939 edition is dramatic. What was floated as local color and cultural diversity in the earlier volume here is either silenced altogether or becomes, much more explicitly and methodically, the documentation of racial segregation. The contrast puts W. T. Couch's worry—that the North Carolina guide did not address the lack of tourist facilities for blacks in the South—and Sterling Brown's objection—that the WPA guides were not written for black users—in new light. In whatever spirit, the 1955 guidebook decisively demonstrates that the 1939 guide did not represent the state as African Americans experienced it, did not acknowledge a reader to whom sites were only partially accessible, provided no guidelines to an apartheid society.

As the guidebooks forgot the federal administration that made them possible, so, as the 1960s unfolded, the WPA Arts Projects generally and the guidebooks specifically slipped out of public view and off publishers' agendas. The terms in which the guides were subsequently recuperated for the public record—terms that had everything to do with public morality, national self-imagery, and what Umberto Eco calls "nostalgic remorse"—then heavily marked the forms of their reissue in the 1980s (10).

What happened between the late 1950s and the 1980s was, of course, a series of national disasters, including the assassinations of John F. Kennedy, Martin Luther King, and Malcolm X, Vietnam, and Watergate. In the same period, a series of bills authorized federal sponsorship of the arts and job creation: in 1965, the National Foundation for the Arts and Humanities came into being, with its two endowments; the Comprehensive Employment and Training Act (CETA) was authorized in 1973 and expanded in 1975. Some of the rhetoric accompanying this federal patronage positioned it as a moral counterweight to the national disgrace of Watergate. In a

Chicago Sun-Times report in 1973, for example, David S. Broder ended his account of a House of Representatives vote to increase appropriations to the National Foundation on the Arts and Humanities (from $80 million to $145 million) with the congressman from Minnesota quoting Alexander Solzhenitsyn on literature protecting "the soul of the nation." Broder commented: "The sight of a Minnesota farmer quoting a Russian novelist to the House of Representatives does not prove the millenium has arrived. But it helps wash out the memory of a former attorney general explaining why he concealed a criminal conspiracy from the President of the United States. And for that, one can be grateful."

This moralistic emphasis was particularly insistent in the public remembering of the WPA and its cultural wing which occurred in this context. When, for example, Richard Nixon vetoed the Employment and Manpower Act with the statement that "the bill . . . would take the country back 35 years by devoting disproportionate sums for 'WPA-type jobs,' . . . 'dead-end jobs in the public sector,'" Robert Roth hotly disputed his definition of the WPA in the Philadelphia *Evening Bulletin*. As evidence of the worthy achievements of the 8.5 million unemployed put to work by the WPA, Roth cited not just the 650,000 miles of road constructed, the 78,000 bridges built, the 46,000 rebuilt, and so on but the guidebooks, "many of which are still in use, for all of the then 48 states and for many cities."

When Jerre Mangione's history of the Federal Writers' Project, *The Dream and the Deal*, was published in 1974, Bernard Weisberger, for one, welcomed the story as a direct antidote to national shame:

We live in another kind of hard times, when pessimism is not easy to avoid. It takes an effort to remember that the United States—its land, its people, its institutions— adds up to something bigger than one generation's troubles and mistakes. It often takes an effort nowadays to remind ourselves that this country is sometimes better than its leaders, always more interesting than its image makers know, and durable enough to outlast the rhetoric of both its critics and its uncritical defenders. But Mangione is really telling us that we were in deep trouble before, and we almost accidentally paid for a self-portrait and we liked and were strengthened by what we saw. ("Reading" 100)

Mangione himself waded into the public debates swirling around the Comprehensive Employment and Training Act in that period. He argued, in a

1975 *New York Times* piece, that the increased funds and more liberal provisions of CETA "could and should mean jobs in every part of the country for needy artists, writers, actors and musicians." He invoked Federal One as the root cause of a more receptive climate to government funding of the arts in recent years and based his appeal on the familiar trope of national morality: the "need for the spiritual strength and national pride that the arts can engender," especially after "the horrors of Vietnam and Watergate."

At the same time, the art historian Francis V. O'Connor was working to revive public awareness of the Federal Art Project, with the initiation, in 1974, of *Federal Art Patronage Notes,* a newsletter designed to create a network of professionals who would bring "the history of federal support for the visual arts in America" to bear on "the development of public art patronage policy."[5] These diverse efforts came together in late 1975, with a conference on the New Deal cultural programs, funded by the National Endowment for the Humanities, spearheaded by O'Connor and including Mangione in its roster of participants.

In the 1980s, attractive reprints of volumes from the American Guide Series began to appear, often packaged in Art Deco–style covers. No longer is information updated and anachronistic social analysis rewritten; instead, introductions and prefaces are added precisely to appreciate the pastness of the contents. In the same decade, three compilations of WPA guidebook material also appeared. In structure and commentary, these samplers make it even clearer that the guidebooks' moral weight depends on their being sealed off both from the history of their own production and from modern America.

When *The WPA Guide to New York City* was reprinted in 1982, for example, William H. Whyte's introduction celebrated the guide as "a precious document to be preserved"; its documentary quality proves the past to be past, inviolate from the great upheavals of modernization during and after World War II (xxi). Alfred Kazin similarly values *New York Panorama* in his introduction to the 1984 reprint because it documents New York's "last age of innocence" (xiii). New York City in the 1930s was, of course, the place of Kazin's own youth, and he was both attracted by and attractive to the Writers' Project; he was one of the rising literati on the left assiduously courted by Alsberg. In Kazin's reading, the guidebook delivers a language of experience (personal and social) that has vanished forever: this is a "period piece" whose left-wing captions are "like going down memory lane" to a "sweet and genuine" civic pride, which he contrasts regretfully with the contemporary commercialism of "I love New York" hats and paper cups (xvi, xv, xvii). The same tack is taken by William S. Powell, professor of history emeritus at the University of North Carolina at Chapel Hill, in his introduction to *North Carolina: The WPA Guide to the Old North State* in 1988. This "State Treasure," as he calls it, gives its reader unmediated access to the historical moment immediately preceding the great changes of contemporaneity ([v]). Promotional materials render the point more bluntly: the jacket blurbs for both the 1982 reprint of *New York City* and the 1988 *North Carolina* use the Wellsian trope: a "tour guide for time travelers." All these rhetorical maneuvers—of preservation, lost innocence, and science fiction—keep the past out of the present, disallowing the kinds of linkages between the 1930s and the present called for by Mangione and Roth in the 1970s.

Not surprisingly, the most textured relationship between the present of the introduction and the past of the guidebook is evoked by the commentator with the greatest project service: Charles van Ravenswaay, former director of the Missouri Writers' Project, in his 1986 introduction to *The WPA Guide to 1930s Missouri* (a title which, again, anchors the content to time past). Musing on his own experience, van Ravenswaay recognizes that the guidebooks' function had much to do with their timing on the very cusp of social change: "In response to the increasing social and economic dislocations and to the related feeling that much of what had given life meaning and stability was being destroyed, people began searching for new ties to the past" (vii). Van Ravenswaay's analysis understands that, as conduits to a "usable past," the guidebooks are as much about present needs as past histories. Significantly, van Ravenswaay develops that analysis not to deconstruct or even critique the cultural process but to reproduce it. He ends his introduction with an invitation to readers to find in the guidebooks a stabilizing version of the past which also guarantees the future: while the guides are a "sort of epitaph" to a period now ended, they "will give today's readers not only pleasure but also an understanding of Missouri's character and traditions whose diversity and basic strengths have not been destroyed by time" (xvii).

In returning the New Deal center stage to the guidebooks, these readings erase the pressures of production, especially the negotiations among federal and local constituencies, thereby consigning guidebook copy to a politically uncomplicated relationship with an idealized past. Van Ravenswaay comes closest to acknowledging the imprint of change on the guidebooks; but none of the introductions concedes the possibility that the guidebooks' very cataloging of social types and systematization of landscapes—a compromise born out of the process of their production—might actively have facilitated mass tourism and its attendant cultural baggage. Perhaps what makes that connection unspeakable for these commentators, what makes them read cultural diversity as meaningful but not its regulation, is at least partly their personal investments in the 1930s.

That entwining of the personal is taken to an extreme by the three personalized compilations of American Guide Series material, which omit not only production record but genre functions. Of the three, one does actually go out on the road, the author using guidebook excerpts to plot his own cross-country journey. None, however, manifests use in the terms hypothesized in Chapter 1: rather than the user negotiating with the guidebook's template in the face of visited sites, these authors, through the process of selection and organization, fit the descriptions to their own agendas, distance them from the testing ground of actual sites. More than ever, the guidebooks become tools for mythologizing the 1930s.

In 1985, Pantheon published *The WPA Guide to America: The Best of 1930s America as Seen by the Federal Writers' Project*, edited by Bernard A. Weisberger, who, ten years earlier, had declared the moral authority of the guidebooks. Weisberger's compilation of selections from the American Guide Series is unabashedly celebratory: "a fiftieth-birthday celebration of a people's treasure" (xi). In line with that impulse, and as the subtitle of his work suggests, he tends to take the teeth out of history. What seems to matter to him about the historical is that it provide reading pleasure: "Readability is the cornerstone of this anthology and tribute. . . . The historical value of the guides is great, but I have given priority to the pure delight that they offer to the committed and curious reader" (xii). And the production history is without tension in this version; specialized and vernacular knowledges, central and local interests are easily coterminous: "Writers and researchers—themselves residents of the states they were describing—visited every spot described, rummaged the record books, and talked long hours with local authorities and plain folk. Thus they brought to their descriptions a unique sense of intimacy—one that involved no sacrifice of accuracy, for all factual statements were meticulously verified or corrected later in the Project's offices" (xii).

Weisberger's guidebook selections smack of a 1930s' regionalist tenet, that a varied landscape bespeaks a rich culture. Like *The American Guide*, he adheres to regional demarcations in his organization; in those sections, he consistently chooses cities and sites most demonstrative of diversity, both in their own characteristics and in contrast with each other. The diversity on show is nicely positioned: it is a harmony of difference that suggests fundamental social stability; there is little sense of the divisiveness that emerged in production, when different interest groups within communities vied for representation. Weisberger, however, also avoids the most monocultural representations: *Idaho* is the only volume virtually absent from the collection.

The problem in framing the guidebooks with such a roseate view of "readable" history is exposed by the representation of race in particular. Presumably on the principle of diversity, Weisberger includes copy from the Mississippi guide, which his own commentary critiques as racist, stereotyping and objectifying difference. Various selections romanticize black manual labor as rhythmic musical activity, sentimentalize ethnic poverty, and celebrate white supremacy: "We Mississippi white folk . . . are bosomed by the earth that conditions us. We think as our land thinks. . . . Our faith is in God, next year's crop, and the Democratic Party" (214). The reproduction of racism is immensely troubling: despite the editor's acknowledgment of "offensive racial and ethnic prejudices" (xiv), the volume fundamentally legitimates its contents with its celebratory framework, refusal to question *which* "people's treasure" is here on show, and assumption that these inequities are of the past, unconnected from present dispositions of social and economic power.

In the same year as Weisberger's compilation, Columbia University Press published *Remembering America: A Sampler of the WPA American Guide Series*, edited by Archie Hobson, with introductions by William Stott. In some ways, this is a more nuanced selection than Weisberger's: Hobson's excerpts on African American life—such as the following copy in the Washington, D.C., guide, by Sterling Brown, the project's national Negro affairs editor—tend to carry their own critique: "The Negro of Washington has no voice in government, is economically proscribed, and segregated nearly as rigidly as in the southern cities he contemns. He may blind himself with pleasure seeking, with a specious self-sufficiency, he may point with pride to the record of achievement over grave odds. But just as the past was not without its honor, so the present is not without bitterness" (77–78). Despite this evidence of a more layered self-consciousness, one of the principal effects of the "sampler" form remains the tidying up of history and politics, partly because the excerpts are removed from the conflicted context of production, composition, circulation, and use, then reorganized into neat thematic categories such as "Work," "Everyday Life," and "The People." This design stabilizes meanings, producing a more culturally diverse, more socially inclusive, and more politically coherent vision than my reading of individual guidebooks can discover.

The design also enables an atypically affirmative reading by Stott, whose sophisticated analyses of the claims of 1930s' documentary—primarily in *Documentary Expression and Thirties America* (1973; rev. ed. 1985)—have been highly influential. Here, Stott's introduction opens by comparing the WPA guides to the public discourse manipulated by totalitarian regimes in 1930s' Europe. This contrast positions the guidebooks as celebrations of "our diversity and our tolerance of diversity. (The political word that characterizes this virtue is, of course, 'democracy,' a very popular word at the time.)" (6). The comparative point is clearly important, but it is also important that the representation of cultural diversity was regulated, social and political identities across the country were fitted to a federally designed and monitored blueprint, to degrees and in ways that mattered, fiercely, to a large range of constituencies.

For example, in the face of a detailed production context, I find it difficult to agree with Stott's analysis that "as always when handling the theme of work, the Guides mean to make us see" (84). In my reading, the archive suggests that there was a fair amount of the social landscape that various architects of the guides meant us *not* to see: there are all the exclusions mandated by the central office as well as Sterling Brown's point about the guidebooks being oriented away from an African American readership, but even some illustrated figures are marginalized by photographic captions (the African American woman sitting in front of "Tenant Cabin, South Carolina," in *The*

Ocean Highway springs to mind). Similarly, when I read Stott's assessment, "Most intellectuals of the 1930s were feminists. . . . The Guides give daily life and 'woman's' work the same patient attention they give industrial labor," I think of *Idaho,* moments in *North Carolina,* even *New York Panorama,* and think that women at work was one of the subjects we are meant *not* to see except in the most contained and apolitical terms.

In both these samplers, "cultural diversity" becomes a kind of mantra, defined as heterogeneous content and distracting attention from the regulatory operations of form and presentation. Jonathan Harris has identified the federal agenda for the Art Project as the representation of "difference without antagonism" (51). This is precisely the rhetoric to which the 1980s' reprints subscribe, along with a rhetorical stabilizing of the record in the re-taxonomizing of information and in the removal of textual material from its application to, and testing by, travel.

Geoffrey O'Gara's book—*A Long Road Home: Journeys through America's Present in Search of America's Past,* published by Norton in 1989—does reconnect the guidebooks with travel. But the reading contract is very different from that offered by individual guidebooks. By resituating excerpts in his own journey across America, O'Gara can control their meanings; he can also displace any evidence of antagonism onto the contemporary scene. His agenda is clear: what he wants, and gets, from guidebook material is familial belonging, at both the personal and the national levels. In their introduction to the 1986 Missouri guide, Howard W. Marshall and Walter A. Schroeder compare the volume to "a good family album with jottings under the snapshots" (xxvi). It is this intimacy and the authority of knowing the lineage of places and people that O'Gara derives from his guidebook pickings.

O'Gara's discovery of the American Guide Series, as he tells it, was tied to his family's move west, from Washington, D.C., to Wyoming, and to his reconstruction of his grandfather's past in California. Reading selectively across several WPA volumes, he first plotted then embarked on a series of cross-country trips between 1984 and 1987—which he condenses into a single narrative from the District of Columbia to Wyoming—all in terms that are heavily familial. He is looking for "that adolescent America" of the past; "I had a curiosity that bordered on hunger for places where the inhabitants felt an indelible kinship with a particular piece of ground" (xiii, xvi).

This route to a sense of place and belonging gives the narrator not just security but moral superiority. At one point, he relates an encounter in the remote Smoke Hole of West Virginia with Georgia tourists who lack both the knowledge of and respect for place that the guidebooks—in O'Gara's excerpting of them—provide. Drinking beer on their meandering ascent up a cave-pocked slope, the two couples become disoriented, vomit and urinate in the caves, stumble around smelling and sounding entirely disharmonious with this place cherished by our informed narrator. When they ask him to take their photograph, he takes an author's revenge, in words and picture: "I looked at them, bobbing against each other in the camera's viewfinder, the pastels of their sport shirts and pants, the bleached hair of the women, the beer-rimmed eyes swimming in the smiling faces. I purposely cut off their heads in the picture, returned the camera, and started back down the creek bed" (50).

The avoidance involved in O'Gara's singularly moral wielding of the guidebooks (and the camera) is suggested elsewhere in the Smoke Hole section. To reconstruct the history and geography of this "remote hollow in the Potomac Highlands" (32), O'Gara stitches together excerpts from the West Virginia guide and from a smaller project publication on the Smoke Hole. This is O'Gara's quintessential destination: hidden from the outside world by its topography, the canyon had bred a distinctively antiquated culture, still remembered in the annual family reunions of former Smoke Holers. O'Gara gains access to these families and their memories through Sarah Kimble, the last of the original inhabitants to make her home in the Smoke Hole, who was removed to a retirement home in the course of O'Gara's trip. The story, then, is of the past changing into the future, locally, and before our traveler's eyes. In reflecting on the mechanisms of modernization that eroded "community culture" in this place, O'Gara comes very close to acknowledging the guides' complicity in this process: "Well-meaning improvement programs—like the Civilian Conservation Corps's construction of a new road into the canyon in the 1930s—had opened these attractive wilds to outsiders, and the visitors who came to hunt and fish introduced the inhabitants to modern conveniences and ideas. The CCC was another program that, like this writers' project, gave jobs to West Virginians, and the road gave Smoke Holers an easy way out as well as in" (61). But he never quite articulates the connection. Even when he visits Paul Becker, former project editor of *West Virginia* and author of *The Smoke Hole*, and describes

Becker's regular trips to Washington, D.C., in his retirement, he never recalls the traffic—literal and metaphorical—between Washington and the states during the project. For O'Gara, as for the other compilers, following "in the footsteps of the WPA writers" means heading in one direction only, away from the administrative center and toward the remote and the antiquated.

The guidebooks' extraction from history is consistent with the disappearance, once again, of the Writers' Project—and the Arts Projects generally—from recent debates about federal art patronage. Typically, the memory of these debates stretches back only as far as the initiatives of the 1960s. When the patronage experiments of the 1930s are remembered, the argument is usually that they are not relevant to current problems because they were job creation schemes. Under the aegis of the America's first national work relief program, art was explicitly funded as *work*, a radical innovation that was breezily rationalized by Harry Hopkins, WPA chief, in his famous line: "Hell, artists got to eat, just like other people!"—a rationale widely repeated in congressional debates by supporters of the Federal Arts Projects (qtd. in Mangione, *Dream* 4 and elsewhere). This categorization brought with it both problems and possibilities regarding labor conditions; it also, on occasion, delivered a very different kind of reading of the guidebooks to that which predominates today. The *Springfield* (Ohio) *News-Sun*, for example, commented: "Great interest in the guide arises from the fact that it is the result of the application of a new sense of governmental responsibility to the citizen, the responsibility to give not a dole, but a job, to the victim of economic depression a job not alone to the manual worker but as well to the professional worker, architect, artist, engineer, writer, a job commensurate with ability and training." Part of what has intervened between the 1930s and now is the 1970s' argument for arts patronage as a moral good in an era of public corruption, rather than a social good in an era of unemployment. That argument has disguised a larger continuity: funding for the arts is always entwined with the long-term economic plight of the vast majority of workers in the arts; reintroducing broader notions of labor into debates over arts funding could only increase the resources for creative activity and its engagement with social change.

In recent years, the WPA guidebooks have been disconnected not just from the story of art-as-labor but from more general historical and social processes. In the postwar period, the guidebooks' perspectives have been overwritten by narrative voices that are much reduced in range, most starkly in the more or less dispassionate documentation of racial segregation. By the 1980s, the cultural work of the guidebooks changed. With the moral argument in place, the guidebooks seem to become available only for celebratory readings. In their recent reissues, their vision is no longer corrected; rather, they are cherished as evidence of the joyful multiplicity of the nation.

In this recuperation of the guidebooks, there is little room for skepticism about their claims to inclusive representation of community, region, and nation. There is no memory of the battles informing production, circulation, and reception, one part of communities' larger struggle to forge their public identities in the face of both internal fissures and the centralized bureaucracies of modernity. The American Guide Series seems not to be read as a window into the cultural processes set in train by federal intervention into local image-making, the cultural fallout from the New Deal mapping of public space. The WPA guidebooks, so laden with competing ideologies and available for an unpredictable range of use, have themselves hardened into articles of faith, incontrovertible evidence of a better America. It is an irony that the Federal Writers' Project, driven by a New Deal "futurological" vision and welcomed for charting "this new America," has been relegated to the sidelines as a nostalgic touchstone of what might have been rather than remembered for its lessons about what could yet be.

Notes

The following archival holdings are cited in the abbreviated form listed here, alphabetically:

Bottolfson Papers: Idaho State Historical Society, AR2/17 Papers of Governor Bottolfson.

Caxton Records: Washington State University Libraries, Manuscript, Archives and Special Collections, Caxton Printers Records, "File 7," the burned remnants of records that survived Caxton's 1937 fire.

Central Correspondence Files: National Archives and Records Administration, Washington, D.C., Record Group 69, Work Projects Administration Central Correspondence Files (entry number followed by box number).

Central Office Records: National Archives and Records Administration, Washington, D.C., Record Group 69, Work Projects Administration Federal Writers' Project Central Office Records (entry number followed by box number).

Clark Papers: Idaho State Historical Society, AR 2/16 Papers of Governor Barzilla Clark (box number followed by folder name).

Clore Collection: Boise State University Library, Clore Collection, Vardis Fisher Papers, MSS2.

Couch Papers: The William Terry Couch Papers, No. 3825 in the Southern Historical Collection, Library of the University of North Carolina at Chapel Hill (folder number).

Division of Information: National Archives and Records Administration, Washington, D.C., Record Group 69, Work Projects Administration Division of Information (box number).

FWP-Couch Papers: Federal Writers' Project, William Terry Couch Papers, No. 3709 in the Southern Historical Collection, Library of the University of North Carolina at Chapel Hill (folder number).

Fisher Papers Idaho: University of Idaho Library, Special Collections and Archives, Manuscript Group 218, Vardis Fisher Papers, 1927-74 (box number).

Notes

Fisher Papers Washington: Washington State University Libraries, Manuscript, Archives, and Special Collections, Vardis Fisher Papers.

Grover Collection: Boise State University Library, Dorys Crow Grover Collection of Papers Relating to Vardis Fisher MSS 120.

Idaho Writers' Project: Idaho State University, U.S. Works Progress Administration Records, Special Collections Series 1: Federal Writers' Project MC 022 (box number followed by folder number).

Kellock Papers: Library of Congress, Manuscripts Division, Katharine Kellock Papers.

Kellogg Papers: University of Idaho Library, Special Collections and Archives, Manuscript Group 57, George Alexis Kellogg Papers, 1940-70 (box number followed by folder number).

Mangione Papers: University of Rochester Library, Department of Rare Books and Special Collections, Jerre Mangione Papers (box number).

Manuscripts: Library of Congress Manuscripts Division, Washington, D.C., Records of U.S. Work Projects Administration: Federal Writers' Project (box number).

NYC Archives: Municipal Archives of the City of New York, Works Progress Administration—Federal Writers' Project Collection.

North Carolina Writers' Project: North Carolina Writers' Project, WPA General Records, Division of Archives and History, North Carolina Department of Cultural Resources.

Oral History Collection: Idaho State Historical Society, Idaho Oral History Center Collection, Interview Transcripts.

Taber Papers: Washington State University Libraries: Manuscript, Archives, and Special Collections, Papers of Ronald W. Taber.

UNC Press: University of North Carolina Press Records, in University Archives, Manuscripts Department, University of North Carolina Library, Chapel Hill.

Van Ravenswaay Papers: Charles van Ravenswaay Papers, Western Historical Manuscript Collection—Columbia, at the University of Missouri, Columbia (Collection Numbers SHS ACC 2788; SUNP 2687).

The following holdings have been consulted but are not directly cited:

C. Jasper Bell Papers, Western Historical Manuscript Collection—Columbia, at the University of Missouri, Columbia (Collection Numbers 2306 f.1634, 1638, 4192).

Correspondence between Vardis Fisher and David Stratton, Washington State University Libraries: Manuscript, Archives, and Special Collections, MS 90-26.

Federal Writers' Project Inventory, Idaho State Historical Society, MS 70.

Vardis Fisher Papers, 1922-70, Washington State University Libraries: Manuscript, Archives, and Special Collections, Cage 229.

Vardis Fisher Scrapbook, Idaho State Historical Society, MS2/468.

Inez Puckett McEwen Papers, 1885-1982, Washington State University Libraries: Manuscript, Archives, and Special Collections, Cage 48.

Letters from Vardis Fisher to Harry Schwartz, University of Idaho Library, Special Collections and Archives, Manuscript Group 5320.

Governor C. Ben Ross Papers, Idaho State Historical Society, AR 2/15.

Viles-Hosmer Papers, Western Historical Manuscript Collection—Columbia, at the University of Missouri, Columbia (Collection Number 3709 f.258).

Sara Lockwood Williams Papers, Western Historical Manuscript Collection—Columbia, at the University of Missouri, Columbia (Collection Number 2533 f.34).

Introduction

1. Work on the Arts Projects includes Billington; Bindas; Brewer; Bustard; Contreras; Craig; Flanagan; Fox; Fraden; Gill; Harris; Hirsch 1973, 1984; Kazacoff; McDonald; Mangione; Mathews; K. McKinzie; R. McKinzie; Melosh; Meltzer; O'Connor, 1972, 1973; O'Connor and Brown; Penkower; Sporn; Taber 1969.

Chapter 1

1. Rosenberg interview, [1968], Mangione Papers 96.

2. Among other places, this title appeared on a 1941 radio program transcription (Division of Information 333/2, "American Guide Week").

3. Alsberg, untitled, undated speech, Mangione Papers 21.

4. Couch to Alsberg, 22 April 1938, FWP-Couch Papers 2.

5. Alsberg [Greene] to A. F. Cleveland, 3 October 1935, Mangione Papers 64.

6. "*Massachusetts: A Guide to Its Places and People*—$2.50—To be published summer 1937," 1937 Central Office Records 2/51.

7. Radio talk, J. D. Newsom, on John T. Frederick's weekly program *Of Men and Books*, 14 June [1941], Manuscripts A994. Whiting makes an important argument about the Regionalist painters' transformation of regionalism into a kind of nationalism and even internationalism with the onset of World War II.

8. "Publishers to Hon. Edward T. Taylor," 19 May 1939, Division of Information 211.721; DeVoto to the Sub-Committee of the Appropriations Committee, House of Representatives, 22 April 1943, Mangione Papers 58.

9. Qtd. in Memorandum, U.S. Commissioner of Education, John W. Studebaker, to Chief State School Officers, 22 October 1941, Division of Information 211.72.

10. [Billie Jensen] to [Charles van Ravenswaay], n.d., Mangione Papers 60.

Chapter 2

1. McGraw interview, [1968?], Mangione Papers 96.

2. Ellison interview, [1968?], ibid.

3. Alsberg interview, 1968, ibid.; Vincent McHugh to Jerre Mangione, 5 September 1978, Mangione Papers 6.

4. This information is compiled from Mangione, *Dream*; Penkower; Hirsch; McKen-

zie, "Writers"; Stella Bloch Hanau to Mangione, 13 August 1969, Mangione Papers 21; Press Release, 26 July 1935, ibid.; "Starving Writers Aid Head Is Named," Washington D.C. *Evening Star,* 27 July 1935.

5. Kellock to Mangione, 29 October 1969, Mangione Papers 58; Harris interview, 1968, Mangione Papers 96.

6. Information on Cronyn is gleaned from Mangione, *Dream*; Penkower; Hirsch; McKenzie, "Writers." In the 1940s, he became a feature writer with the Office of War Information and writer-editor with the United Nations. Subsequently, he worked for the State Department, then the United States Information Agency 1950–64 (Obituary, *Washington Post*, 10 May 1969).

7. Information on Harris is gleaned from Mangione, *Dream*; Penkower; Hirsch; McKenzie, "Writers." By 1953, Harris was deputy administrator of the State Department's International Information Administration, forerunner of the U.S. Information Agency, when he was hauled up before Joseph McCarthy's House Un-American Activities Committee. Harris gave a stinging rebuke to McCarthy's method of innuendo and defied the committee (Carl T. Rowan, "Why the 'Safe Guys' Never Write a Book," Washington D.C., clipping, Mangione Papers 63). In 1966, Harris was cited as the top official in the USIA's book division, making decisions about which books would do the most to forward foreign policy aims of the U.S. government—which books to distribute, which to translate, which textbooks to support ("U.S.I.A. Will Spend $6-Million on Books in Next 12 Months for Propaganda," *New York Times*, 3 October 1966, Mangione Papers 63).

8. Kellock to Mangione, 26 June 1969, Mangione Papers 58. Kellock handled all the tour copy, prepared plans for *US One, The Ocean Highway, The Oregon Trail, Tourists of Eastern Idaho*, and *Intracoastal Waterway* and planned the details of the *Death Valley Guide*. She completed for press the tour sections of thirty-three state guides, or approximately half the copy in nearly two-thirds of the project's major series, and did prefinal work on the remaining fifteen (Kellock to Mangione, 22 May 1969, Mangione Papers 58). By 1951, Kellock was a policy officer in the State Department and was pursued by McCarthy because of her husband's Russian connections (a lung tumor prevented her from testifying) (Kellock to Mangione, 26 August 1972, Mangione Papers 58).

9. Collier to Mangione, 7 September 1969, Mangione Papers 68.

10. Larry [Morris] to Mangione, 19 June 1969, Mangione Papers 58; Kellock to Mangione, 24 November 1971, Mangione Papers 68.

11. Alsberg to Editor or Publisher, 27 November 1935, Central Office Records 2/50; *School Executive* magazine, qtd. in "Excerpts from Review Comment on the American Guide Series," the American Guide Series catalog, Central Office Records 12/82.

12. Editorial responses to manuscript details are in "Supplementary Instruction #11 to The American Guide Manual," Appendix A, General Information and Miscellaneous Notes, 5 May 1936, Central Office Records 11/69.

13. Kellock to Mangione, 29 October 1969, Mangione Papers 58; Kellock to Esther Greer, 24 November 1937, Central Office Records 13/103.

14. Coy to Mangione, 7 February 1968, Mangione Papers 68.

15. Harris, "Notes on the Federal Writers' Projects with Special Reference to the American Guide," 17 September 1936, Central Office Records 5/50.

16. Alsberg [Howard Greene] to Edwin Bjorkman, 6 June 1936, Central Office Records 1/37

17. Report, Mr. J. M. Scammell to Alsberg, 26 January 1938, Central Office Records 6/57.

18. Field Report, Kellock to Alsberg, 2 February 1936, Central Office Records 6/61.

19. Kellock to Grace Kellogg, 8 May 1937, Mangione Papers 64.

20. Billington to Mangione, 28 January 1969, Mangione Papers 1.

Chapter Three

1. Fisher to Alsberg, 15 August 1936, Central Office Records 1/11.

2. HRS typescript by John Ryan, "Federal Writers Project District #1 Counties: Bear Lake, Franklin, Oneida, Bannock, Gingham, Caribou, Power, Bonneville, Butte, Clark, Fremont, Jefferson, Lemhi, Madison, and Teton"; and by Mr. Enke, "Literature; Region Consisting of Bonneville, Butte, Clark, Fremont, Jefferson, Lemhi, Madison and Teton Counties," Idaho Writers' Project 2/11; Straus to James Dunn, 8 November 1935, Idaho Writers' Project 1/5; Merriam to Mangione, [1969], Mangione Papers 68.

3. Fisher to Gipson, 16 April 1936, Caxton Records.

4. Mangione, *Dream* 78, 201; Penkower 40; Taber, "Project" 123, 154; Fisher to Cronyn, 18 December 1935, Central Office Records 1/11; Fisher to Laney, 26 March 1936, Fisher Papers Idaho 1.

5. Gipson to Fisher, 5 February 1936, Caxton Records; Gipson to Dick Lake, 27 September 1936, and Fisher to Gipson, 29 September 36, Caxton Records Series II/"Vardis Fisher, Idaho Guide, Old Correspondence, 1936."

6. Fisher to Alsberg, 30 June 1936, Central Office Records 13/87; CoC and local press letters qtd. in Taber, "Fisher" 72; Fisher to Gipson, 1 December 1936, Caxton Records.

7. Cronyn to Fisher, 19 September 1936, Central Office Records 13/87; Alsberg to Fisher, 20 October 1936, Central Office Records 1/11; Fisher to Cronyn, 29 September 1936, Central Office Records 13/87.

8. Cronyn to Gipson, 27 November 1936, Central Office Records 13/87; Kellock to Mangione, 22 May 1969, Mangione Papers 58; Fisher to Cronyn qtd. in Taber, "Project" 141; Fisher to Cronyn, 25 November 1936, Central Office Records 13/87; Cronyn to Fisher, 19 October 1937, Central Office Records 28/2; Holmes qtd. in Taber, "Project" 142, n 70; Isham to Woodward, 5 June 1937, Central Office Records 1/11; Fisher to Harris, n.d. [rec'd 24 March 1937], Central Office Records 1/11.

9. Milton 3–4, 40; letter by Fisher, n.d., Central Office Records 12/3.

10. Cronyn to Fisher, 1 October 1936, and Alsberg [Kellock] to Fisher, 10 August 1936, Central Office Records 13/87; Alsberg [Kellock] to Fisher, 29 October 1936, Central Office Records 1/11.

11. Fisher to Cronyn, 5 March 1937, Central Office Records 1/11.

12. Alsberg [Kellock] to Fisher, 2 July 1936, Central Office Records 13/87.

13. An instructive contrast can be made with the 1996 National Park Service Guide to Craters of the Moon. Although that pamphlet uses language similar to Fisher's, it also provides a modern, human-scale account by telling the story of Robert Limbert's trek across the lava in 1920 and the instrumentality of his reports and photographs in securing the site's protection as a national monument in 1924. This story would undoubtedly have been available for Fisher's use, if he had so chosen. See DeVoto, "WPA" 8; "Idaho," Crawford to Alsberg, n.d., Central Office Records 13/87; Milton 14.

14. Cronyn to Fisher, 22 September, 4, 19 October 1937, Central Office Records 28/2.

15. "Preliminary Report on Idaho Guide," June 1936, Central Office Records 13/87.

16. Fisher to Ryan, 6 February 1936, and Ryan to Fisher, 8 February 1936, Idaho Writers' Project 1/5; Fisher to Alsberg, 27 April, 5 May 1936, Central Office Records 13/87.

17. Fisher to Alsberg, 30 June 1936, and Fisher to Cronyn, 30 July 1936, Central Office Records 13/87; Fisher to E. L. Hockett, Secretary, Chamber of Commerce, Idaho Falls, 19 October 1938, and Fisher to Hon. Barzilla Clark, Governor of Idaho, 15 January 1937, Clark Papers 18/WPA-FWP; "Author Claims Idaho Is Ruined," *Statesman*, 20 March 1936, Kellogg Papers 2/10.

18. Fisher to Lathen, 11 January 1937, Caxton Records, Series II/"Vardis Fisher, Idaho Guide, Old Correspondence, 1936–37."

19. Gipson to Fisher, 11 January 1937, ibid.

20. AP Release to Idaho newspapers, 26 February 1937, Central Office Records 13/87; Fisher to Alsberg, 7 August 1936, and Fisher to Harris, 23 February 1937, Central Office Records 1/11.

21. Alsberg to Fisher, 25 April 1936, Central Office Records 13/87.

22. Fisher to Seidenberg, 25 April 1936, and Alsberg [Kellock] to Fisher, 29 October 1936, Central Office Records 1/11; Fisher to Alsberg, 30 June 1936, and Editorial Report, n.d., Fisher to Cronyn, 30 July 1936, Central Office Records 13/87; Workers of the WPA Writers' Program, Idaho, "Idaho Digest for Travelers," September 1939, Bottolfson Papers 7.

23. Alsberg [Charles Smith] to Fisher, 21 July 1938, Central Office Records 1/11.

Chapter 4

1. One of her colleagues characterized her, retrospectively: "A compulsive talker and worker, often tactless, given to encroaching on the domain of Essays, reluctant to surrender a City, but possessed of enormous vitality. She added more than we liked to

concede at the time to the guidebooks. Her range of interests was wide, and it is due to her insistence that thousands of sites of battles, feuds, significant events and curious happenings appear along the highways and byways. She had a healthy hunger for the economy of a region: when avocados are picked, how automobiles came to be made in Michigan, why beaver hats went out of fashion, etc. She was a demon, and rightly so, for accurate mileage and fought like a mother lion for wordage, holding that Tours, being the raison-d'etre of a guidebook, deserved the larger part of the space" (Harold Coy to Mangione, 7 February 1968, Mangione Papers 68).

2. "Supplementary Instruction #11E to The American Manual: Complete Summary of Tour Form, 17 October 1938," Central Office Records 11/69.

3. Kellock to Grace Kellogg, 27 October 1936, Central Office Records 13/98; Alsberg [Kellock] to Irene Fuhlbruegge, 6 May 1936, Central Office Records 13/108. Biographical sources on Kellock are Fourth U.S. Civil Service Region Investigation Division: Report of Special Hearing, 10 February 1944, and Memo, Kellock to John Newsom, n.d., Kellock Papers; "About Our Authors," *American Scholar* 9 (1940): 510; Mangione, *Dream*, passim; K. McKinzie, passim; Penkower, passim; and personal correspondence and taped interviews in the Mangione Papers. The most extensive information about her visits to the Soviet Union appears in an FBI report on Kellock, 19 May 1943, Kellock Papers.

4. Kellock to Alsberg, 20 January 1936, Kellock Papers.

5. Alsberg [Kellock] to Greer, 25 May 1937, Central Office Records 13/90; Alsberg [Kellock] to Wainger, 6 October 1936, Central Office Records 13/113; Alsberg [Kellock] to Mabel Montgomery, 28 November 1938, Central Office Records 13/122; Alsberg [Kellock] to Wainger, 28 October 1938, Central Office Records 13/113.

6. Kellock to Mangione, 26 August 1972, Mangione Papers 58.

7. Kellock to Alsberg, 7 July 1938, Central Office Records 16/182.

8. Innumerable, very detailed letters of correction, signed by Alsberg but written by Kellock, can be found in Central Office Records 13.

9. Kellock to Fisher, 28 February 1938, Central Office Records 28/202, and Kellock to Alsberg, 12 September 1938, Central Office Records 16/182; Arthur Scharf, WPA Writers Notes #2, August 1967, Pittsburgh, Pa., 3, Mangione Papers, unsorted; Kellock to Spring, 8 December 1938, Central Office Records 13/132.

10. Alsberg [Kellock] to Fisher, 28 February 1939, Central Office Records 28/202; Alsberg [Kellock] to T. J. Edmonds (via E. J. Griffith), 23 March 1939, Central Office Records 13/118.

11. Alsberg [Kellock] to Gable, 22 March 1938, Central Office Records 13/105; Alsberg [Kellock] to Mark Christensen, 26 April 1938, Central Office Records 13/132.

Chapter 5

1. Initially, Orrick Johns was director of the New York City Reporters' Unit (a section of the Writers' Project dedicated to reporting WPA activity). He then replaced Wal-

ter K. Van Olinda as director of the Writers' Project proper. The Reporters' Unit was dissolved after about a year (Mangione, *Dream* 160-63).

2. Robert W. Bruere to Paul U. Kellogg, 23 June 1937, 7, Central Correspondence Files 651.317 NYC/2125.

3. The New York City project survived for three more years, under the state reorganization into the Work Projects Administration after 1939; in that period, it had two more directors (Mangione, *Dream* 83).

4. Characterization of 1930s' political debates, within and beyond New York City, draws on Aaron, Bloom, Cooney, Gilbert, Pells, Susman, and Wald.

5. To say that the project recognized and foregrounded the category of racial difference is not to say that there was no racism on the project: witness Alsberg's and Hopkins's recurrent warnings to the project; the initiation of the Harlem Joint Conference Against Discriminatory Practices in May 1936, Press Clippings Concerning Negro Affairs, Division of Information 313; and the complaint of the *Pittsburgh Courier*, 14 January 1937: "The original group of the writers project under Orrick Johns, resigned director, made no provision for important work now being done by Negro writers on the New York City Guidebook. It remained for the Negroes themselves to point out the inconsistency of a guide book without including the innumerable interesting phases of Negro life." These measures finally led to the situation boasted of in an undated publicity release: "The work of gathering and writing the material to be used in the section [of *New York Panorama*] on the Negro was done almost exclusively by Negro WPA writers. The Guide presents, for the first time, a comprehensive and unbiased picture of the Negro as he lives, works, and plays, and its study represents a distinct advance over the distorted material offered by most available books on the Negro" (Manuscripts A538).

6. Bruere to Kellogg, 23 June 1937, 2, 12, Central Correspondence Files 651.317 NYC/2125; "How It Was Done," August 1938, Central Office Records 1/30.

7. One of the New York City rewrite editors, for example, advised his staff: "The Columbia University story, after a dignified discussion of Columbia's most important features, averts boredom by a note on what the male students prefer in drinks and women" (Arthur Halliburton to Staff, 4 May 1936, Central Office Records 13/111).

8. "The Fair of the Future 1939: Social Theme, Physical Concept, Design Organization, Summary," Submitted by the Committee formed at the Dinner at the City Club, Wednesday, December 11, 1935, 1, Manuscripts A557.

9. The records of the Sirovich bill hearings are in the *Congressional Record*, House Joint Resolution 79, 1938; those of the Coffee-Pepper bill hearings are in the *Congressional Record*, Senate 3296, 1938.

10. Alsberg to Shaw, 5 November 1938, and Levenson to Alsberg, 2 August 1938, Central Office Records 1/30; Evelyn H. Hersey, American Committee for Christian Refugees, to Newsom, 11 December 1939, National Refugee Service to Newsom, 19 December 1942, and Levenson to Alsberg, 17 November 1938, Central Office

Records 1/28. Florence Kerr wrote to Albert E. Austin that she was pleased that *New York Panorama* had sold 3,279 copies in three months (27 May 1939; Central Correspondence Files NYC 651.3178/2117). Cecil L. Rutledge, Major, Infantry, Acting Adjutant, to Works Progress Administration, 25 March 1940, Central Correspondence Files NYC 651.3178/2127.

11. Correspondence about the Abbott book is in Central Office Records 13/111. The quotation comes from Alsberg to Lawrence S. Morris, 25 February 1938; the plagiarism charge is recounted in Alsberg to Thomas Parker, 22 October 1938.

12. Technically, he was found guilty of falsifying his record as noncommunist by the Division of Investigation, FWA, 1940 (Central Correspondence Files 651.317 NYC/2126; Division of Information 2116).

13. Publicity Release, 8 June 1939, Central Office Records 1/30.

14. Alsberg to Strauss, 10 February 1939, Manuscripts A534; Alsberg to Strauss, 20 February 1939, Central Office Records 13/111; Gaer to Alsberg, January 1939, Central Office Records 6/59A. Two New York City directors—Harry Shaw and Harold Strauss—came and went during the most intense period of the guidebook's production; Joseph Gaer, one of Alsberg's most effective troubleshooters, took over editorial supervision of the volume at a crucial juncture, yet Lou Gody is credited as editor in chief in the published volume; and at least half a dozen assistant editors were involved.

15. Bruere to Kellogg, 23 June 1937, 2, 12, Central Correspondence Files 651.317 NYC/2125; Publicity Release, August 1936, Division of Information 83; Alsberg [Harris] to Kirk, 3 March 1937, and Kirk to Hopkins, 23 February 1937, Central Correspondence Files 651.317 NYC/2124.

16. Alsberg to Strauss, 28 January 1939, Manuscripts A534.

17. Mumford to Alsberg, 5 October 1937, Central Office Records 5/50; "American Guide Manual," 1935, Central Office Records 11/69; Alsberg to Shaw, March 1938, Central Office Records 2; Alsberg to Joseph Gaer, 20 January 1938, Manuscripts A543.

18. Publicity Release, 6 June 1939, Manuscripts A796. The New York City project was particularly committed to representing ethnicity: it produced several works in the field, including *Italians of New York* (1938), *The Jewish Landsmanschaften of New York* (1938), and the Foreign-Language Press Project, and Alsberg frequently reminded employees to be knowledgeable and professional on this topic (for example, Alsberg to Shaw, Central Office Records 2/30).

19. Alsberg to Shaw, 23 April 1938, Manuscripts A535; Supplementary Instructions No. 15 to "The American Guide Manual," 15 September 1936, Central Office Records 11/70.

20. Shaw to Alsberg, 19 May 1938, Central Office Records 1/29.

21. Publicity photographs in "WPA Activities—FWP Publicity," NYC Archive; details of games show, Malmberg to Alsberg, 25 April, 12 June 1939, Central Corre-

spondence Files 651.317 NYC/2126. Alistair Cooke request, 1938, and clipping of Eleanor Roosevelt presentation, Division of Information 2117.

Chapter 6

1. Yancey, Jottings [December 1967], 2, Mangione Papers 61. Hendricks, who was from Indiana, was forty-six years old at the beginning of the project. He had probably moved to North Carolina after his service in World War I, serving as managing editor and city editor of the *Asheville Times*, 1919–26, and editor of the *Asheville Advocate*, a newspaper supported by the American Federation of Labor ("Biographical Notices, FWP: NC," Central Office Records 12/3; Hirsch, "Culture" 14). In 1936, Kellock judged that Hendricks was doing "the major editorial work—the real guide work" (Field Report, Kellock to Alsberg, 8 February 1936, Central Office Records 6/61). Bjorkman gave Hendriks primary credit for the final look of the guidebook: he called him "my chief editorial assistant" (Bjorkman to Alsberg, 27 July 1938, Central Office Records 1/37.)

George L. Andrews was forty-nine years old at the start of the project, having been born in North Carolina, worked as a teacher, then as a full-time fiction freelancer, 1929–35. Bjorkman said that Andrews was a writer of state renown ("Biographical Notices, FWP: NC," Central Office Records 12/3); "on his own time he aided young project workers eager to publish their personal work" (Hirsch, "Culture" 13). In 1936, Andrews was slated to write the guidebook for the eastern end of the state (Kellock to Alsberg, 3 February 1936, Central Office Records 6/61). In 1938, he became heavily involved in gathering local legends: according to Bjorkman, "It seems that Andrews and his gang can do fine work the moment they get away from the Guide. What they are doing now is short story work, and in that field Andrews really counts" (Bjorkman to Couch, 2 May 1938, FWP-Couch Papers 2). In 1937, both Hendricks and Andrews had relief status.

2. Bjorkman to Alsberg, 18 March 1937, 17 January 1938, Central Office Records 1/37; Bjorkman to Alsberg, 17 March 1937, Central Office Records 13/114; Kelly to Couch, 21 October 1939, FWP-Couch Papers 8.

3. Bjorkman to Santford Martin, 4 March 1937, and Bjorkman to Alsberg, 19 June 1936, FWP-Couch Papers 1.

4. Mrs. Samuel H. Hines to Alsberg, 10 November 1936, Central Office Records 1/37; McKay to Alsberg, 15 September 1936, Central Office Records 1/37.

5. Alsberg [Kellock] to Bjorkman, 19 March 1936, and North Carolina Bulletin 17, Edwin Bjorkman to All District Supervisors, 13 February 1936, Central Office Records 13/114; Kellock to Alsberg, 4 February 1936, Central Office Records 6/61; Yancey, Jottings [December 1967], 2, Mangione Papers 61; Harriss to Hopkins qtd. in Hirsch, "Culture" 37–38.

6. Kellock to Alsberg, 4 February 1936, Central Office Records 6/61; Bjorkman to Alsberg, 10 February 1936, Central Office Records 13/114.

7. Couch to Daniels, 21 October 1937, FWP-Couch Papers 2. Once federal sponsorship was under attack, both Couch and Bjorkman tried to marshal forces in support of the federal office and its high standards: Couch to William R. McDaniel, 20 June 1939, and Bjorkman to Hon. Alva Adams, 26 June 1939, FWP-Couch Papers 7; Couch to Senator J. W. Bailey, 27 April 1939, UNC Press. Innumerable letters from Couch, accusing Washington of centralization, obfuscation, censorship, and propaganda, are held in Couch Papers 8 and UNC Press. With the devolution of the federal project in September 1939, the Department of Conservation and Development became the sponsor of the North Carolina project, with one hundred security and ten nonsecurity workers. In August 1941, Bjorkman resigned, and the office moved to Raleigh, with eighteen workers.

8. Bjorkman to Couch, 8 January 1938, FWP-Couch Papers 2.

9. Field Report for 18–24 December [1936?], Frank B. Well to Henry Alsberg, Central Office Records 6/61; Bjorkman to Cronyn, 9 September 1937, FWP-Couch Papers 2.

10. Bjorkman to Alsberg, 5 July 1938, Central Office Records 13/114.

11. Bjorkman to Alsberg, 10 November 1938, Central Office Records 13/114, Alsberg [D. C. Kline] to Hall, 18 November 1938, and Alsberg [Kellock] to Bjorkman, 14 November 1938, Central Office Records 13/114.

12. Couch to Alsberg, 25 January 1939, FWP-Couch Papers 5.

13. Office on Negro Affairs to Couch, 19 October 1938, FWP-Couch Papers 3; Bjorkman to Couch, 29 December 1938, FWP-Couch Papers 4.

14. Editorial Report on Elizabeth City, S[terling] A. B[rown], 23 October 1937, and Editorial Report on Wilmington, S[terling] A. B[rown], 25 October 1937, Manuscripts A323; Editorial Report, "The Negroes," G. B. R[oberts], 24 February 1938, Manuscripts A325; Bjorkman to Alsberg, 1 September 1938, FWP-Couch Papers 3.

15. Editorial Report on Arts and Handicrafts Essay, 30 July 1938, Manuscripts A325. This case has been made more recently by Gilroy and Levine, among others.

16. Couch to Alsberg, 22 April 1938, FWP-Couch Papers 2.

17. Couch to Alsberg, 16 June 1939, FWP-Couch Papers 7; Field Report, Darel Mc-Conkey, 2 November 1936, Central Office Records 6/61, and Loretto Carroll Bailey to Bjorkman, 19 November 1936, 28 April 1937, FWP-Couch Papers 1, 2; Bjorkman to Alsberg, 6 November 1936, Central Office Records 1/36.

18. A print run of 7,500 is cited by Couch (Couch to Andrews, 15 November 1939, UNC Press); by 1944, however, the initial print run was put at 8,280 (7,384 sold, 131 complimentary distribution, 663 damaged); a second printing of 3,500 was under way (Lucille Varner to Donald E. Strout, 21 August 1944, UNC Press). In its first year, the guide sold 4,134 copies; by 1953, it had sold 13,514 copies ("Sales for North Carolina Guide," UNC Press). In 1953, Lambert Davis characterized these sales: "There was a good institutional sale but the vast majority of the copies were sold through bookstores to individuals. While the book sold well in North Carolina, most of the sales were outside of the State" (Davis to William Carmichael, 11 August 1953, UNC Press).

19. Bjorkman to Couch, 13 January 1937, FWP-Couch Papers 1.

20. Alsberg to Couch, 15 June 1937, FWP-Couch Papers 2.

21. Couch to Bjorkman, 5 June 1936, FWP-Couch Papers 1; Couch to Bjorkman, 3 August 1938, FWP-Couch Papers 3.

22. Harriss to Hopkins, 19 December 1936, Central Office Records 1/37.

23. G. B. Roberts, Editorial Report, 16 February 1938, Manuscripts A325.

24. This reading is indebted to information provided by David Wright, a social historian at the University of Massachusetts, who is studying the Pea Island Life Savers.

25. Alsberg to Bjorkman, 28 January 1936, Central Office Records 1/37; Bjorkman to Alsberg, 4 September 1937, Central Office Records 13/114.

26. I am grateful to Professor Gerald Schwartz of Western Carolina University for this information about contemporary practices.

27. North Carolina Bulletin 11, Edwin Bjorkman to All District Supervisors, 24 January 1936, Central Office Records 1/36; Bjorkman to Alsberg, 2 November 1936, Central Office Records 1/36; Yancey, Jottings [December 1967], 3, Mangione Papers 61.

28. Frank P. Graham to Alsberg, 12 July 1938, UNC Press; Couch to Tarleton Collier, 14 September 1938, FWP-Couch Papers 3.

29. Couch to Bjorkman, 17 July 1936, FWP-Couch Papers 1; Couch to Bjorkman, n.d., FWP-Couch Papers 2.

30. This response was what Bjorkman had sought: he hoped that having sponsors publicize the guidebook "will emphasize the more or less official status of the work" (Bjorkman to Alsberg, 27 April 1939, FWP-Couch Papers 6). Sixteen years later, Lambert Davis judged, "The Federal Writers' Project was a federally subsidized venture and as there was some initial doubt as to the reception of these volumes, every effort was made to get the highest state sponsorship for the individual volumes. . . . I believe that all the original state guides included a letter of recommendation from the governor as an additional device for emphasizing state sponsorship" (Davis to Ben E. Douglas, 5 November 1954, UNC Press).

31. Adelaid L. Fries to Andrews, 20 February 1936, FWP-Couch Papers 1; *Asheville Times* 13 September 1939, NC Writers' Project.

32. Parker to Sharpe, 9 February 1955, UNC Press.

33. Local reviews are in FWP-Couch Papers 8 and in NC Writers' Project. Couch to Kelly, 18 October 1939, Couch to Bjorkman, 20 October 1939, and Kelly to Couch, 19 October 1939, UNC Press.

34. Isaac S. London to Alsberg, 10 October 1939, UNC Press; "Subsidy for Slander," *Greensboro Daily News*, 13 October 1939; "Ignorant Writers," *Richmond County Journal*, 18 October 1939.

35. Compendiums of local and national reviews of *These Are Our Lives*—as well as original press clippings—are available in "Excerpts from reviews of THESE ARE OUR LIVES"; "Additional excerpts from reviews of THESE ARE OUR LIVES"; "Comments from letters on THESE ARE OUR LIVES," UNC Press.

36. Providence review in "Excerpts from reviews of THESE ARE OUR LIVES," UNC Press; Laughlin, "Chapter II North Carolina," NC Writers' Project; Alsberg to Couch, 20 June 1939, FWP-Couch Papers 6; Couch to Alsberg, 10 August 1939, FWP-Couch Papers 7.

37. Personal interview, 3 September 1992.

Chapter 7

1. Letters and telegrams from Alsberg to Balch and Parker survive which show the director's hand at work in the hiring process (Central Office Records 1/22, 23; see also Mangione, *Dream* 76, 103). In person, however, Alsberg disavowed his role: in one telephone conversation, for example, Parker said, "I took your man Balch and also Brown"; Alsberg prevaricated: "That is very nice. Do they fit in? I don't want you to think that recommendations coming from here must be taken on" (Mangione Papers 20).

2. One description of Parker's censorship is provided in Lawrence Morris's Field Report to Alsberg, 28 May 1936, Central Office Records 6/60; Conroy, "Writers"; letters and telegrams of support from numerous national and state organizations are gathered in Central Office Records 1/22, 23, 31; transcriptions from numerous telephone conversations and meetings are held in Mangione Papers 21.

3. Many clippings from local newspapers covering the strike are gathered in Mangione Papers 60. Alsberg to Kerr, 30 October 1936, 7 November 1936, Mangione Papers 21; Balch interview, 1968, Mangione Papers 96.

4. I have culled the details of van Ravenswaay's biography and his responses to the project from the Van Ravenswaay Papers. Van Ravenswaay, "The Making of the Missouri Guidebook: Reminiscences of the One-time State Supervisor," 5 November 1985, Van Ravenswaay Papers 8.

5. "MFS Member Honored—Charles van Ravenswaay," *Missouri Folklore Society Newsletter*, February 1988, 13, Van Ravenswaay Papers 6.

6. Jensen to Mangione, 28 January 1969, Mangione Papers 68.

7. Balch interview, 1968, Mangione Papers 96.

8. Beard to Harris, 11 August 1937, Central Office Records 13/103.

9. Conroy, "Literature," n.d., and "Literature and Drama," 18 March 1937, 3–4, Manuscripts A221; Conroy, "Art," 19 April 1937, Manuscripts A218; Conroy, "Music," 17 April 1937, Manuscripts A221. Other manuscripts by Conroy include "Kansas City," 19 April 1937 (the piece that most clearly demonstrates his attention to class), "Moberly," n.d., and "Ste. Genevieve," 6 April 1937, Manuscripts A219; "Drama," n.d., Manuscripts A222.

10. Editorial Report on "Missouri: Literature," by L. D. A., 25 March 1937, Manuscripts A221; Summary Criticism on "Missouri: Kansas City," by J. W. M., 20 July 1937, and Editorial Report on "Missouri: Kansas City," by J. C. R., 27 April 1937,

Manuscripts A219, and Editorial Report on "Missouri: Music," anon., 20 April 1937, Manuscripts A221.

11. Editorial Report on "Missouri: Columbia," by S. G. S., 27 April 1937, Manuscripts A220; Harris to Greer, 11 March 1937, Central Office Records 13/102.

12. Balch, "St. Louis," 19 April 1937, Manuscripts A219.

13. Balch, "Springfield," 21 April 1937, Manuscripts A220.

14. Cronyn to Greer, 22 May, 29 April 1937, Manuscripts A220; Editorial Report on "Missouri: St. Louis," by N. M. G., 19 May 1937, Manuscripts A219; Harris to Murray, 30 April 1937, Central Office Records 22.

15. Alsberg [Kellock] to Parker, 19, 29 October 1936, Central Office Records 13/103; Parker, "Folkways," n.d., Manuscripts A220; Parker et al, "Racial Elements and Folklore," 16 December 1936, Manuscripts A220.

16. Morris to Alsberg, 25 March 1936, Central Office Records 6/60; a voluminous and sometimes contradictory correspondence on the Springfield guide is sprinkled throughout Central Office Records 1/22, 6/60, 13/102, 103; Alsberg [Lomax] to Parker, 19 October 1936, Central Office Records 13/103.

17. Van Ravenswaay to Irving Dilliard, 27 May 1941, Van Ravenswaay Papers, Addition; van Ravenswaay, "The Making of the Missouri Guidebook: Reminiscences of the One-time State Supervisor," 5 November 1985, Van Ravenswaay Papers 8.

18. Rosenberg interview, [1968], Mangione Papers 96; van Ravenswaay "The Making of the Missouri Guidebook," 5 November 1985, Van Ravenswaay Papers 8; [Jensen] to van Ravenswaay, [28?] April 1941, [Jensen] to [van Ravenswaay], n.d., [van Ravenswaay] to Jensen, 31 March [1941], and Jensen to van Ravenswaay, n.d., Van Ravenswaay Papers, Addition.

19. Various letters and memorandums concerning Washington's selection of photographs for the Missouri guide are held in Manuscripts A220.

20. Jensen to Mangione, 28 January 1969, Mangione Papers 68.

Conclusion

1. Two-minute transcription, "Americans Discover America," and untitled transcription for Kate Smith program, Division of Information 333/2, "American Guide Week."

2. The editorial team was composed of Mary Barrett, Edward Dreyer, Dora Thea Hettwer, William R. McDaniel, Walter McElroy, H. H. Miller, Joseph Miller, Dale L. Morgan, Montana Lisle Reese, and Ellen M. Rollins. See Alsberg interview, 23, 24 May 1968, Mangione Papers 96.

3. George Willison, in an interview with Mangione, suggests that McElroy, in fact, did most of the work on the new volume (Mangione Papers 69). Although Alsberg later remembered the book as having been adopted by the Book-of-the-Month Club, he also admitted that Walter Friese, senior editor at Hastings House, if asked about sales, "makes a face" (Alsberg interview, 23, 24 May 1968, Mangione Papers 96). By

the 1970s, Kellock had either forgotten or never knew that the 1949 volume existed (John Fondersmith interview with Katharine Kellock, 31 August 1973, provided by Fondersmith from his files on the WPA Guides).

4. Davis to George Ross, 22 April 1953, and Helen Parker to Bill Sharpe, 9 February 1955, UNC Press.

5. "Federal Art Patronage Notes" 1, no. 1 (September 1974): 1. In this initiative, O'-Connor was following the lead of Dorothy C. Miller, widow of Federal Art Project director Holger Cahill, who organized the traveling show, "The U.S. Government Art Projects: Some Distinguished Alumni," for the Museum of Modern Art in 1962.

Works Cited

Aaron, Daniel. *Writers on the Left*. New York: Harcourt, Brace, and World, 1961.

Abbott, Berenice. *Changing New York*. New York: E. P. Dutton, 1939.

"About Our Authors." *American Scholar* 9 (1940): 510.

Alexander, Charles C. *Nationalism in American Thought, 1930–1945*. Chicago: Rand McNally, 1969.

Alsberg, Henry. "New Guide to America." *New York Times*, 9 February 1936.

———, ed. *The American Guide: A Source Book and Complete Travel Guide for The United States*. New York: Hastings House, 1949.

"The American Guide in the Schools." *Journal of the National Education Association* 27 (May 1938): 140–41.

"The American Guide Puts Wichita on 'Crossroads of Nation.'" *Wichita* (Kans.) *Eagle*, 27 December 1936.

Anderson, Benedict. *Imagined Communities: Reflections on the Origin and Spread of Nationalism*. 1983. Rev. ed. New York: Verso, 1991.

Anderson, Katherine McClure. "Today's Books." *Macon* (Ga.) *Telegraph*, 7 April 1938.

Asch, Nathan. *The Road: In Search of America*. New York: Norton, 1937.

Asheville (N.C.) *Times*, 13 September 1939.

Attebery, Louie W. "Vardis Fisher." In *A Literary History of the American West*, edited by J. Golden Taylor et al. Fort Worth: Texas Christian University Press, 1987.

"Author Claims Idaho Is Ruined." *Statesman*, 20 March 1936.

Baigell, Matthew. *The American Scene: American Painting of the 1930's*. New York: Praeger, 1974.

Bal, Mieke. "Telling, Showing, Showing Off." *Critical Inquiry* 18 (Spring 1992): 556–94.

Balch, Jack S. *Lamps at High Noon: A Novel*. New York: Modern Age Books, 1941.

————. Review of *Idaho*. *New Republic*, 19 May 1937.

Banks, Ann, ed. and intro. *First-Person America*. New York: Knopf, 1980.

Barkley, Frederick R. "W.P.A. Catalogs America." *Washington Star*, 25 April 1937.

Barthes, Roland. "The *Blue Guide*." In *Mythologies*, translated by Annette Lavers. London: Granada Publishing, 1973.

————. "The Eiffel Tower." In *The Eiffel Tower and Other Mythologies*, translated by R. Howard. New York: Hill and Wang, 1984.

Belasco, Warren James. *Americans on the Road: From Autocamp to Motel, 1910–1945*. Cambridge, Mass.: MIT Press, 1981.

Benét, Stephen Vincent. "Patchwork Quilt of These United States." *New York Herald-Tribune*, 28 December 1941.

Benton, Thomas Hart. *An American in Art: A Professional and Technical Autobiography*. Lawrence, Kan.: University Press of Kansas, 1969.

Billington, Ray Allen. *The American Frontier Thesis: Attack and Defense*. Washington, D.C.: American Historical Association, 1971.

————. "Government and the Arts: The W.P.A. Experience." *American Quarterly* 13 (1961): 466–79.

Bindas, Kenneth J. *All of This Music Belongs to the Nation: The WPA's Federal Music Project and American Society*. Knoxville: University of Tennessee Press, 1996.

Bishop, John Peale. "The Strange Case of Vardis Fisher." *Southern Review* (Autumn 1937): 355.

Blake, Casey Nelson. *Beloved Community: The Cultural Criticism of Randolph Bourne, Van Wyck Brooks, Waldo Frank, and Lewis Mumford*. Chapel Hill: University of North Carolina Press, 1990.

Bloom, Alexander. *The New York Intellectuals and Their World*. New York: Oxford University Press, 1986.

Boorstin, Daniel J. *The Image: A Guide to Pseudo-Events in America*. New York: Harper & Row, 1961.

Boyer, M. Christine. *Dreaming the Rational City: The Myth of American City Planning*. Cambridge, Mass.: MIT Press, 1983.

Bradley, Van Allen. "Vardis Fisher and the West." [1968]. (Clipping, Clore Collection 12).

Brewer, Jeutone. *The Federal Writers' Project: A Bibliography*. Metuchen, N.J.: Scarecrow Press, 1994.

"Brilliant Idaho Encyclopedia Completed by WPA Writers." *Boise* (Idaho) *News*, 26 January 1938.

Broder, David S. "The Unfamiliar Show of Conscience." *Chicago Sun-Times*, 22 July 1973.

Bromfeld, Louis. "Guides Better Than Baedeker's." *New York Herald Tribune*, 16 February 1941.

Bustard, Bruce I. *A New Deal for the Arts*. Washington, D.C.: National Archives and Records Administration/Seattle, University of Washington Press, 1997.

C. J. P. "North Carolina Guide Book." Raleigh (N.C.) *News and Observer*, 29 October 1939.

Cassidy, Frederic G., ed. *Dictionary of American Regional English*. Vol. 2. Cambridge, Mass.: Belknap Press of Harvard University Press, 1991.

Catton, Bruce. "A Book a Day." *Bristol* (Va.) *News-Bulletin*, 2 February 1937.

Chadbourne, Horace. Review of *Idaho*. *Frontier and Midland*, undated clipping, 294. (Central Office Records 2/51).

Clark, Thomas D. Review of *Idaho*. *Lexington* (Ky.) *Leader*, 14 March 1937.

"Concerning a Book." *Greensboro* (N.C.) *News*, 14 October 1939.

Conrad, Peter. *The Art of the City: Views and Versions of New York*. New York: Oxford University Press, 1984.

Conroy, Jack. "Writers Disturbing the Peace." *New Masses* 17 (November 1936): 13.

Considine, Bob. *Ripley, the Modern Marco Polo*. Garden City, N.Y.: Doubleday, 1961.

Contreras, Belisario R. *Tradition and Innovation in New Deal Art*. Lewisburg, Pa.: Bucknell University Press, 1983.

Cooney, Terry A. *The Rise of the New York Intellectuals: Partisan Review and Its Circle*. Madison: University of Wisconsin Press, 1986.

Couch, W. T. Review of *Idaho*. *Raleigh* (N.C.) *News and Observer*, 18 April 1937.

———, ed. *Culture in the South*. Chapel Hill: University of North Carolina Press, 1934.

Craig, E. Quita. *Black Drama of the Federal Theatre Era: Beyond the Formal Horizons*. Amherst: University of Massachusetts Press, 1980.

Cutler, Phoebe. *The Public Landscape of the New Deal*. New Haven: Yale University Press, 1985.

Daniels, Jonathan. "The Old North State." *Saturday Review of Literature*, 13 March 1940.

Darst, Katharine. "Here and There." *St. Louis Globe-Democrat*, 13 June 1941.

Denning, Michael. *The Cultural Front: The Laboring of American Culture in the Twentieth Century*. London: Verso, 1996.

DeVoto, Bernard. "The First WPA Guide." *Saturday Review of Literature*, 27 February 1937: 8.

———. "U.S. One." *Saturday Review of Literature*, 19 March 1938: 8.

———. "The WPA Guides." *Saturday Review of Literature*, August 1937: 8.

———. "The Writers' Project." *Harper's Magazine* (January 1942): 221–24.

Doig, Ivan. "The Baedeker of Idaho." *Pacific Search: Northwest Nature and Life* 12 (June 1978): 21–23.

Dos Passos, John. *U.S.A.* 1937. Harmondsworth, U.K.: Penguin, 1966.

Duffus, R. L. *New York Times Sunday Magazine*, 11 January 1937.

Du Von, Jay. "Idaho Is First to Publish State Guide by WPA Writers." *Des Moines* (Iowa) *Register*, 7 March 1937.

Duncan, James S., and Nancy G. Duncan. "Ideology and Bliss: Roland Barthes and the Secret Histories of Landscape." In *Writing Worlds: Discourse, Text and*

Metaphor in the Representation of Landscape, edited by Trevor J. Barnes and James S. Duncan. London: Routledge, 1992.

Eco, Umberto. *Travels in Hyperreality*. Translated by William Weaver. London: Pan/Picador, 1987.

Estavan, Lawrence. "The Bookman's Daily Notebook." *San Francisco Chronicle*, 28 May 1941.

The Federal Writers' Project of the Federal Works Agency, Work Projects Administration, for the State of North Carolina. *North Carolina: A Guide to the Old North State*. Chapel Hill: University of North Carolina Press, 1939.

Federal Writers' Project of the Works Progress Administration. *The Ocean Highway: New Brunswick, New Jersey, to Jacksonville, Florida*. New York: Modern Age Books, 1938.

——. *The Oregon Trail: The Missouri River to the Pacific Ocean*. New York: Hastings House, 1939.

——. *U.S. One: Maine to Florida*. New York: Modern Age Books, 1938.

Federal Writers' Projects [*sic*] of the Works Progress Administration. *Idaho: A Guide in Word and Picture*. Caldwell, Ida.: Caxton Printers, 1937. Rev. ed. New York: Oxford University Press, 1950.

Federal Writers' Project of the Works Progress Administration in New York City. *New York Panorama: A Comprehensive View of the Metropolis, Presented in a Series of Articles Prepared by the Federal Writers' Project of the Works Progress Administration in New York City*. New York: Random House, 1938.

——. *The WPA Guide to New York City: A Comprehensive Guide to the Five Boroughs of the Metropolis—Manhattan, Brooklyn, the Bronx, Queens, and Richmond—Prepared by the Federal Writers' Project of the Works Progress Administration in New York City*. New York: Random House, 1939.

Federal Writers' Project of the Works Progress Administration in North Carolina, Tennessee, and Georgia. *These Are Our Lives: As Told by the People and Written by Members of the Federal Writers' Project of the Works Progress Administration in North Carolina, Tennessee, and Georgia*. Chapel Hill: University of North Carolina Press, 1939.

Fisher, Philip. *Making and Effacing Art: Modern American Art in a Culture of Museums*. New York: Oxford University Press, 1991.

Fisher, Vardis. "An Essay for Men." *Esquire*, September 1936: 35, 187–90.

——. *Children of God: An American Epic*. New York: Harper, 1939.

——. *Orphans in Gethsemane: A Novel of the Past in the Present*. Denver: Alan Swallow, 1960.

Flanagan, Hallie. *Arena: The Story of the Federal Theatre*. 1940. Rpt. New York: Limelight, 1985.

Flora, Joseph M. *Vardis Fisher*. New York: Twayne, 1965.

"44 Publishers Ask WPA Writing Go On." *New York Times*, 22 May 1939.

Foucault, Michel. *The Order of Things: An Archaeology of the Human Sciences*. New York: Pantheon Books, 1971.

Fox, Daniel M. "The Achievement of the Federal Writers' Project." *American Quarterly* 13 (1961): 3–19.

Fraden, Rena. *Blueprints for a Black Federal Theatre, 1935–1939*. Cambridge: Cambridge University Press, 1994.

Galloway, Janice. *Foreign Parts*. London: Jonathan Cape, 1994.

Gannett, Lewis Stiles. "Books and Things." *New York Herald Tribune*, 5 March 1938.

———. "Books and Things." *New York Herald-Tribune*, 22 December 1937.

———. "Idaho, No 'Gem' but a Dawn!; Books and Things." *New York Herald-Tribune*, 9 July 1937.

———. "Reading about America." *Publishers Weekly* 134 (3 May 1941): 1818-19.

Geertz, Clifford. *Local Knowledge: Further Essays in Interpretive Anthropology*. New York: Basic Books, 1983.

Gelernter, David. *1939: The Lost World of the Fair*. New York: Avon Books, 1995.

Gilbert, James Burkhart. *Writers and Partisans: A History of Literary Radicalism in America*. New York: Wiley, 1968.

Gill, Glenda E. *White Grease Paint on Black Performers: A Study of the Federal Theatre, 1935–1939*. New York: Lang, 1988.

Gilroy, Paul. *The Black Atlantic: Modernity and Double Consciousness*. Cambridge, Mass.: Harvard University Press, 1993.

Gitelman, Lisa. "Negotiating a Vocabulary for Urban Infrastructure, Or, The WPA Meets the Teenage Mutant Ninja Turtles." *Journal of American Studies* 26 (August 1992): 147–58.

Gray, Richard. *Writing the South: Ideas of an American Region*. Cambridge: Cambridge University Press, 1986.

Grover, Dorys C. *Vardis Fisher: The Novelist as Poet*. New York: Revisionist Press, 1973.

Gutheim, Frederick. "America in Guide Books." *Saturday Review of Literature*, 14 June 1941: 3–5, 15.

Hansen, Harry. "The First Reader." *New York World Telegram*, 5 March 1938.

Harris, Jonathan. *Federal Art and National Culture: The Politics of Identity in New Deal America*. Cambridge: Cambridge University Press, 1995.

Haskell, H. J. "The 'Show Me' State." *New York Herald-Tribune*, Book Section, 6 July 1941.

Hirsch, Jerrold Maury. "Culture on Relief: The Federal Writers' Project in North Carolina, 1935–42." M.A. thesis, University of North Carolina at Chapel Hill, 1973.

———. "Portrait of America: The Federal Writers' Project in an Intellectual and Cultural Context." Ph.D. diss., University of North Carolina at Chapel Hill, 1984.

Hobson, Archie, ed. *Remembering America: A Sampler of the WPA American Guide Series*. Introductions by Bill Stott. New York: Columbia University Press, 1985.

Hofstadter, Richard. *The Progressive Historians: Turner, Beard, Parrington.* New York: Knopf, 1968.

Hopkins, Harry. "They'd Rather Work." *Collier's,* 16 November 1935: 9.

Horlings, Albert. "Guidebooks to America." *New Republic,* 13 April 1942: 501–2.

"Idaho Guide Off the Press; Fine Exposition of State's Romance, History, Beauty." *Boise News,* 26 Jan 1938.

"Ignorant Writers." *Richmond* (N.C.) *County Journal,* 18 October 1939.

"Is It History?" *Chowan* (N.C.) *Herald,* 12 October 1939.

Jacksonville (Fla.) *Journal,* 13 January 1941.

Jakle, John A. *The Tourist: Travel in Twentieth-Century North America.* Lincoln: University of Nebraska Press, 1985.

Jameson, Fredric. *The Political Unconscious: Narrative as a Socially Symbolic Act.* Ithaca: Cornell University Press, 1981.

Jenkins, Henry R. "A Guide to North Carolina." *Opportunity,* October 1939.

Jones, Alfred Haworth. "The Search for a Usable American Past in the New Deal Era." *American Quarterly* 22 (1971): 710–24.

Kammen, Michael. *Mystic Chords of Memory: The Transformation of Tradition in American Culture.* New York: Knopf, 1991.

Kazacoff, George. *Dangerous Theatre: The Federal Theatre Project as a Forum for New Plays.* New York: Lang, 1989.

Kazin, Alfred. "Introduction." *New York Panorama.* By the Federal Writers' Project of the Works Progress Administration in New York City. 1938. New York: Pantheon Books, 1984.

———. *On Native Grounds: An Interpretation of Modern American Prose Literature.* New York: Harcourt, Brace, 1942.

Keller, Ulrich. *The Highway as Habitat: A Roy Stryker Documentation, 1943–1955.* Santa Barbara, Calif.: University Art Museum, 1986.

Kellock, Katharine. "The WPA Writers: Portraitists of the United States." *American Scholar* 9 (Autumn 1940): 473–82.

Kendall, M. Sue. *Rethinking Regionalism: John Steuart Curry and the Kansas Mural Controversy.* Washington, D.C.: Smithsonian Institution Press, 1986.

King, Richard. *A Southern Renaissance: The Cultural Awakening of the American South, 1930–55.* New York: Oxford University Press, 1980.

Kolodny, Annette. *The Lay of the Land: Metaphor as Experience and History in American Life and Letters.* Chapel Hill: University of North Carolina Press, 1975.

Lancaster (Pa.) *News,* 19 July 1936.

Levine, Lawrence. *The Unpredictable Past: Explorations in American Cultural History.* New York: Oxford University Press, 1993.

Lindeman, Eduard C. "Farewell to Bohemia." *Survey Graphic,* April 1937: 207–8.

MacCannell, Dean. *The Tourist: A New Theory of the Leisure Class.* New York: Schocken Books, 1989.

McCardell, Lee. "Sees Rt. No. 1 Guide, Hopes Maryland One Is Better." *Baltimore Evening Sun*, 1 March 1938.

McDonald, William F. *Federal Relief Administration and the Arts: The Origins and Administrative History of the Arts Projects of the Works Progress Administration.* Columbus: Ohio State University Press, 1969.

McHugh, Vincent. *I Am Thinking of My Darling: An Adventure Story.* New York: Simon and Schuster, 1943.

McKinzie, Kathleen O'Connor. "Writers on Relief, 1935–42." Ph.D. diss., Indiana University, 1970.

McKinzie, Richard C. *The New Deal for Artists.* Princeton: Princeton University Press, 1973.

MacLeod, Norman. *You Get What You Ask For.* New York: Harrison-Hill Books, 1939.

"Me. to Fla." *New York Herald Tribune*, 20 March 1938.

Mangione, Jerre. *The Dream and the Deal: The Federal Writers' Project, 1935–1943.* 1972. Rpt. Philadelphia: University of Pennsylvania Press, 1983.

———. *An Ethnic at Large: A Memoir of America in the Thirties and Forties.* Introduction by Bernard A. Weisberger. Philadelphia: University of Pennsylvania Press, 1983.

———. "The Federal Writers' Project: What a Relief It Was!" *Philadelphia Inquirer*, 8 December 1972.

———. "It's Time for a New W.P.A. for Artists." *New York Times*, 27 April 1975.

Marling, Karal Ann. *The Colossus of Roads: Myth and Symbol along the American Highway.* Minneapolis: University of Minnesota Press, 1985.

———. *George Washington Slept Here: Colonial Revivals and American Culture, 1876–1986.* Cambridge, Mass.: Harvard University Press, 1988.

———. "A Note on New Deal Iconography: Futurology and the Historical Myth." In *Prospects: An Annual of American Cultural Studies* 4. New York: Burt Franklin, 1979.

———. *Wall-to-Wall America: A Cultural History of Post-Office Murals in the Great Depression.* Minneapolis: University of Minnesota Press, 1982.

Marron, Jas. F. "Going My Way?" *Jacksonville* (Fla.) *Sunday Times-Union*, 10 July 1938.

Mathews, Jane De Hart. *The Federal Theatre, 1935–1939: Plays, Relief, and Politics.* Princeton: Princeton University Press, 1967.

Meany, Edmond S. Jr. "Route One." *Washington Post*, 8 April 1938.

Melosh, Barbara. *Engendering Culture: Manhood and Womanhood in New Deal Public Art and Theater.* Washington, D.C.: Smithsonian Institution Press, 1991.

Meltzer, Milton. *Violins and Shovels: The WPA Arts Projects.* New York: Delacorte Press, 1976.

Mertz, Paul E. *New Deal Policy and Southern Rural Poverty.* Baton Rouge: Louisiana State University Press, 1978.

"Millions Spent to Advertise Nation's Distress, Says Taber." *New York Sun*, 4 May 1939.

Milton, John. *Three West: Conversations with Vardis Fisher, Max Evans, Michael Straight*. Vermillion, S.D.: University of South Dakota Press, 1970.

"Mirror to America." *Time*, 3 January 1938: 55.

"A Misguided Guide." *Jackson* (Mich.) *Citizen Patriot*, 19 May 1941.

"Missouri's Guide Book Rich in Lore." *St. Louis Globe-Democrat*, 14 June 1941.

Mitchell, W. J. T., ed. *Landscape and Power*. Chicago: University of Chicago Press, 1994.

Morrison, Toni. *Playing in the Dark: Whiteness and the Literary Imagination*. New York.: Random House–Vintage, 1993.

Mosse, George L. *The Nationalization of the Masses: Political Symbolism and Mass Movements in Germany from the Napoleonic Wars through the Third Reich*. New York: H. Fertig, 1975.

Mumford, Lewis. *The Culture of Cities*. 1938. Westport, Conn.: Greenwood, 1971.

———. "Writers' Project." *New Republic*, 20 October 1937: 306–7.

"Nation Writes Autobiography with American Guide Series." *Durham* (N.C.) *Herald-Sun*, 9 November 1941.

Natanson, Nicholas. *The Black Image in the New Deal: The Politics of FSA Photography*. Knoxville: University of Tennessee Press, 1992.

Nettels, Curtis. "Frederick Jackson Turner and the New Deal." *Wisconsin Magazine of History* 17 (1934): 257–65.

Nisbet, Robert. *A History of the Idea of Progress*. New York: Basic Books, 1980.

"North Carolina Guide and Blackbeard." *Greensboro* (N.C) *Daily News*, 29 October 1939.

"North Carolina Guide Is Delightful Adventure; Elizabeth City Has Prominent Place in Book and in Its Making." *Elizabeth City* (N.C.) *Daily Advance*, 13 October 1939.

Norton, Albert Charles. "Idaho: A Guide in Word and Picture." *Social Studies* (May 1937): 230.

O'Brien, Michael. *The Idea of the American South, 1920–1941*. Baltimore: Johns Hopkins University Press, 1979.

O'Connor, Francis V., ed. *Art for the Millions: Essays from the 1930s by Artists and Administrators of the Works Progress Administration Federal Art Project*. Greenwich (Conn.): New York Graphic Society, 1973.

———. *The New Deal Art Projects: An Anthology of Memoirs*. Washington, D.C.: Smithsonian Institution Press, 1972.

O'Connor, John, and Lorraine Brown, eds. *Free, Adult, Uncensored: The Living History of the Federal Theatre Project*. Washington, D.C.: New Republic Books, 1978.

Odum, Howard W., and Harry Estill Moore. *American Regionalism: A Cultural-Historical Approach to National Integration*. New York: Henry Holt, 1938.

O'Gara, Geoffrey. *A Long Road Home: Journeys through America's Present in Search of America's Past*. New York: Norton, 1989.

"Only Director and Supervisor Left—200 Once on Payroll." *St. Louis* (Mo.) *Post-Dispatch*, 15 May 1938.

Pathfinder, 17 December 1938.

Patton, Phil. *Open Road: A Celebration of the American Highway*. New York: Simon and Schuster, 1986.

Pecora, Vincent. "The Limits of Local Knowledge." In *The New Historicism*, edited by H. Aram Veeser. New York: Routledge, 1989.

Peeler, David P. *Hope Among Us Yet: Social Criticism and Social Solace in Depression America*. Athens: University of Georgia Press, 1987.

——. "Unlonesome Highways: The Quest for Fact and Fellowship in Depression America." *Journal of American Studies* 18 (1984): 185–206.

Pells, Richard. *Radical Visions and American Dreams: Culture and Social Thought in the Depression Years*. New York: Harper & Row, 1973.

Penkower, Monty Noam. *The Federal Writers' Project: A Study in Government Patronage of the Arts*. Urbana: University of Illinois Press, 1977.

Pittsburgh Courier, 14 January 1937.

Powell, William S. "An Introduction to a State Treasure." *North Carolina: The WPA Guide to the Old North State*. Columbia: University of South Carolina Press, 1998.

——, ed. *Dictionary of North Carolina Biography*. Vol. 1. Chapel Hill: University of North Carolina Press, 1979.

Putnam, Jared. "Guides to America." *Nation* 24 December 1938: 694.

Review of *Idaho*. *London Times*, 22 July 1939.

Review of *Missouri*. *Missouri Historical Review* 36 (October 1941): 108–10.

Review of *Missouri*. *St. Louis Globe-Democrat*, 11 June 1941.

Review of *Missouri*. *St. Louis Post-Dispatch*, 10 June 1941, 20 June 1941.

Review of *North Carolina*. *Roanoke Rapids Herald* n.d. (North Carolina Writers' Project).

Review of *Virginia*. *New York Times*, 29 September 1940.

Robinson, Blackwell P., ed. *The North Carolina Guide*. Chapel Hill: University of North Carolina Press, 1955.

Rorty, James. *Where Life Is Better: An Unsentimental American Journey*. New York: Reynal & Hitchcock, 1936.

Rosenberg, Harold. "Anyone Who Could Write English." *New Yorker* 20 January 1973: 99–102.

Roskolenko, Harry. "I Went into the Country." *American Stuff*, Special Issue of *Direction* 1 (February 1938): 68.

——. *When I Was Last on Cherry Street*. New York: Stein and Day, 1965.

Roth, Robert. "Spirit of Old WPA Might Help Nation Stave off Serious Slump." *Evening Bulletin* (Philadelphia), 22 December 1970.

Rowan, Carl T. "Why the 'Safe Guys' Never Write a Book." *Washington Sunday Star,* 14 May 1967.

Rukeyser, Muriel. *U.S. 1*. New York: Covici Friede, 1938.

Rushmore, Howard. "Land of Trails." *Sunday Worker* (New York City), 2 April 1939.

Russell, Don. "A Guide for WPA Guidebooks." *Chicago Daily News,* 9 February 1937.

Rydell, Robert. *All the World's a Fair: Visions of Empire at American International Expositions, 1876–1916.* Chicago: University of Chicago Press, 1984.

"Saga of Mary Read." *Greensboro* (N.C.) *Daily News,* 5 November 1939.

Said, Edward. *Culture and Imperialism.* New York: Knopf, 1993.

Scharf, Arthur. "Selected Publications of the WPA Federal Writers' Project and the Writers' Program." In Jerre Mangione, *The Dream and the Deal: The Federal Writers' Project, 1935–1943.* 1972. Rpt. Philadelphia: University of Pennsylvania Press, 1983.

"Shameful." *Rockingham* (N.C.) *Post Dispatch,* 12 October 1939.

"'Show Me, Missouri' Shows Well in the American Guide Series." *Kansas City Star,* 21 June 1941.

Simpson, David. "Being There?: Literary Criticism, Localism, and Local Knowledge." *Critical Quarterly* 35 (1993): 3–17.

Singal, Daniel Joseph. *The War Within: From Victorian to Modernist Thought in the South, 1919–1945.* Chapel Hill: University of North Carolina Press, 1982.

Snell, George. "Candid Book Summarizes Results of Idaho Project." *Salt Lake City Tribune,* 14 February 1937.

Sontag, Susan. *On Photography.* New York: Farrar, Straus & Giroux, 1977.

"Speaking of Pictures—Road Signs." *Life,* 27 June 1938: 4–6.

Spearman, Walter. "University Press Comes Out." *Raleigh* (N.C.) *News and Observer,* 8 October 1939.

Spivak, John L. *America Faces the Barricades.* New York: Covici Friede, 1936.

Sporn, Paul. *Against Itself: The Federal Theater and Writers' Projects in the Midwest.* Detroit: Wayne State University Press, 1995.

Springfield (Ohio) *News-Sun,* 5 January 1941.

"Starving Writers Aid Head Is Named." *Evening Star* (Washington, D.C.), 27 July 1935.

Steinbeck, John. *Grapes of Wrath.* 1939. Rpt. New York: Viking, 1958.

Stott, William. *Documentary Expression and Thirties America.* 1973. Rev. ed. New York: Oxford University Press, 1985.

Stryker, Roy Emerson, and Nancy Wood. *In This Proud Land: America 1935–1943 as Seen in the FSA Photographs.* Greenwich, Conn.: New York Graphic Society, 1973.

"Subsidy for Slander." *Greensboro* (N.C.) *Daily News,* 13 October 1939.

"Supervisor Bjorkman Writes Letter about North Carolina Guide." Elizabeth City (N.C.) *Daily Advance,* 10 November 1939.

Susman, Warren I. *Culture as History: The Transformation of American Society in the Twentieth Century.* New York: Pantheon Books, 1984.

Taber, Ronald Warren. "The Federal Writers' Project in the Pacific Northwest: A Case Study." Ph.D. diss., Washington State University, 1969.

———. "Vardis Fisher and the 'Idaho Guide': Preserving Culture for the New Deal." *Pacific Northwest Quarterly* 59 (April 1968): 68–76.

Tafuri, Manfredo. "The Creation of Rockefeller Center." In Giorgi Cucci et al., *The American City: From the Civil War to the New Deal*. Translated by Barbara Luigia La Penta. Cambridge, Mass.: MIT Press, 1979.

———. "The Regional Plan of New York and Its Environs and the Problem of Congestion." In Giorgi Cucci et al., *The American City: From the Civil War to the New Deal*. Translated by Barbara Luigia La Penta. Cambridge, Mass.: MIT Press, 1979.

Thompson, Ralph. "Books of the Times." *New York Times*, 25 May 1937.

Trachtenberg, Alan. "From Image to Story: Reading the File." In *Documenting America, 1935–1943*, edited by Carl Fleischhauer and Beverly W. Brannan. Berkeley: University of California Press, 1988.

"The Traveler's Notebook." *Washington Sunday Star*, 8 November 1936.

Tugwell, Rexford Guy, Thomas Munro, and Roy E. Stryker. *American Economic Life and the Means of Its Improvement*. 3rd ed. New York: Harcourt, Brace, 1930.

Ulrich, Mabel S. "Salvaging Culture for the WPA." *Harper's Magazine* 178 (May 1939): 653–64.

"'U.S. One: Maine to Florida' Tells Tourists Where to Go, What to See And What to Eat." [Unidentified clipping, Kellock Papers].

"U.S.I.A. Will Spend $6-Million on Books in Next 12 Months for Propaganda." *New York Times*, 3 October 1966.

Van Ravenswaay, Charles. "Foreword." In *The WPA Guide to 1930s Missouri by Workers of the Writers' Program of the Work Projects Administration in Missouri*. Introduction by Howard Wight Marshall and Walter A. Schroeder. Lawrence: University Press of Kansas, 1986.

Vardis Fisher: A Critical Summary with Notes on His Life and Personality. Caldwell, Ida.: Caxton, 1939.

Vaudagna, Maurizio. "Summary Introduction." *L'Estetica della politica: Europa e America negli anni trenta*. Turin: Biblioteca di Cultura Moderna Laterza, 1989.

"WPA Guide Series to Be Celebrated." *New York Daily Worker*, 22 October 1941.

"The WPA in the World of Tomorrow." *Philadelphia Inquirer*, 14 March 1939.

"WPA Writers Seem Unfamiliar with Hyde." *Dare County* (N.C.) *Times*, 27 October 1939.

Wald, Alan M. *The New York Intellectuals: The Rise and Decline of the Anti-Stalinist Left from the 1930s to the 1980s*. Chapel Hill: University of North Carolina Press, 1987.

Ware, Susan. *Beyond Suffrage: Women in the New Deal*. Cambridge, Mass.: Harvard University Press, 1981.

Washington Post, 10 May 1941.

Weisberger, Bernard. "Reading, Writing, and History." Review of Jerre Mangione,

The Dream and the Deal: The Federal Writers' Project, 1935–1943. American Heritage 25 (February 1974): 98–100.

Weisberger, Bernard A., ed. *The WPA Guide to America: The Best of 1930s America as Seen by the Federal Writers' Project*. New York: Pantheon Books, 1985.

White, Hayden. *Tropics of Discourse: Essays in Cultural Criticism*. Baltimore: Johns Hopkins University Press, 1978.

Whiting, Cecile. "American Heroes and Invading Barbarians: The Regionalist Response to Fascism." *Prospects* 13 (1988): 295–324.

———. *Antifascism in American Art*. New Haven: Yale University Press, 1989.

Whyte, William H. "Introduction." In *The WPA Guide to New York City* by the Federal Writers' Project of the Works Progress Administration in New York City. New York: Pantheon Books, 1982.

Wilson, Alexander. *The Culture of Nature: North American Landscape from Disney to the Exxon Valdez*. Cambridge, Mass.: Blackwell, 1992.

Wilson, Charles Regan, and William Ferris, eds. *Encyclopedia of Southern Culture*. Chapel Hill: University of North Carolina Press, 1989.

Winston, Robert Watson. "North Carolina: A Guide to the Old North State." *New York Herald Tribune*, 28 January 1940.

Wolff, Janet. "On the Road Again: Metaphors of Travel in Cultural Criticism." In *Resident Alien: Feminist Cultural Criticism*. New Haven: Yale University Press, 1995.

Workers of the Writers' Program of the Work Projects Administration in the State of Missouri. *Missouri: A Guide to the "Show Me" State*. New York: Duell, Sloan and Pearce, 1941.

"Writers' Project: 1942." *New Republic*, 13 April 1942: 480.

Yezierska, Anzia. *Red Ribbon on a White Horse*. 1950. New York: Persea Books, 1981.